CW00485551

IN HARDSHIP
AND HOPE

This book is dedicated to all those who have had to leave
home to make their life in another country.

© Greg Quiery 2017
Published by G & K Publishing
Printed and bound by W&G Baird
Book design by March Design, Liverpool

ISBN 978-1-9998038-0-3

This book is copyright under the Berne Convention. All rights are reserved. Apart from any fair
dealing for the purpose of private study, research, criticism or review, as permitted under the
Copyright Act 1956, no part of this publication may be reproduced, stored in a retrieval system, or
transmitted in any form or by any means electronic, electrical, chemical, mechanical, optical,
photocopying, recording or otherwise without the prior permission of the copyright owner. Enquiries
should be sent to the publisher at the undermentioned address.

www.liverpoolirishhistory.com

IN HARDSHIP
AND HOPE

A History of the Liverpool Irish

Greg Quiery

G&K

ACKNOWLEDGEMENTS

My thanks to Simon Rahilly who edited this book. His advice and support were invaluable. His editing was insightful and rigorous. Dr Kevin McNamara also went through the manuscript in great detail, correcting errors and suggesting improvements. Sadly he did not lived to see it published. A special thanks to Mandy Vere who was an extremely patient and meticulous proof reader. They have each been very thorough. However, I must make it clear that any errors and inaccuracies are entirely my responsibility.

I have had much assistance over the years from local libraries. My thanks in particular to Roger Hull and colleagues at the Liverpool Record Office, and to Helena Smart the archivist there. Thanks to staff at Sydney Jones library, especially Andrew Willan, who was a great help digging out parliamentary papers, to Meg Whittle, and Mary Borg before her, at the Metropolitan Cathedral Library for access to Catholic parish records, to staff at Hope University where the Nugent Papers are kept, and to Sr. Annie Lunny for access to the archives of the Poor Servants of the Mother of God.

I have had valuable assistance and advice from Michael Kelly who has written so much about the Liverpool Irish. Kathleen McKeating read the document and provided valuable comment. I must also thank specialist readers Tony Birtill, Mike Hogan, Ritchie Hunter, and Marie Quiery. Jimmy McGovern provided very useful observations on the concluding section. Ian McKeane provided encouragement, support and inspiration at the outset. He is very much missed. Frank Boyce not only provided encouragement and guidance but also gave me access to his manuscript of oral interviews. Thanks also to Laura Marie Brown, Marij Van Helmond, Peter King, Professor Mary Hickman, Bishop Tom Williams, Joe Farag and His Honour Dr David Lynch.

The individuals I interviewed for the closing pages gave their time generously, and were prepared to discuss with me their personal experiences. The final section could not have been completed without them. Many thanks.

Cover photographs from the Thomas Burke collection at Liverpool Public Record Office.

ABBREVIATIONS

AOH   Ancient Order of Hibernians
BPP   British Parliamentary Papers
CWMA   Conservative Working Men's
       Association
CYMS   Christian Young Men's Society
ELA   Employer's Labour Association
HC   House of Commons
HO   Home Office
INA   Irish Nationalist Association
IRB   Irish Republican Brotherhood
ISDL   Irish Self-Determination League
LC   *Liverpool Courier*
LIRA   Liverpool Irish Republican Army

LRO   Liverpool Record Office
LUP   Liverpool University Press
LWMCA Liverpool Working Men's
       Christian Association
NUDL   National Union of Dock Labourers
PRO   Public Record Office
RIC   Royal Irish Constabulary
RTE   Raidio Teilifis Eireann (Ireland's
       national public broadcaster)
SVP   Society of Saint Vincent De Paul
THSLC The Historical Society of
       Lancashire and Cheshire
UCD   University College Dublin

CONTENTS

PART THREE FROM 1914 TO 1960s

PREFACE

'Hope is a good thing. Maybe the best of things.'
Andy Dufresne in Stephen King's *The Shawshank Redemption.*

When I came to Liverpool in the early 1970s I was aware of the city's unique character and world-wide reputation. In time I came to realise that this character was rooted in a dramatic and turbulent past. I was gradually drawn to explore the history of the city, and especially that of the Irish, one of the many communities in the Liverpool melting pot. I became fascinated by the story. 'In Hardship and Hope' is the result. I hope it will engage the reader in an account which is direct in style and enjoyable to read. The book is concerned mainly, but not exclusively, with the Catholic Irish. Whilst the core of the book concerns the Irish in nineteenth and early twentieth century Liverpool, it also examines the early years of the Irish community in the eighteenth century and, in the closing section, the process of integration and assimilation which took place in the nineteen fifties and sixties. It is an attempt to do justice to a dramatic story of courage and hardship. I also hope it will illuminate, for the reader, one aspect of the story of our city – Liverpool – through a better understanding of one of its many communities, and the difficulties that community has overcome. I also hope it casts light upon the migrant experience, so common in today's world. The Irish in Liverpool endured hostility and remained isolated for generations. This book examines the factors behind this relative isolation and why it persisted for so long.

A focal point of the book is the Irish Famine, and its dramatic impact on Liverpool. I examine how this catastrophic event resulted in profound and permanent changes in the social structure of Liverpool. To present a picture of everyday life in nineteenth century Liverpool, I have examined a number of topics including employment, education and housing conditions as they affected both female and male members of the community. There is also an account of the role played by the Catholic Church, which was engulfed by the arriving Irish and found itself thrust into the centre of affairs in the city. The arrival of the Irish, with their alien values, religion and culture, generated friction and conflict. The book analyses the consequent political developments, along with Irish nationalism, Irish revolutionary movements, sectarianism and the related public disorder.

The closing section concerns the tightly-knit Irish communities of the inter-war years and how they eventually began to break up. There is a discussion of the distinctive Irish Catholic culture which persisted in the satellite estates and how new communities, often centred around a Catholic parish, were established in the post war era. In the final chapter I examine how this culture declined and why. Here I use interviews with individuals

– some of them from other ethnic backgrounds – who grew up in Liverpool's Irish Catholic environment, and have seen it transformed.

I have included reference to Irish Protestants where I have information about them. Whilst it is estimated that Irish Protestants formed about 20% of the total coming to Liverpool, their story is more difficult to trace. They made a significant contribution to many aspects of life in the city. They integrated with less difficulty, having common religious and political beliefs with the resident population. Their story awaits further research.

An understanding of the Liverpool Irish, how they came to be here, what their values and culture were, and how they influenced the character of the city, is essential if we are to understand contemporary Merseyside. This book examines the consequences of migration for both the migrants themselves and for the host community, the tensions which can result from migration and the process of resolution. In the case of the Liverpool Irish this process of integration was to take an extremely long time. Why this should have been so is one of the central themes of this book.

A number of other themes are reflected in contemporary politics. Exploiting fear of migrants to secure votes, and the reliance on private sector housing to meet the needs of the most deprived are two examples. Researching the book I was struck by the scale of inequality. Many of the wealthy paid little heed to the condition of the poor. Whether contemporary Britain can learn anything from such events is for the reader to judge.

There are a number of books concerning the Liverpool Irish and related topics which I would recommend. John Belchem's *Irish Catholic and Scouse* is a detailed and comprehensive account. Frank Neal's *Sectarian Violence, the Liverpool Experience* covers the issue of sectarian conflict and related politics in detail. Waller's *Democracy and Sectarianism* is a magisterial work which is immensely detailed and informative. Tony Birtill's *Irish In Liverpool,* relates the history of the Irish language in Liverpool. Michael Kelly has produced a number of books, mainly focused on biographical accounts, each of them of great interest. Tommy Walsh's *Being Irish in Liverpool* is a vivid insider's account by one who was at the forefront of the community for a generation. Having read each of these I had the feeling that there was a need for a narrative account for the general reader, providing a clear sense of how events and their consequences unfolded in chronological order, explaining movements in Ireland, which so influenced Liverpool, and relating events in Liverpool to the wider political and social context. I hope you find it an enjoyable and informative read.

IN HARDSHIP AND HOPE **PART ONE** THE IRISH IN LIVERPOOL BEFORE 1847

CHAPTER ONE

THE FIRST ARRIVALS

The overwhelming mass migration of Irish people during the years of the Irish Great Hunger, 1846-53, rightly occupies a prominent place in the imagination of Liverpool people to this day. However, this horrendous time and the events associated with it should not distract our attention from the more significant and long term pattern of steady and continuous arrival and departure of Irish people in every era, from the earliest days of the port through to the twenty-first century. Commercial and business links with Ireland, along with family and social connections, have remained strong in every decade of the city's history.

The 16th century writer, Leland, noted when referring to 'Lyrpole' that, 'Irish merchants cum thither as to a good haven'.[1] He remarked that these merchants were attracted by local concessions. 'At Lyrpole is small custom paid, that causeth merchants to resort thither.' Amongst the merchandise was, 'good Irish yarn that Manchester men do by (sic) there.'

Contact was not confined to trading links. Soldiers and supplies making their way to Ireland to take part in the Elizabethan conquest there, occasionally passed through Liverpool, though Chester was more often used. In 1599 the Earl of Essex used Liverpool for the transport of troops. 'The port was one of the places of embarkation for Cromwell's troops on the way to Ireland.'[2] In the 1690s King William of Orange camped on the banks of the Mersey, before making his way to Ireland, and victory at the Boyne.

As trade increased so did the Irish community. During the Elizabethan era (1533-1603), 'many families came from Ireland to Liverpool and laid the foundation of an extensive commerce between the two countries,'[3] establishing warehouses and businesses which were essential to the early development of the town. Following the eventual conquest and colonisation of Ireland during the 1600s there were closer economic and commercial ties. Amongst other things the language barrier was being eroded, as more people in the area around Dublin, known as The Pale, and along the Irish east coast, began to speak English. Those Irish traders who were Catholic carried on their business in the face of considerable difficulty, because of the operation of the oppressive Penal Laws, which, to give a few examples, barred them from holding public office, or owning a horse worth more than £5, and fined them for not attending Anglican services.[4] Such restrictions were also applied to other non-Anglicans, such as Presbyterians. Trade with Ireland continued, and included such items as feathers, fish, wool, and linen cloth. When in the 1690s King William allowed the import of hemp and flax from Ireland duty free, trade increased substantially. Estimates put the number of Irish-born residents at this time at around 1,800.[5] The baptism register of St Mary's Catholic Chapel in Lumber Street (off Old Hall Street) showed a 'striking predominance of Irish surnames and several places of residence given as 'of' or 'from' Ireland.'[6]

Trade increased steadily during the more settled period of the 1700s. When the first slaving ships set out from Liverpool in the late 1690s the town's population was less than 10,000. In 1717 the opening of the wet dock, designed by Thomas Steers – who had fought with King William at the Battle of the Boyne – greatly increased the port's capacity. During the following century Liverpool rose to become not only a major trading power, but also the world's largest slaving centre, providing the finance, ships and crew which transported hundreds of thousands from West Africa to the Americas. Many thousands of Irish people had been victims of the trade in the 1600s when they were transported to the Caribbean and sold into slavery. The attitude that the Irish were an inferior race, suited to such treatment, persisted in the public domain in succeeding centuries. There is little evidence that Irish merchants became involved in the trade, probably because they did not have the money to invest. One who did was Felix Doran who lived in Lord Street, and whose ship *The Blossom* was used to sell three hundred Africans into slavery, earning Doran and his partners £28,000 (equivalent to over £2.5 million in today's value). With such rewards on offer, Liverpool became one of the world's leading financial and trading centres, making it an attractive destination not only for Irish merchants, but also for the daring and the desperate in search of opportunity. Liverpool maintained the atmosphere of a frontier town. Fortunes were made quickly and lost just as easily. Young men on the streets after dark or drinking in taverns were liable to be pressed into service on a slaving ship or navy vessel. In 1793 Felix McIlroy, a ship's captain on a routine trip from Newry in Co Down was shot dead in Water Street whilst resisting a press gang.[7]

The Catholic Irish remained at a severe disadvantage throughout the eighteenth century, being excluded by law from certain areas of public life. In addition, suspicion of Catholicism and hostility towards it was a significant factor. Catholic chapels were destroyed by mob violence in Liverpool on several occasions. St Mary's was burned to the ground in 1746, in reaction to the 1745 Jacobite Rising in Scotland. It was rebuilt as a more robust and discreet premises, but was again destroyed in 1759.[8] The Jesuit Order was present in Liverpool with a mission to continue to offer Catholic services. Amongst those who benefitted from this often clandestine ministry were Irish seamen, for whom the Jesuit Father Price said mass in premises in the city centre.[9]

By 1751 'Liverpool now controlled the great bulk of the Irish trade.'[10] Later in the century regular package services were opened and trading links strengthened. In 1770 Liverpool imported from Ireland 14,000 firkins (a barrel of about nine gallons capacity) of butter, 26,000 cow hides, and over 3,000 barrels of beef. In 1778, 988 vessels 'entered from Ireland' rising to about 1,376 by 1801, that is about 26 per week. Smithers records that 'nearly one fifth part of the export trade of Liverpool is with Ireland.'[11] New arrivals also increased. Family names such as O'Connor and Maguire occur more frequently in records. 'Irish' names in Gores Directory – a listing of business and professional men – rose from 15 in 1766, to 80 in 1781.[12] Some – such as Captain O'Connor and Captain O'Mara – were seafarers, whilst others were merchants and traders. The transport service each morning to Warrington and Manchester was run by a Mr James Maguire. Few were in professions, as Irish Catholics were still excluded by law.

In the 1790s 'the great influx of Irish and Welsh' was remarked on.[13] The Irish republican rising of 1798 also impacted on Liverpool. Troughton[14] complains that 'in the summer of 1798, so great was the influx of persons of every description into this town from Ireland that house rents and the price of lodgings were greatly advanced, and have continued exorbitantly high.' Many people 'came to Liverpool as a place of refuge from the horrors of rebellion and martial law.' He notes that they 'contributed at once to the wealth and population of the place.' Apart from an influx of the relatively well-to-do at this time, Troughton also remarked upon the arrival of 'many immoral characters of the lower class.' Liverpool had a direct ferry link with Wexford, one of the key centres of the rising, and focal point of disturbances. Names common in Co Wexford, such as Dwyer and Byrne, appear in Liverpool at this time.[15]

Many of the new Irish arrivals were Protestants, descendants of the colonisers of previous generations, bearing names already familiar in England. When Troughton mentions that many of those arriving in 1798 were 'loyal Irish', these are the people to whom he is referring. Because these Irish Protestants merged so easily into English society, it is difficult to monitor their impact.

In politics, 18th century Liverpool was not liberal. City governance remained under the archaic freeman system established more than a century earlier. Only freemen could stand for or vote in local and parliamentary elections. Predominantly members of the established Anglican Church, they had the power to add other freemen to their number, leaving local political power in the hands of this small self-selected group. If Englishmen of a more liberal mindset had little chance of political influence, the Irish were even further removed, by nationality and religion, from civic power and influence.

For those with limited resources, life in Liverpool was not going to be easy. The tenfold expansion of the city population to 77,000 by 1800 was unplanned.[16] Public health was undermined by poor housing, uncontrolled development, limited water supply and inadequate or non-existent sewage services. The opportunities presented by the slave trade and its voracious appetite for risky investment starved manufacturing of resources. Although Liverpool, with its shipping and, from 1720 onwards, canal networks, was well positioned for the nurturing of manufacturing, in reality the thriving pottery and chemical industries declined, leaving the population with few opportunities for skilled work.

TIMELINE – EIGHTEENTH CENTURY

1700	Liverpool Merchant begins first slaving voyage from Liverpool.
1716	Thomas Steers completed first wet dock.
1726	Gullivers Travels published.
1775	American War of Independence begins.
1789	French Revolution

After the Act of Union

In 1801 the Act of Union abolished the Irish parliament. The purpose was to integrate Ireland and Britain into one political and economic unit – the United Kingdom. However, the Irish economy declined steadily under the Union, and the resultant emigration made a steady impact on Liverpool. During the years following the Union, the population of Ireland rose substantially, from about 5 million in 1800 to over 6.8 million in 1821, and then to 7.7million by 1831.[17] This placed intolerable strains on the predominantly rural Irish economy. Most Irish land was in the possession of a small elite of Protestant landlords, whose families had been put in place during colonisation – a process completed in the 1690s – and the plantations which followed. They were alienated by culture, religion and politics from their numerous and resentful Catholic tenants. Since one of the effects of the Union was to postpone land reform, rural distress became more acute as years passed. Poverty and hunger became endemic in certain areas, particularly the western counties. This situation was compounded by the decline of manufacturing. Having few raw materials, and little capital, Irish industry – other than in the predominantly Protestant north eastern counties – found it impossible to compete with the scale and sophistication of British industrial development. For those who could not make a living in this environment, Liverpool – a city of growing prosperity and just a short distance away – was a tempting prospect.

In rural areas some landlords offered incentives to tenants to leave, while others evicted those who could not afford rent increases. There were recurring instances of regional famines.[18] The Poor Law, designed to provide support for the most desperate in Britain, was not established in Ireland until 1838, and even then was not an entitlement. As time passed, seasonal labourers, those hoping to be soldiers – more than 40% of those in the British army were Irish[19] – and an increasing number of the destitute poor could now be added to the businessmen and traders already coming to Liverpool.

From the latter half of the eighteenth century onwards, increasing numbers of Irish labourers regularly passed through Liverpool, finding jobs building canals – the Irish navvies – or as harvesters in Lancashire and Cheshire, some going as far east as Lincolnshire. With the arrival of the first Irish steamship service on the Mersey – *The Waterloo* in July 1822 – the traffic increased rapidly.[20] Whilst they may have come in a spirit of adventure, the harvesters often endured great hardship, and provided a remarkable spectacle. They assembled in groups in their native town or village in Ireland before setting off on foot for the nearest port, arriving in Liverpool after sitting out on deck, and then marching off into the neighbouring countryside. One observer at the time described these hardworking people as: 'hundreds of squalid creatures … without shoes, stockings or shirts … with rags hardly sufficient to cover their nakedness.'[21] Whilst another, John Denvir, noted: 'The vast armies of harvest men, clad in frieze coats and knee breeches, with their clean white shirts with high collars, and tough blackthorn sticks, who might be seen … marching, literally in their thousands, from the Clarence Dock, Liverpool and up the London road to reap John Bull's harvest.'[22]

It is estimated that by 1840 about 57,000[23] were making this annual trip, one in seven of them being women. At the peak harvest period fares were reduced to as little as three pence, in contrast to ten pence or more at other times of the year.[24] It was convenient for English farmers to make use of this labour, as it was cheap and seasonal. When the work was finished they made their way back through Liverpool and other ports, bringing with them valuable wages to sustain families back home during the winter. Failure to obtain harvest work would be a disaster, and in years of poor harvest the streets of Liverpool became congested with those who could not find their return fare.

Work on the construction of canals, and later railways, was also to some extent seasonal, since it often slowed down or ceased altogether during winter. Some labourers found work in Liverpool itself, as a programme of dock construction initiated in 1819 with the building of the Princes Dock, continued into the middle of the century and beyond. As these docks were dug out by pick and shovel, the magnitude of the task was such that a great number of labourers were required.

Others came to settle permanently. During the early years of the century the passenger traffic to and from Ireland formed a large proportion of the total annual traffic through Liverpool, and represented a substantial boost to the town in commercial terms. Amongst those arriving were increasing numbers of the poorest Irish peasants. Smithers remarks that in 1801 the 'state of Ireland caused numbers to flock over to Liverpool in such a distressed state that a violent dysentry ensued followed by numerous deaths'.[25]

This new wave of arrivals often travelled on foot from their village to the nearest Irish port, and then on to Liverpool, in the same manner as the agricultural labourers. A large number settled in the predominantly Irish area near to the docks, centred on present day Whitechapel. Some found work or accommodation through family and friends. Many Irish migrants travelled to nearby towns and cities – such as Manchester, where there was a large Irish community – in search of work.

There was a substantial and influential Irish middle class. Self-made business people, attracted by the commercial success of the city, found opportunities in warehousing and export, livestock trading, retailing and brewing. Many of these enterprises were branches of existing family concerns in Irish east coast towns such as Dundalk or Drogheda. Families such as those of Daniel O'Connell and Richard Lalor Sheil had survived the ban on Catholics owning property or transacting business by making use of Protestant agents or having a family member convert. Laws excluding Catholics from higher education were finally repealed during the 1790s, allowing admission to universities. As a result there was an emergent professional class, which included doctors, journalists, teachers and lawyers. Many left Ireland for Britain to further their careers. Such people played an important role in the Irish community in Liverpool and in the life of the city during the first half of the nineteenth century. Examples include Richard Sheil, a wealthy merchant, Terence Bellew McManus who had warehouses in Liverpool, the Cullens, who were cattle dealers, and journalist Michael J. Whitty, who not only became Liverpool's first Chief Constable, but was also owner and editor of the *Liverpool Daily Post.*

By the early 1800s there were a number of areas of distinctive Irish settlement. Outside the modern John Lewis store in the Liverpool One shopping district, it is possible to look down through a glass spy hole to see the walls of the old dock, Liverpool's original 'pool'. In the early nineteenth century, in the area around this dock, right on the waterfront and extending into Cleveland Square and Canning Place, a high proportion of the resident population was Irish. South John Street and Canning Place were 55% Irish at this time. Burke refers to 'the dense Irish population which within living memory was to be seen in and around Whitechapel, Paradise Street and South John Street.'[26] It was a bustling area, where migrants looked for hostel accommodation before boarding ship. They mingled with discharged sailors, dock workers, street traders, businessmen, officials and hangers-on. Irish people worked as dockers, took up the profitable trade of running hostels, or became pub landlords and shop keepers. From this area residents began moving southwards to the streets on either side of Park Lane, as far as the intersection with Parliament Street including New Bird Street, and Crosbie Street,[27] an area of poor housing close to the docks. This settlement continued to expand southwards into Park Place, following the building of a new Catholic chapel, St Patrick's, there in 1827. Some of Liverpool's first sectarian rioting took place along Parliament Street as these Irish residents came into conflict with the carpenters who worked in the nearby shipyard and were almost exclusively Protestant.

In the 1830s many Irish settlers lived off Dale Street and in the side streets beyond Moorfields. This area, a mixture of solid residences and poor housing, leads down a gentle slope to the damp and unhealthy area around Fontenoy Street and present day Byrom Street, where the poorest lived. There was also an Irish settlement at Regent Road alongside the docks in the north end. This area expanded with the opening of the Clarence Dock in 1830.[28] The original gates of this dock, through which Irish ferries discharged their passengers each year from 1830 until 1932, still stand as silent witness to over a century of Irish migration. The area is close to the head of the Leeds Liverpool canal, where there was plenty of economic activity and opportunity for casual work. James Muspratt, the Dublin born chemist, had a large workforce in this area, almost all of them Irish. Later this community continued to expand eastwards towards Scotland Road.

Whilst these were areas where there were streets with a concentration of Irish-born people, many individuals, including middle class merchants, and Protestant Irish, were scattered across other districts of the rapidly growing town. In total there were about 20,000 Irish-born living in Liverpool in this period.[29]

Herman Melville came to Liverpool in 1839, and described it as follows: *'In the evening, especially when the sailors are gathered in great numbers these streets present a most singular spectacle, the entire population of the vicinity being seemily turned into them. Hand-organs, fiddles and cymbals, plied by strolling musicians, mix with songs of the seamen, the babble of women and children and the groaning and whining of beggars. From the various boarding houses, each distinguished by gilded emblems outside – an anchor, a ship, a windlass or a dolphin – proceeds the noise of revelry and dancing: and from the open casements lean young girls and old women, chattering and laughing with the crowds in the middle of the street.'*[30]

The numbers of Irish Catholics arriving in Liverpool can be

determined through census returns, the study of typical Irish names and returns for attendance at Catholic schools and churches. It is more difficult to come to an estimate of the numbers of Irish Protestants coming to Liverpool and their impact upon the town. They have been described as 'the invisible seventh' of the Liverpool Irish population.[31] Irish Protestants were predominantly from Ulster, the northerly Irish province, and undoubtedly many Ulster people came to Liverpool. Ulster Protestants found it less difficult to integrate in Britain. Although arriving in Liverpool from a rural area or even from the industrial city of Belfast would have been a shock to them, Irish Protestants had much more in common with the majority population in Liverpool than did their Catholic fellow countrymen and women. They had similar religious beliefs and political convictions, including a strong commitment to empire and crown. They were not distinguished from the existing population by their surnames. They would usually join religious congregations made up predominantly of local people. In the case of Anglicans they would have found that many of their fellow Ulstermen – such as the Reverends Hume, Auld and McNeile – were clergy in the local churches. Church membership gave them a social introduction to Liverpool society, and eased the process of integration. Many were tradesmen who had the appropriate skills to find well paid employment.

There was also an established Ulster Protestant middle class. William Brown from Co Antrim is perhaps the best example of a wealthy and successful Ulster Protestant in Liverpool. The family firm opened offices in Philadelphia, New York and Liverpool, dealing first in linen, a product common in Ulster, but then expanding into cotton. They acquired such wealth that they went into banking. They survived the great financial crash of 1837, a crisis caused by unregulated banks lending too much money on a poorly secured basis, thus inflating land prices. The resulting crash shook the international economy. Richard Cobden said of Brown: 'There is hardly a wind that blows, or a tide that flows in the Mersey, that does not bring a ship freighted with cotton or some other costly commodity for Mr Brown's house.'[32] Another was James Muspratt, who pioneered the LeBlanc process (producing soda ash, which was widely used in making soap and other products) and established a thriving chemical industry on Merseyside. His works on Vauxhall Road caused such pollution that he was taken to court on a number of occasions, and was eventually forced to move his operation to other districts, including Runcorn and St Helens. His giant chimney on Vauxhall Road – designed to carry the poisonous fumes out of the area – was said to have provided a useful navigation aid for ships approaching the Mersey.

CHAPTER TWO

LIFE IN THE IRISH COMMUNITY

Amongst the many issues facing the reforming Whig government in the 1830s was the condition of the Irish poor, whose situation was considered more desperate than that of any other population in Europe. They appointed a commissioner – Cornewall Lewis – to investigate.[1] In 1834 he turned his attention to the condition of the Irish resident in Britain. The evidence presented to Cornewall Lewis is a rich source of anecdotal information. Most of the witnesses were middle or upper class English gentlemen, who were shocked by conditions in the poorest city slums in which so many of the Irish lived. As many of the witnesses had a political axe to grind, or were writing for newspapers, their accounts must be taken with a pinch of salt.

Many of their statements served to reinforce existing stereotypes. In some cases the Irish were portrayed as feckless, with poor habits as regards cleanliness. They were frequently regarded as dishonest and pugnacious. One witness before Lewis remarked that: 'their mode of life is in general on a par with that of the poorest of the native population, and inferior to it.' Another stated, 'The Irish emigration into Britain is an example of a less civilised population spreading themselves … beneath a more civilised community.' And again, 'I consider that the influence of the poor Irish on Liverpool has been decidedly bad; they are less cleanly in their habits, more addicted to drink, and the women are less industrious; I think it would be advantageous to Liverpool if no more were to settle in it'.[2]

On the other hand there were more positive stereotypes; the Irish were simple folk, welcoming, humorous and fond of jokes and conversation. Whatever the pre-conceptions and prejudices, it came as a shock for both English and Irish when the two cultures met. Irish people came from a predominantly rural background. Their mode of dress was more casual than that of the city dweller. For most it was their first time in an urban environment, since at this time fewer than one in twenty Irish people lived in a town. They came from rural districts where keeping a pig in or near the house, for example, or stacking dried animal waste for fuel were often good ideas. Living in close proximity with neighbours was new to them. The majority, who had come to Britain to better themselves, were very poor indeed. And for most it was their first experience of living in a society where Catholicism was not the dominant religion. 'When the Irish come, the change from their own society and from a country where their religion is held in respect, makes many of them wish to return.'[3]

Amongst those giving evidence to Cornewall Lewis's Committee was the Reverend Thomas Fisher, who was the resident Catholic priest at St Mary's, Edmund Street. Of his 3,000 communicants, about two thirds were Irish.

'A large proportion of the Irish in my flock are in a very low state, living in cellars and garrets.'[4] The cellars in particular were cold, damp and unhealthy. The Irish were living in them because they were the cheapest accommodation, and perhaps could not otherwise be rented. Many were later to be closed under health regulations. Overcrowding was common. Families were large and new arrivals from Ireland – often relatives or friends – were frequent.

'The poor relations of those settled in England frequently come over to them, and are supported by their friends until they find employment. They come over from all parts, especially the north and west.'

They had few possessions. Father Fisher tells us that ' their furniture is very poor. A pallet of straw, a stool sometimes a table, an iron pot and a frying pan, a jug for water, a few plates and a leaden or pewter spoon.'[4] These are the possessions of those who arrived with nothing, and found only poorly paid work upon arrival. 'Persons of this class live on potatoes, or stir-about (porridge). Now and again perhaps they may get a herring or a little bacon; they neglect their children and send them out begging.'[4]

On a more positive note: 'the circumstances of the Irish are better than those of the same class in Ireland,' said Dr Collins, a Maynooth educated Irish medical practitioner, working in Liverpool at the time.[5] 'All the adults have shoes but not necessarily the children.' Since it was said that amongst the poor in Ireland, 'a bed or blanket was a rare luxury,' it seems that the Irish in Liverpool would have considered themselves better off than those at home.[6]

Community feeling was strong, as one would expect in a poor, tightly-knit emigrant group. 'They marry early and have large families; and they assist one another a good deal, both those who are resident here and those just come from Ireland, whether relations or not.'[7] And another witness to the same committee remarked: 'they are also generous to one another to a great extent. They assist one another in sickness and misfortune.'

A local priest, Reverend Peter Wilcock, of St Anthony's, a native of Lancashire, gave evidence. On Irish family life he noted that 'the Irish have a wish to marry early.' On the question of sexual promiscuity amongst them he was of the opinion that: 'there is not much intercourse amongst the Irish before marriage. In general pregnancy is the consequence and not the cause of marriage.'[8]

Many of those travelling in Ireland at this time remarked upon the nature of the Irish character, even in times of extreme privation. 'It would not be right to omit the fact that in all their misery, the Irish demonstrated time and again to visitors, commissioners, journalists and so forth, a seemingly inexhaustible reserve of gaiety and lightheartedness, that were duly noted …' Woodham-Smith notes that: 'good manners and hospitality were universal amongst the Irish.'[9] 'The neighbour or the stranger finds every man's door open, and to walk in without ceremony at meal times and to partake of his bowl of potatoes is always sure to give pleasure to everyone of the house,' wrote Sir John Carr, who toured Ireland soon after the Union. Sir Walter Scott noted in 1825 that: 'their natural condition is turned towards gaiety and happiness'.[9] Those in Liverpool also seem to have shared these characteristics, being generous to others, and enjoying the lighter side of life.

Most Irish saw Liverpool as a place of opportunity. Certain families, over time, worked their way up into the more prosperous well-to-do classes. 'Many of those who come over, by their general conduct and industry, realise something more comfortable; and many of them have got into business as tradesmen, clerks and especially as publicans.'[8] As one would expect, they also had hopes that the rising generation would achieve higher standards of living. Dr Collins again: 'They have a greater facility of getting their children bound in trades than they have in their own country,' making the point that Liverpool could provide the opportunity of advancement for the poor Irish.

'And it is a well known fact that many who settle as paupers, by putting their children to school … frequently get them taken on as clerks into merchants and attorneys offices, and by time and industry they have become comparatively influential members of society, whereas no such facilities of rising in the world occur in their own country.' Seeking apprenticeships, they become 'mates, stewards or even merchant masters'.[5]

Certainly drinking was common. 'The Irish are bad managers. They make a large sum go a very short way. They also spend a very great deal of money in drinking, even those who are not confirmed drunkards.' William Parlour, Superintendent of Police in Liverpool, stated that 'assaults are extremely frequent amongst the lower class of Irish; and in almost every case that arises from drunkenness.'[10]

Michael James Whitty, Superintendent of the Night Watch and himself an Irishman testified 'as to crimes against the person … aggravated assaults are frequent amongst them, arising from some sudden provocation and drink. These are the result of the drunken rows in which men and women are indiscriminately engaged; I never knew an Irish row in which women were not concerned.'[10] Rowdiness and disruption in Irish areas, not just in Liverpool, but across Britain, were common.

On this topic Whitty didn't mince his words: 'The Irish give infinitely more trouble and are infinitely more riotous and disorderly in the streets than any other class of persons, or than all others put together; they make a great deal of noise, they are in fact more accustomed to a country than a town life; I do not think that because they make so much noise in the streets they get more credit for drunkenness than they deserve; hundreds, I might say thousands of them spend all their wages on a Saturday night.'[11]

These two senior police officers were also in agreement on another matter. 'Certain classes of crimes are almost exclusively Irish in Liverpool, viz, illicit distilling and passing of counterfeit coin,' according to Parlour. For his part Whitty stated: 'As to offences against the revenue, the illicit distillation and smuggling of whiskey are very frequent among the Irish of Liverpool'.[11] It was not an easy community to police. The Irish stuck together, especially in the case of police actions. To close down a still or to enter an Irish street to make an arrest required a considerable number of officers.

The front of St Patrick's chapel, Park Place, which opened in 1827, showing Celtic Cross, statue of St Patrick and dedication plaque.

Ribbonism and Politics

Finding themselves in a foreign city, with little opportunity to participate in civic or political life, the Irish developed networks of their own. Significant among these were the ribbon clubs. Secret societies were extremely influential in Ireland at this time. They were a product of a political environment in which the majority existed outside the law, and had no opportunity for redress within it. The notorious Six Acts of 1819 – the year of the Peterloo Massacre in Manchester – were designed to suppress any dissent, and amongst other things prohibited public meetings of more than fifty, driving underground many activities which today would be considered perfectly legitimate. It was in this hostile environment that the ribbon societies functioned. They were exclusively male, and have been given various names such as ribbonmen or whiteboys. In Ireland they had generally come into being to address a specific issue, such as a landlord evicting tenants or charging exorbitant rents. Moving usually by night they destroyed crops on landed estates, cut the tendons of cattle, and attacked landlord agents and tithe collectors.

The societies also provided a degree of emergency social support in an era well before the state had any thought of doing such a thing. They were secret because the Combination Acts had outlawed any such activity however innocent. Rural unrest was one of the reasons martial law was imposed in Ireland throughout most of the first half of the century. Irish migrants soon brought the ribbon networks to Liverpool. Government was concerned that these societies could provide a platform for more widespread rebellion.

Ribbon networks in Liverpool included the Molly Maguires, the Northern Union and the Irish Sons of Freedom. To access the benefits available a new arrival had to confirm his membership with a secret signal such as a password or handshake, or even a card or certificate. The societies undoubtedly provided mutual support. Contributions were collected from members, held by a treasurer, and distributed by an officer. They were used to assist those in hardship – such as evicted tenants or those fleeing from the authorities. They would also meet other costs, especially funeral expenses. The system assisted those arriving in Liverpool, providing connections to work and short-term accommodation. Generally, officers were elected at regular meetings, which were held in the only available public spaces – public houses – leading to regular drinking sessions. The societies were monitored by the authorities, and penetrated by informers. Arrests were frequent. Abuse of funds was also a recurring problem, hardly surprising in secret societies in a poor community with no legal structure, whose officers had little means of their own. The Irish Sons of Freedom had their headquarters in the Hibernian Tavern, Newton Hill Street. Members paid six pence quarterly. This was used to send their elected 'President' to regular meetings of the Society leadership in Ireland, to assist fugitives, to provide legal assistance for members in jail, and to pay benefits to members. Evidence of their activities came to light through police records. In October 1839 police arrested Richard Jones and found his shorthand notes, which provided details of ribbon activities.[12] The notes contained information not only on the membership, but about power struggles within the organisation, together with evidence of hostility towards rival organisations such as the Oddfellows or Friendly Societies. (In any ribbon society there was generally a prohibition against belonging to any other mutual organisation.) The Catholic Church was keen to maintain a monopoly on social organisations in Catholic communities. The taking of a secret oath was in direct contravention of church law. The ribbon societies themselves remained determined to avoid clerical interference.

There were also frequent tensions between the Liverpool societies and the Dublin leadership. The Liverpool associations found it difficult to make ends meet. There were just too many demands for their assistance, with such large numbers of Irish migrants passing through the city in search of casual work. Societies often relied upon the larger contributions of better off tradespeople and retailers to stay afloat. When such members left the associations, as happened, for example, following arrests in the late 1830s, their numbers and capability were much reduced.

Ribbon associations gave impetus to the existing pub culture, but also brought a sense of local and regional pride, a common feature of life in Ireland. As a result 'faction fights' became common. The strong ribbon networks from areas of sectarian conflict in Ireland – such as Co Armagh – may well have injected sectarian feelings into the community in Liverpool.

Perhaps the best known organisation to have emerged from this era is the Ancient Order of Hibernians (AOH), whose admission rituals, subscriptions, ceremonies and welfare brief testify to its ribbon origins. In the words of John Denvir: 'Members must be Catholic and Irish, or of Irish descent. They must be of good moral character, and were not to join in any secret societies contrary to the laws of the Catholic Church. They were to exercise hospitality towards their emigrant brothers and to protect their emigrant sisters from all harm and temptation.'[13] One of the key Hibernian objectives was to allow individual members to pay subscriptions towards burial costs, as there was a charge for burial in Catholic land. Another such society was the Orange Order, founded in Armagh in the 1790s, also with its own rituals and subscriptions, commitment to defend Protestant freedoms against Roman Catholicism and to support fellow members.

Irish participation in conventional politics was led by Kerryman Daniel O'Connell, the dominant figure in Irish politics in the first half of the nineteenth century. He was charismatic, a powerful and eloquent speaker, who built a nationwide network of local organisations, and an effective newspaper propaganda machine. His campaign for Catholic Emancipation – the right of Catholics to sit in Parliament – was supported by mass meetings in Ireland. In 1829 the movement succeeded – in the teeth of persistent opposition from George IV and the Duke of Wellington (Irishman Arthur Wellesley, the victor at Waterloo) – in winning for Catholics and other non-Anglicans, the right to sit in Parliament. He became known variously as 'the uncrowned King of Ireland', or 'The Liberator'. Despairing of the Whigs ever introducing reform in Ireland he now began campaigning for Home Rule (what we today would call devolution). Mass meetings agitating for constitutional change continued to be central to his campaign. The Repeal Association was to become another significant network within the Irish community in the 1830s. In contrast to the ribbon societies, it was an avowedly constitutional organisation, committed to acting within the law. It famously gathered funds through the 'repeal rent', collected outside churches each Sunday. The 'rent' went towards funding O'Connell's newspapers and campaign activities. Whilst Irish Catholic clergy held him in very high regard, the English Catholic clergy – many of them Empire supporters hostile to constitutional change – were often suspicious. In one famous incident in February 1841[14] the parish priest of St Patrick's, Park Place, Englishman Father Parker came into conflict with the Liverpool Repealers, and turned over their table outside the church, where they collected donations after mass. However powerful O'Connell may have been, Father Parker was determined to maintain his parochial authority.

O'Connell was popular in Liverpool and visited a number of times. He stayed at the Adelphi Hotel, went to mass in St Nicholas church nearby, and would address crowds from the hotel balcony.[15] On other occasions he lodged in Old Swan or with the Rathbones at Greenbank, in a house still standing near the present day Greenbank Park. On more than one occasion the monthly Liverpool contributions to his fund were higher than those of all equivalent groups in Ireland. His peaceful campaign for equal treatment under the law was met with derision in the Tory press. *The Liverpool Mail*, in an editorial on O'Connell, made the following assertion: 'One of the many obnoxious vices of popery is that where it prevails, it generates hosts of filthy and importunate mendicants – the vermin of the human race.'[16]

When he died in Italy in 1848 his body was eventually brought back to Ireland. In response to requests from the authorities – who feared widespread disorder should the body pass through Liverpool on its way to Dublin – his corpse rested in Chester before being transferred to a ship on the Birkenhead side of the Mersey. Many thousands crossed the river to pay their respects.

Irish Language

The Irish language was in daily use amongst many of the Irish in Liverpool in this period, though it is difficult to establish how widespread it was. Irish was the first language generally in the south and west of Ireland – encompassing at least half of the population – and a significant number of migrants came from those areas. Whilst many could speak both English and Irish, those facing the greatest challenge were those from more remote areas who could speak only Irish. This topic is dealt with in detail by Tony Birtill in his book *A Hidden History, Irish in Liverpool*.[17] He records that in 1842 a petition with some 24,000 signatures of Liverpool Irish Catholics was sent to the Vatican department known as the Congregation for the Propagation of the Faith. The petition had been organised by three Liverpool based Irishmen, cattle dealer Charles Leonard, publican Jack Langan – a champion boxer whose premises were close to the Clarence Dock gates – and Edmund Griffin, a customs officer.

'The petition claimed that very little was being done to help the Irish spiritually and that some English Catholics were even putting obstacles in the way of the few Irish priests who tried to help.'[18] One of the issues raised in the petition was the question of use of the Irish language.

'The main lack, the petitioners claimed, was of priests who could speak Gaelic, so that large numbers could not go to confession; even the mission of St Patrick's, built specifically for the Irish, had no Irish priest.'[19] Eventually Father Francis Murphy was appointed to meet the needs of Irish speakers in the area.

Abraham Hume was a Church of England clergyman who worked in the Vauxhall area from 1847 to 1884. He himself was Irish, a scholar and prolific writer. He carried out detailed research in the district, examining poverty, deprivation and family life. On finding that there were large numbers of Irish speakers he decided to learn the language himself, so as to be able to engage with this portion of the population. In his book 'Missions at Home', he published some detailed figures. He found that in the St Stephen's district 'out of 1,580 Catholic households … 869 of them spoke Irish and 711 English.' In the adjoining Vauxhall district of 1,142 families, 487 spoke Irish. At the heart of the Irish community in the north end, Lace Street, he found that 'out of 89 households, 78 were Irish speaking.' Of 90 families living in the courts running off Lace Street he found that 75 were Irish speaking.[20]

There was another Irish speaking area, in the south end of the city in the early and middle nineteenth century, centred on the core district around Crosbie Street. John Denvir remarks that 'nearly all in Crosbie Street were from the west of Ireland, and amongst them there was scarcely anything but Irish spoken.'[21] As to the extent to which Irish was in everyday use in Liverpool, Irish speakers have left no record. In the two 'core' Irish areas identified above, Irish undoubtedly was common, and it is likely that the language was spoken on the street amongst neighbours. In local shops and markets traders would no doubt have found it beneficial to be able to use the language, but there is no evidence of spoken or written Irish penetrating any deeper into mainstream Liverpool culture, administration or commerce.

Catholicism

The new arrivals from Ireland greatly increased the numbers of practising Catholics in Lancashire. The existing Catholic chapels in Liverpool were unable to meet the demand. The sight of crowds congregated around the outside of a chapel during Sunday mass was not unusual. The Irish Catholics were a stark contrast to the established Lancashire Catholic tradition, in which a small number of families – some with landed wealth – had remained committed to the old Catholic faith during the upheavals of the reformation and the passing of laws expunging Catholic rights. The more demonstrative Catholicism of the increasing numbers of Irish was often regarded with suspicion by the English Catholic community, which had, over generations, learned survival strategies within the English political environment. The often boisterous behaviour of the Irish raised the Catholic profile in public to a greater degree than the settled community would have wished. The largely middle class and well integrated local Catholic population was now outnumbered by the influx of poorer less well educated co-religionists, often bringing their own distinctive devotional practices.

By 1815 there were two large Catholic chapels, St Anthony's in Dryden Street and St Nicholas on Copperas Hill. Relations with the city authorities were on a better footing than had previously been the case. The consecration of St Nicholas – which was later to serve as a pro-cathedral until a more appropriate building was constructed in the twentieth century – was a remarkably harmonious affair, with the Lord Mayor attending High Mass. St Patrick's, Park Place, was opened in 1827, the new St Anthony's on Scotland Road in 1833 and St Oswald's, Old Swan in 1842. New arrivals continued to outpace these developments, and chapels remained overcrowded. Ad hoc premises were used to meet the needs, as new parishes were established, known in the first instance as 'missions'. Father Parker of St Patrick's, for example, in 1843 rented a 'penny theatre' on the corner of Blundell Street to say mass. Holy Cross parish also began in temporary premises. Once a congregation was established, fundraising and church building could follow.

Education

In the early nineteenth century there was little provision for the education of children, and what provision there was, was often no more than containment. Most received no formal education at all. Many children were working or engaged in family tasks during the day. Their only sight of education was at religious Sunday school once a week. It was estimated that about 60% of children aged five to fifteen were not attending week-day schools at this time.[22] One estimate from the 1830s was that 'there were then in Liverpool 244 dame schools'.[23] These were usually set up by women who used their home or any local rooms which became available. In return for a daily contribution small groups of children received basic tuition. There were about 5,000 children in these schools.

There were some more formal schools, usually with a male headteacher, who charged a fee for each pupil. Standards varied greatly from one institution to the next. Some schools were established and managed by charities, often in conjunction with churches. The first Catholic school was in Gerard Street off Byrom Street. It was opened in 1803 by the Benedictines. Such religious orders could provide education on a low budget, as they drew teaching staff from their own members, who were supported by the order. By 1821 the Catholic Charity Schools in Copperas Hill were well established, with 300 children in regular attendance. As the name suggests, this provision relied on donations from wealthy benefactors to construct or rent premises, provide equipment and meals, and employ staff. Dr Collins, giving evidence to Cornewall Lewis in 1833, stated that there was a large school being prepared at the north end, but that further provision was needed. However the additional schools could not be built 'for lack of funds.'[24] Reformers such as Robert Owen and the Liberal William Rathbone advocated an expansion of quality provision with state assistance, but most funding was left to voluntary organisations and churches.

In 1807 the Benevolent Society of St Patrick was established by wealthy benefactors to provide education for the children of Irish people in the city. (Their school building in Pleasant Street is standing to this day.) This school, though not under the management of any denomination, had the approval of both Catholic and non-Catholic clergy. By 1824 there were 504 children in attendance. In 1831 Thomas Wyse, MP visited the school. He was preparing education proposals for the elementary education system to be established in Ireland. The problem in Ireland was how could a government – Protestant in ethos – establish a state supported education system in Ireland, where the majority was Catholic? Wyse was very impressed by the system operated by the Benevolent Society.

'At Liverpool there exists a school, and it has existed for twenty years. Catholic and Protestant have been educated in perfect harmony together. Five thousand have issued from it; all provocation to religious dissention and rancour was sedulously kept away. Yet was their religious education neglected? Far from it; they were taught the Scriptures and catechism by their parents and pastors.'[25]

Originally established by the Benevolent Society of St Patrick, Pleasant Street School building is still standing. Photo: G. Quiery.

But such well managed schools could only cope with a minority of children. Church authorities were concerned that the Catholic education of the next generation was being neglected. Philanthropic campaigners were dismayed that there was so little provision for the education of the great majority. Liverpool Corporation was persuaded to establish provision, at the rate-payers expense. They opened the North and South Corporation Schools in the 1820s. However, the Anglican dominated Corporation insisted that only Anglican teaching would be permitted, with the result that parents who were not Anglican kept their children away. Calls for the system to be reformed were not addressed until after the Reform Act of 1832.

Employment

The Irish in Liverpool took up a wide variety of occupations. A significant proportion were single men and women, a group more inclined to migrate. Many harvest workers – a good number of them women – passed through the city each year, causing considerable commotion in the Irish quarters, on their way home 'with their pockets full'. For these rural folk there was the added excitement of their annual visit to a large city. Other migrants settled in the city for months, or even years before either returning home or staying permanently. One commentator tells us that: 'Irish unmarried men sometimes go back in the winter, and take their wages to their parents.'

An important source of employment for the Irish was the army. Travellers to Ireland were often asked whether there was 'any chance of a good war breaking out', and young Irish men were constantly arriving in Liverpool hoping to enlist. During the Napoleonic Wars Irish men responded to the call for increased enlistment for the expedition against France. Thus, only two years after the most widespread rebellion of the century in Ireland in 1798, large numbers were enlisting in the British army to fight for British interests on the Continent. Amongst the most distinguished regiments in the Peninsular War (1807-14) were the Connaught Rangers, who were later to be stationed in Liverpool.

For most Irish males in Liverpool the prospect was unskilled or semi-skilled labouring. One gentleman told the Cornewall Lewis committee that: 'The kind of work at which they are employed is usually of the roughest, coarsest and most repulsive description, and requiring the least practice.'[26] And again it was said that 'The bulk of the Irish population is formed of common-day labourers.' The building contractor Samuel Holme carried out a survey amongst those he described as 'the lowest sort' of Irish men, in 1834, in order to discover their occupations.[27] His findings are in the chart below.

Mechanics	780
Brickmakers	270
Sugar-boilers	200
Mason's labourers	350
Bricklayer's labourers	850
In chemical works and soaperies	600
Sawyers	80
Labourers employed in smithies and lime kilns plasterers yards and by paviors	340
Lumpers about the docks who discharge vessels and reload	1,700
Porters employed in warehousing goods etc	1,900
Coalheavers and other sundry employment	430
TOTAL	7,500

How accurate or inclusive this survey was is difficult to say. However it does provide a snapshot of occupations, almost all unskilled and involving strenuous labour. Many of these occupations were in very poor and unhealthy working conditions, including sugar-boiling and chemical works. Dock work could often be extremely dangerous, especially in wet weather when material was shifted along narrow gang planks from ship to shore. Lumpers were people who worked in sub-contracting gangs on the docks, the group being paid a lump sum per job however long it took to complete. Lumpers might also include those working on digging out new docks. Here gangs were paid by the amount of soil they shifted. Curiously there is no account of the numbers employed at sea, possibly because so many were absent. Occupations such as coal heavers, and many of the jobs on the docks, could only be carried out by men who were young and fit. As the unskilled worker grew older his options decreased considerably. The effect of so many men arriving to compete for these unskilled or semi-skilled jobs was to increase competition for work, and depress wages. One witness to Cornewall Lewis stated that the Irish, being used to living on so little, could manage better on poor wages.

Most Irish workers did not have the appropriate skills for the urban environment. Many specialist occupations, such as carpenters in the ship yard, were effectively a closed shop, with positions passing from father to son. There were skilled Irish workers, such as weavers, who moved to England in increasing numbers as Irish industry continued to decline, but such workers were unlikely to find work matched to their abilities in Liverpool, and headed for the cotton mills of Lancashire.

In the casual environment on the docks there was never a regular work routine. There was no financial security under the system, little opportunity to plan or save, no unionisation, and little possibility of achieving higher status jobs or additional skills. Families trapped in these occupations were very slow to advance in the world or improve their prospects. It was a marginalised and precarious existence.

Most Irish women found work where they could as casual or semi-skilled workers. We can derive some idea of the hardships endured by such women through examination of the life of Kitty Wilkinson.[28] She was born in Derry in 1786 and came to Liverpool in 1804. She was capable and educated, but could only find work as a domestic servant. Her income was used to support her mother who had fallen ill. She then opened a school where she taught reading and sewing – a dame school; the sort of place where the children of poor Irish emigrants could gain a basic education. The school did not succeed. Her mother was living on the premises and the nature of her illness proved too distracting. Kitty resorted to collecting manure, which she stored in a hole in a field, before selling it to farmers. Her first husband was a sailor, who later died at sea. He was away at the time of the birth of their first child, while she was working as a domestic char woman. At the time of the birth her employer found her starving at home, having had nothing to eat for two days. She returned to work, this time in a nail factory, where hot metal was picked by hand and hammered into shape. Her hands became so blistered and disfigured from the heat of the nails she had to leave. Kitty not only endured hardship, with nothing by way of public provision to assist her, but was also forced to turn her hand to a wide variety of unpleasant and often unhealthy occupations. Her experience typifies the life of many women at this time, surviving on their own, relying on others in the locality for support. There were those whose husbands, faced with the challenge of rearing a family in such tough conditions, simply left, or never returned from a sea voyage. Many lost their partner in life through accident and disease. Others had become pregnant outside marriage and were forced by social conventions to leave their native parish in Ireland. Many such came to Liverpool, where they took their place amongst the very poorest. Some single women sought domestic work, but it was not an easy option, nor was it to everyone's taste. Opening up hostel accommodation, or taking in lodgers was another source of income.

Women looked for any opportunity to supplement the family income, including piecework – such as needlework or laundering – which would be collected by an agent from their door. Setting up a market stall was another option, hawking fish, vegetables or cheap goods. There was work for women in laborious physical tasks, such as the processing of cotton or the repetitive oakum picking (pulling apart old ropes so that the material could be used for caulking (blocking) the holes in ships). To allow women to take up such work, neighbours co-operated over child minding and caring for the sick and elderly.

Housing and Health

Liverpool was a seaport with a large transitory population. There were many hostels close to the waterfront catering not just for those preparing to board ship, but also those – particularly single persons – working locally. Accommodation was cheap, conditions basic. Census returns show that many householders had longer term lodgers who shared the premises, paid a rent and had meals with the family. Those arriving from Ireland were frequently accommodated by relatives already settled in Liverpool. Elderly relatives, or brothers and sisters – often with their wife or husband – were found a bed in a room somewhere in the house. In addition there were commercial lodging houses, where landladies would provide accommodation and a daily meal in a large dwelling house. There were several thousand of these in Liverpool, many of them run by Irish people. Though licensed, they were seldom inspected and were frequently overcrowded.

Those with steady skilled employment lived in terraced housing with reasonable facilities, including running water and fireplaces in each room. In Seel Street for example, in the 1830s Ellen McDonough had a cooperage (making barrels) at number 53, while Thomas Carey at number 48 was described as a gentleman.

The least fortunate were those who lived in the notorious court and cellar dwellings. These were designed to extract as much income as possible from a small patch of land, in a city where people could not afford high rents. Court housing had only been profitable through squeezing the greatest number of tenants into the smallest possible space. In the early 1840s there were about 3,000 courts in Liverpool, with about 55,000 people living in 18,000 dwellings. Duncan estimated that in the early 1840s there were about 87,000 people in Liverpool living in about 2,000 courts, and that there were about 8,000 inhabited cellars with 35,000 living in them.[29] Rooms in Liverpool were smaller than those in Birmingham or Bristol, and in the districts where courts were common, overcrowding was greater than anywhere else in Britain. The Unitarian J.H. Thom observed that 'there are more courts in Liverpool than in other towns … the average size of a court in Birmingham is twelve times the size of a court in Liverpool.'

'Our corporate bodies as well as private individuals have been accessory to the cutting up of the ground by square inches in order to make money by packing human beings together as if they were cotton bales. The highest possible price has been screwed out of building land … The supreme right of property is at all events in towns an evil of the most enormous magnitude.'[30] 'Hence arose subdivisions of mean narrow streets filled with close gloomy courts, into which as many dwellings as possible were packed, irrespective of light or air.' A large proportion of those living in such conditions were Irish.

Typically a court would be accessed via an alleyway squeezed between two warehouses or workshop buildings. Often these alleys were covered, giving the impression of entering a damp cave. At the end of the alley – sometimes so narrow that those entering had to squeeze past anyone coming in the opposite direction – the high walls on either side would eventually open out to terraces of five or six dismal houses in facing rows, each house two or three storeys high, with a roughly paved court area between rows. There might be a family in each house, making some ten to twelve families in total. Many courts were even more densely packed, sometimes with a family to each floor, and even in the cellars.

Many courts, whilst accommodating large numbers of residents, were constructed without a proper water supply. Residents were expected to share one water pump in the centre of the court. All water for drinking, washing and food preparation had to be collected in vessels at this tap and carried indoors. There were frequent crises in the provision of water, and it was not unusual for the water supply to a court to be cut off for extended periods. Although the city council had had the power since 1786 to supply water, they had little interest in the courts. In most cases extending supply to the courts would have been a comparatively simple matter, as often there was already piped water in the houses nearby. The sharing of just one or two toilets by all the men and women in the court was another problem, as residents suffered the indignity of queueing, paper in hand, for their turn. Some toilets were based on a seepage system, even though seepage was limited in Liverpool clay. Others relied on the scavengers, whose duty it was to remove toilet waste. Liverpool's first Medical Officer of Health, Duncan stated: 'Ashpits and privies were infrequently emptied and their contents consequently often spread over the court. I do not know of a single court,' he says, 'which communicates with the street or sewer with a covered drain.'[31]

With diseases such as diarrhoea and dysentery – a similar but more severe illness – being common,[32] we can only guess at the conditions endured by the population. In addition there was the problem of disposing of waste material, including food scraps. Rats were endemic. The court houses had no back doors, and often no windows at the rear of the house. Everything had to go through the front and down the alley. The dwellings were dark, damp and cold.

However, even the miserable courts had their own hierarchy of deprivation. Appalling though conditions were above ground, those who lived in the cellars endured even greater hardships. In addition to the cold and dark, drainage was often a problem.

The campaigner Dr Duncan described these cellars in 1844, as follows: 'The cellars are ten or twelve feet square, generally flagged – but frequently having only the bare earth for a floor, and sometimes less than six feet in height. There is frequently no window; so that light and air can gain access to the cellars only by the door, the top of which is often not higher than the level of the street … There is sometimes a back cellar, used as a sleeping apartment, having no direct communication with the external atmosphere, and deriving its scanty supply of light and air solely from the first apartment.'[33]

Rainwater would on occasions flood the cellars, and was often slow to seep away. On occasion, landlords were told that cellars were condemned because the ceiling was too low. The solution to this problem was to lower the floor level by digging deeper into the clay. There are many accounts of visits to cellars where residents are found lying on damp bedding, which could only be reached by crossing the pools of water permanently on the floor. Often bricks were positioned to allow people to avoid pools by hopping from one to another. If there was a heavy downpour during the night, rain water from the rooftops would often find its way through the drainage system down into the cellar, often drenching the residents sleeping there. In those cellars next to the privy, raw sewage would seep through the walls. Illness was rife. Life expectancy was low.

Calls for reform were resisted by the landed interest. There was scrutiny of a sort from The Poor Law Commissioners who published their landmark Report on the Sanitary State of the Labouring Classes of Great Britain in 1842, revealing the scandalous conditions in towns, including Liverpool. Campaigners such as Edwin Chadwick and Dr Henry Duncan had been working for years to highlight the problem. Population density in parts of Liverpool – calculated to be the equivalent of 460,000 per square mile – was twice that of London.

This sketch by Bruce Scott of a court in 1950s Liverpool illustrates the open drainage, the narrow passageway and density of housing.

In such conditions infectious diseases spread quickly. In 1832 cholera broke out. It is a disease of the intestine, which causes severe diarrhoea and vomiting. Transmission is through infected drinking water or food products. The advent of the disease spread terror in Liverpool, as the way in which it spread was not then known. Mortality rates were high, and everyone feared for their lives. The authorities had no effective method of combating the disease. About 5,000 persons were affected, with 1,500 deaths, before the epidemic receded. It was during this crisis that Kitty Wilkinson initiated a common sense public health practice which saved many lives. Using only a small boiler in her house in Dennison Street, near the Clarence Dock, she began thoroughly washing clothing and bedding in hot water, believing this might well combat whatever it was that was causing the disease. She was correct. Those in her street escaped the worst of the epidemic. Public policy eventually caught up with her initiative, as public washing and bath facilities were opened, first in Liverpool and then across the country. (See biographical details – Appendix One.)

Detail from the stained glass window in the Lady Chapel, Liverpool Anglican Cathedral, commemorating Agnes Jones who was appointed Superintendent of the Liverpool Workhouse Infirmary in 1834, at the instigation of the Rathbones. She transformed conditions there before falling fatally ill from exhaustion in 1868. See biography in Appendix One. Photo: Simon Rahilly.

During the outbreak the authorities were convinced that the dead bodies of infected persons carried a risk. Local laws required the bodies to be immediately removed from residential areas for quick burial. Within the Irish community there was a custom of 'waking' the dead. The body would remain in the house for a number of days, while neighbours and relatives gathered around to reminisce and pay their last respects. In some cases police were required to enforce the regulation that bodies be removed. Apart from the violation of custom and practice, there was a suspicion that the bodies would be sold on to 'bodysnatchers' who would profit by selling them to medical institutions. Such fears were not without substance, as just a few years before William Gill had been found guilty of running a grave robbing network around Liverpool, following the discovery of no less than thirty-three bodies at the docks, a shipment intended for the dissecting rooms in the anatomy school in Edinburgh. The confiscations of bodies led to disorder, known as the 'cholera riots' which pitted the Irish community against the police.[34] The epidemic eventually receded, but as insanitary conditions persisted in the city, the disease was destined to return.

Kitty Wilkinson's head stone in the shadow of Liverpool Anglican Cathedral. Photo: G. Quiery.

Sectarian Conflict

The arrival of Irish Catholics in large numbers created tensions in the city, and raised the likelihood of open conflict. Whilst there had been isolated sectarian incidents – such as the burning of the Edmund Street chapel in 1775 – sectarianism as a built-in component of political life and public discourse, along with provocative annual rituals, did not flourish at first.

Both Protestant and Catholic communities were vulnerable to the exploitation of their fears and beliefs. The majority had little or no education, were subject to poverty and economic hardship, and lacked job security. The Catholic Irish had a deep regard for their religion which many practised regularly. Any affront to their beliefs was experienced as a personal insult. Having come from an environment which was exclusively Catholic they were at first shocked by the open, vigorous and enthusiastic assaults in the press and at public meetings upon beliefs which they held sacred and whose immutability they took for granted. They were hostile towards the established church in any case. They had been forced to pay taxes to support the Anglican Church of Ireland at home, whilst their own church went without funding. The established church was part of the British state which was the instrument of their subjection in Ireland. Expressions of nationalism, closely linked to sectarian feeling, ran deep and were easily aroused.

At the same time the Irish community did not have an organised political structure through which to respond to local issues affecting them. They were locked out of the politics of the city, as were the majority of citizens, through the exclusiveness and patronage of the existing electoral system. The frustration brought about by such impotence led to a political vacuum, which was easily filled by secret organisations and ad hoc activity on the streets.

Many Protestants were fearful. Catholics were seen as disloyal, having historically been involved in attempts to subvert the existing order. Their first loyalty was to Rome rather than to the institutions of the British Protestant state – the Crown, the Church and the Empire. Priests were believed responsible for the duping and exploitation of a gullible, compliant and superstitious peasantry.

These fears are succinctly and vigorously expressed in the following: 'The priests are the authors and instigators of this abominable system. The peasant is merely the priest's dupe and tool ... These men in every social and political relation of life are the enemies of England. Driven by an incendiary and rapacious priesthood, they usurp the power of law, laugh at Acts of Parliament, create votes by perjury, and glory in the increased power they derive from flagitious corruption and demoralisation'.[35]

Many harboured or promulgated even stranger attitudes towards Catholicism. A Protestant group active in Liverpool at this time was the Ladies Irish Island Society, founded with the purpose of spreading the true word of God amongst 'our deluded Irish fellow subjects'.[36] They were once addressed by a speaker who asserted that inhabitants of an island off the west coast of Ireland worshipped the Virgin Mary as a fish.[37]

Those working class and artisan Protestants who felt threatened by social and economic change were the ones most vulnerable to anti-Catholic rhetoric. For them associations such as the Orange Order offered a secure place in society, commitment to traditional values, and political and economic protection. Many feared that the Irish were taking jobs, driving down wages and competing for housing.

Political events, especially anything seen as advancing the Catholic cause, were often the catalyst for trouble. In 1807 the sitting MP, William Roscoe was defeated in the parliamentary election by Banastre Tarleton, whose campaign slogan was 'Church and slave trade forever'. The slogan appealed to the narrow self-interest of artisan voters, such as shipyard workers. Catholic rights was another emotive issue. In the same election Roscoe was attacked by unemployed sailors, who feared for their livelihood and were wary of the power of Catholicism. The prolonged and ultimately successful campaign for Catholic emancipation, which Roscoe supported, served to raise the profile of sectarian conflict, confirmed Protestant fears and required politicians to take sides. Daniel O'Connell's meetings in Liverpool – where he was often the guest of Liberals – did nothing to quell these fears.

The anti-Catholic Orange Order was built up in Liverpool over a long period of time, and was an important contributory factor in exacerbating religious tensions. The Order was founded in Co Armagh in the north of Ireland in 1795, at a time of growing sectarianism and advancing republicanism. Orange lodges began appearing in Lancashire in the early 1800s. Most were associated with regiments which had been involved in Ireland at the time of the 1798 Rising. They were founded on a fear of the power of Catholicism, and the Catholic powers on the continent. Lodges were also founded in the Lancashire cotton towns, perhaps as a result of Irish Protestant workers coming there for jobs. The first Orange march in Liverpool took place in 1819,[38] and resulted in a riot. The march was organised by Ralph Fletcher and his colleagues, Manchester based Orangemen. Fletcher had a lifelong association with extreme groups around Lancashire, and frequently advocated violence for political ends. The marches, which had been openly provocative to the Catholic community, were attacked by Irish crowds. The Orange Order in Liverpool, though now established, stagnated for the following decade. However, regular conflicts between Protestants and Catholics continued, especially around 12 July, Orangemen's Day. Certain public houses – such as the Wheatsheaf on Scotland Road – became associated with Orange meetings. The large annual Irish marches on St Patrick's Day were also an occasion for communal tension.

Whilst inter-communal street violence was the most obvious way in which sectarian tensions became evident, sectarian attitudes permeated every aspect of life in the city. Public appointments were a regular battleground. In Liverpool the oddly named Select Vestry was the body which administered the Poor Law and the Workhouse. The Board was exclusively Anglican. In one incident Father Parker – Catholic priest at St Patrick's – testified that he: 'had heard the master of the workhouse school addressing the children in the school room, saying that every Catholic would go to hell'.[39] Catholic services were forbidden. Catholic residents, many of them ill, were required to leave the building on Sundays to attend mass at the nearest Catholic church. One side effect of this rule was that additional numbers declared themselves Catholic, in order to have the opportunity to get out, some returning later in the day in a state of drunkenness. Dr McNeile, the Anglican clergyman renowned for his illiberal views, was extremely influential in the Vestry decision that no Catholic service of any kind be allowed on the premises. Protestant ultras such as McNeile felt a sense of betrayal when Catholic emancipation was finally granted in the Catholic Relief Act of 1829.

As sectarian animosity steadily increased, the Reform Act of 1832 was to create a situation in which tensions and divisions were further exacerbated, and sectarian practice was to become more deeply embedded in Liverpool life and politics.

TIMELINE – NINETEENTH CENTURY

1807	Abolition of Slave Trade Act passed. UK.
1813	Pride and Prejudice published.
1815	Battle of Waterloo.
1818	Black Ball Line begins regular package sailing to America.
1830	Opening of Liverpool – Manchester railway.
1837	Samuel Morse patents his electrical telegraph.
1847	Publication of Wuthering Heights – Emily Bronte.
1854	St George's Hall, Liverpool, opened.
1858	First trans-Atlantic cable laid.
1859	Origin of Species by Charles Darwin published.
1865	Louis Pasteur patents his method of killing bacteria.
1865	Aerial panorama map of Liverpool created by local artists.
1867	Alfred Nobel patents dynamite.
1872	George Eliot (Mary Evans) published Middlemarch.
1876	Alexander Bell patents telephone.
1886	Railway tunnel under the Mersey opened.
1886	Benz patents motor vehicle driven by internal combustion engine.
1889	First motion picture.
1893	New Zealand introduces votes for women.
1895	Oscar Wilde imprisoned for gross indecency.
1898	War of the Worlds by H.G. Wells published.

CHAPTER THREE

THE 1832 REFORM ACT AND ITS CONSEQUENCES

Before the 1832 Reform Act, politics in Liverpool was under the control of the city's Freemen, a self-perpetuating group comprising about 10% of the male population, who served for life, passed on the right to vote to their sons, and elected new Freemen to their own ranks. They elected 41 councillors, almost all Anglican in religion. Only Freemen could vote in local elections or stand for office. They enjoyed substantial concessions – such as exemption from local taxes and port dues – and they were invariably Tory. It was an outdated and corrupt system, a relic of an earlier age, redundant now in a city of over 300,000. It wasn't only in the electoral system that reform was urgently needed. Water supply, sewage, housing, cellar dwellings, education and poor law provision all needed root and branch reform.

It was not just in Liverpool that change was demanded. There was a restless, even rebellious mood across the country. Although the coercive Combination Acts were used to suppress organised opposition, protest and disorder were becoming more common. There was widespread dissatisfaction with the narrowness of the franchise. In 1828 O'Connell's vocal campaign and mass meetings had won for Catholics the right to sit in parliament. Yet only a tiny minority could vote. Many important towns and cities had no representation at all in a parliament which had remained unreformed since before the industrial revolution. Birmingham and Manchester, for example, had no MPs. Lords of the manor, landed gentry, Anglican clergy and other establishment figures dominated the legislature. When Wellington spoke out against reform in 1832 he was defeated in parliament. The new reforming group – the Whigs (fore runners of the modern Liberal Party) – with a majority of just one, decided to call an election. They won, with a large majority, and brought forward an electoral reform bill which was rejected by the Lords. Protests and rioting followed. Bristol town hall was burned down. The King – himself opposed to reform – wanted to bring Wellington back. It was the last time a British monarch made such an autocratic appointment. He was advised to submit to public opinion, and yielded. The House of Lords, threatened with an avalanche of new Whig peerages to wipe out the Tory majority in the unelected chamber, allowed the Representation of the People Act to pass, thus opening the way for a very different parliament.

The wave of reforming legislation which followed was to have a great and lasting impact on Liverpool, though not always in the ways that might have been anticipated.

The appointment of new government commissioners to carry out an investigation into corruption in Liverpool resulted in a reformed council structure, with a wider franchise to include rate payers. The next decade saw not only the reform of Liverpool Corporation, but also a series of Acts of Parliament, sponsored by the city authorities, to improve housing, sanitation and water supply. Poor law administration – in Liverpool the Select Vestry – was also overhauled.

When the first elections under the new system took place in 1835, there was the distinct possibility that for the first time control of the council would be wrested from the Tory establishment. The Liberals, mainly self-made business people, merchants and traders, were the opposition. Their support included non-conformists such as Baptists, Methodists, Unitarians, Quakers and Moravians. These were all minority groups who felt themselves excluded. The Irish were certainly in this category, and generally had hopes that Liberal rule would improve their lot. But Liberal support for the abolition of slavery earlier in the century had made them unpopular amongst certain sections of the electorate, as many in Liverpool – such as seamen and ship builders – considered that slavery was in their economic interest. When the new administration at Westminster abolished slavery in the Empire (1833) they alienated many Liverpool voters.

There was intense excitement leading up to the first ever open election of city councillors. Leaflets and posters were distributed widely, reform songs were written and sung, and there was much activity on the streets. This excitement was transmitted into the Irish community. The Liberals were keen to make the point that the Irish were not a menace to public safety or a threat to the existing order. But the activities during the weeks before 12 July that year undermined this argument.

Rumours that there was to be an Orange procession swept the Irish districts. Although no Orange march took place, the protest against it went ahead anyhow. Large crowds gathered in the Irish area around Tithebarn Street and Vauxhall. There was little trouble during the day, but that night, after people had been drinking and milling around, disorder broke out. It spread quickly to the Great Crosshall Street area, and soon there was a full-scale riot.[1] The night watch was reinforced, but the number and ferocity of the crowd was too great for them. The watchmen took refuge in the Bridewell, which was surrounded by an estimated 2,000. The superintendent of the night watch, Michael Whitty, was nearby in the fire station at Hatton Garden. He was 'a Catholic Irishman of powerful build and great courage'.[2] He arrived with watch officers from other parts of the town. He succeeded in driving the rioters away from the Bridewell, but they soon regrouped and attacked again. Whitty was later joined by 100 men of the dock police, and 200 troops before the situation was brought under control.

The following day crowds gathered again in the Irish area in the south of the town, around Park Lane. Many were armed with sticks and other weapons. There were skirmishes with the police. Those arrested the day before were moved to the comparative security of the main Bridewell, as it was feared that the crowd might try to release them. Batches of special constables were sworn in – some 500 in all – and more troops were called upon. By that evening the situation was again brought under control, and the worst disturbances Liverpool had seen until that point had come to an uneasy conclusion.

The *Liverpool Mercury*, the more moderate of the local papers averred: 'The peaceful inhabitants of the town were endangered by a most lawless and savage excitement leading up to the election, by a series of riots, in which the lowest orders of the Irish residents were the principal, or indeed the only actors.'[3]

When the elections took place the following December, the Liberals, so long excluded from municipal control, swept to power, winning 45 out of the 50 available seats.[4] One of those elected was the wealthy Irish Catholic Richard Sheil, who stood in the Scotland Ward. A new era was ushered in. The new Council had a broad programme of reforms. On the agenda were sanitation, housing, policing and reorganisation in education.

The Schools Dispute
The new Liberal administration was to be short lived. A significant factor in its eventual defeat was the issue which arose from its education policy, and in particular their determination to include all children – the children of Irish Catholics amongst them – in the city's school provision. A new education committee was established, with William Rathbone in the Chair. In addition to the Liberal majority, there were Anglican, Catholic and dissenter representatives. They seemed unaware of the hornet's nest they were about to disturb. They decided on a new curriculum in the corporation schools.

Although provided for from the public purse, the two schools – opened in 1827 – had long been dominated by Anglican clergy, with the result that in time almost all the children in the schools were of the Anglican persuasion. Other denominations were effectively excluded.

Rathbone now oversaw negotiations between representatives of the various denominations – Anglicans included – to establish an agreed set of scriptural and religious readings which could be used in school assemblies. It was to be a system very similar to that in use in the Benevolent Society of St Patrick's school, Pleasant Street, referred to earlier. Children were to receive religious instruction in the faith nominated by their parents, in the hour immediately after school on certain days. The Irish Commissioners of Education obliged with a selection of readings already in use there. Arrangements were made to allow clergy from each denomination to come into the schools to teach children of their faith at times set aside for religious instruction.

Once these measures were adopted there was uproar amongst the

Anglican clergy. They withdrew their services from the two schools and initiated a campaign against the new system. Irishman Hugh McNeile 'the O'Connell of Protestantism'[5], a vocal founder member of the recently formed Protestant Association, led the charge. He objected to versions of the bible other than the Anglican being used in the schools. It was through his letters to the press and campaign pamphlets rather than through publicity circulated by the Education Committee, that most people first learned about the new system. The Liberals, lacking the political 'nous' of the Tories, were outflanked by opposition propaganda – a pattern that was to be repeated many times in Liverpool politics in the years to come.

At an excited public meeting in the Amphitheatre – where the Royal Court theatre stands today – shortly after the Liberals established the new school regulations, Hugh McNeile boldly appealed for funds to open rival schools, and £3,000 was promised on the spot, an amount which in a few days increased to £10,000. Anglican parents were persuaded to withdraw their children. North and South Corporation schools were left almost empty. The temporary buildings which the churchmen had taken instead were crowded to the doors. In time the vacant places in the Corporation schools were filled by the children of parents from other denominations, including Irish Catholics.

The parliamentary election the following year became known as 'the bible election'. Tories were quick to see the potential of the issue, with the result that a vigorous and ruthless campaign was initiated, which was to have far reaching social and political effects. McNeile's catch phrase was that 'the bible has been expelled.' This was of course patently untrue, and for this reason the Liberals – inexperienced in politics – assumed that it would not be believed. They considered that the self-evident truth of their case would be enough to confound McNeile and the Tories. McNeile and his coterie carried their campaign forward from the pulpit, at public meetings and in the press. 'In numerous pamphlets, newspaper articles and speeches, the policy of the Council was attacked or defended. Some of the pamphlets were little more than prolonged diatribes against the Roman Catholic Church, conventionally described as the whore of Babylon, the mother of harlots etc.'[6]

Charles Trevelyan, when visiting Liverpool in 1840 heard McNeile preaching, and was horrified. According to Trevelyan, McNeile's theme was that: 'The time has come when everyone must choose between God's side and the devil's. We must fight even unto death. We must lay down our lives rather than submit. The struggle was to end only in the subjection either of Catholics or Protestants.'[7]

McNeile's beliefs can be summarised in his own words: 'Popery is a double evil. It is a political evil, for it enslaves instead of giving liberty. It is a religious evil, for its creed is false and it withholds the scriptures from the people …'[8]

McNeile always maintained that his inflammatory speeches were directed against the Catholic religion, and not against individual Catholics, but it is evident that this subtle distinction was not well understood by large numbers of his followers. The less intemperate Anglican clergy were motivated by a genuine belief in the evils of Catholicism. Such was their political influence that Tory politicians had to align with them at election times. In the words of Frank Neal: 'No potential Tory councillor could hope to achieve public office unless he established himself in McNeile's eyes as a 'sound Protestant'.[9]

The Tories were unscrupulous in their use of the schools issue at parliamentary and local elections during the following years. Samuel Holme, for example, a wealthy builder, in an address to the Liverpool Operative Conservative Association in 1836 asked his audience,

'Did they wish that the children of their poorer neighbours should be educated upon strict scriptural principle, or did they wish that the word of the eternal God should be expelled from their schools?'[10] The issue gained national publicity. It came to be generally believed that the bible was now not to be used in Liverpool schools.

By 1837 the atmosphere had deteriorated to such an extent that rioting broke out during the general election in July. Large crowds of Irish gathered in both the Vauxhall and Park Lane areas. As in 1835, the police were led by Irishman Michael J. Whitty. Rioting continued throughout the day. To make matters worse Protestant gangs from the area around Parliament Street went on the rampage around the mainly Irish Catholic areas of Crosbie Street and New Bird Street 'attacking anyone who wore Liberal colours and, more ominously, seeking out Irishmen for special treatment.'[11]

In 1839 the ultra-Conservative Dr Sleigh, who had been appointed editor of the conservative minded Liverpool Standard, was dismayed to learn that Protestants were withdrawing their children from the 'unscriptural' schools. He wrote a number of editorials denouncing the Liberals, only to discover later – through William Rathbone – that not only was the Bible not excluded, but it was actually taught in the schools. When he had the good grace to withdraw his former remarks, he was dismissed from his editorship of the Standard.

During this prolonged campaign against the Liberal schools policy, links were cemented between the fundamentalist preachers, Protestant organisations and the Tory Party. Such links were to contribute to long term Tory dominance, and long term sectarian tensions. Branches of the Protestant Association were formed, largely through McNeile's efforts. The importance of Protestant democracy was emphasised, and increasing numbers of local Tory politicians would come to rely upon membership of the Orange Order to secure advancement. No Popery campaign speeches became a regular feature of local elections.

A guided walk outside the remains of the North Corporation School. October 2015.

During the Corn Laws agitation of the early 1840s street disorder broke out once more. Churches became targets, as did public houses frequented by one side or the other. Individuals were attacked in the street. Provocative gestures such as Orange bands and the wearing of party colours became more common. In the election campaign of that year with the Tories on the verge of regaining control of the council, Protestant and Irish mobs turned on the police. The Irish first introduced the tactic – which was to be a feature of Liverpool rioting in years to come – of mounting the roof tops, to hurl slates down on the police below, resulting in the death of a Protestant man.[12] Frank Neal describes some of the incidents which took place on 12 July 1841.

'Throughout the day there were small but vicious confrontations. Characteristic was the incident in which two men known to be Protestants were pursued by an Irish mob who assumed they were Orangemen. The two took refuge in a house of a courageous Irishwoman, but the door was beaten down. One man escaped over the back wall, but the other, a carpenter, was dragged out and badly beaten up. Elsewhere gangs of carpenters were roaming the town looking for Irishmen who, when found, were given similar treatment. Another carpenter was badly beaten in Lime Street by a large gang of Irish while a large mob of Protestants ran down Mount Pleasant shouting, 'We're Orangemen – we'll have No Popery – down with the Popery Bible'.[13]

Even little children, '… were seen running about the street with red paper flags containing mottoes about the Church, the Queen and scriptural education.' When the rioting was finally quelled, the police were exhausted. Whitty had spent most of the day on his horse being pelted with bricks and stones. When the Conservative Councillor Holmes levelled criticism at Whitty in the Watch Committee, it was suggested that in future elections Mr Holmes be appointed superintendent of police, an offer Mr Holmes was quick to decline.

'The No Popery campaign, initiated in 1835, had paid handsome political dividends.'[14] The Conservatives finally won back control of the council in 1841. In January 1842 they introduced new rules for the Corporation Schools, providing for the instruction of the children in the doctrines of the Church of England. 'As soon as the regulations of the new Committee came into force … almost all of the 936 Roman Catholic children in attendance were withdrawn.'[15]

Sectarianism was now a permanent mechanism in Tory politics, and a feature of local elections. There was an ultra-Protestant caucus on the council, a vigorous group of evangelical clergy and a growing Orange Order. Those who had so assiduously fanned the embers of sectarian bigotry now found that the flames, which at times threatened to engulf the city, could not be so easily doused.

In the words of the Liberal inclined *Liverpool Mercury*: 'Such are the fruits of the 'no Popery' harangues whereby week by week the pulpits of some of the churches of this town are desecrated. Such are the fruits of the seeds of discord which have been sown by those who profess to be followers of 'The Prince of Peace'.[16] Year by year sectarian violence continued in the city, stimulated by inflammatory preachers and social and political events. The magistrate Edward Rushton, the son of a well-known Liverpool radical: 'made himself unpopular with Orangemen by taking a tough line on Orange Parades'.[16] The annual processions associated with 17 March (St Patrick's Day) and 12 July were invariably occasions of tension.

The newly inflamed sectarian attitudes also permeated the Select Vestry elections. In a city where inequality was so stark, one might have thought that reform would introduce more generous provision. Yet the Poor Law Amendment Act of 1834 was passed because of concerns that existing provision was too generous. Claimants would now have to be destitute, rather than just poor, and would have to reside in the workhouse, where conditions were so appalling that very few would consent. The Liverpool Select Vestry were able to show the commissioners that they were already paying an extremely low rate to claimants. While the national average in 1832/3 was 9s 9d per head, in Liverpool it was only 4s.[17]

In the more divisive political atmosphere, elections to the Vestry committee were now keenly contested. McNeile was determined to ensure that Catholicism did not get a foothold. It was 1845 before an alliance of Liberals and Catholics managed to get three candidates elected. That year the Vestry decided 'in obedience to Dr McNeill (sic) that no religious service of any kind for the Roman Catholics should be permitted inside the workhouse.'[18] Irish Catholics worked in alliance with the Liberals as their campaign against such attitudes continued. They secured 11 Vestry places at the next election, with one of their number John Yates becoming the first Catholic Poor Law Guardian. In 1850 there were about 3,300 in the workhouse, of which about 1,300 were Catholic. Proposals put forward by Mr James Whitty, a leading member of the Catholic group on the Vestry board, that a room be set aside for Catholics to hear mass in the workhouse, that a Catholic version of the bible be allowed, and that a teacher be engaged to instruct Catholic children, were all rejected with regularity.

Sectarianism was also evident in the police service. A career in the police provided secure and relatively well paid work, making the service an obvious target for networks such as the Orange Order, based as they often were on mutual advancement and preferential treatment for members. Many suspected Orange infiltration of the police. Following repeated attacks on St Patrick's church, Park Place in the 1840s, the magistrates became concerned that the police were not doing enough to protect Catholic premises. The leading magistrate, Rushton, and the Liberal William Rathbone became involved in a stand-off with the Watch Committee. Rushton was committed to working to achieve fair play before the law. His father, also Edward Rushton, although blind, had been extremely active in local affairs, campaigning against slavery and in favour of the republican cause in the 1790s. Rushton junior made himself unpopular with Orangemen by taking a tough line on the holding of Orange parades and the flying of flags and banners which could be offensive to Catholics.[19] He worked in conjunction with the Mayor, often by-passing the Watch Committee which oversaw the police. There were frequent allegations of police bias against the Irish. The Grand Master of the Orange Order was an influential member of the Watch Committee. In 1844 he instructed the committee to ascertain the religion of each police officer. Why he took this step was not clear, but the suspicion was that it was with a view to removing those who were Catholic.

Rushton responded with a threat to remove from the force: 'all members of illegal societies'. There were allegations that over 60 police officers were in the Orange Order. Following a meeting between Rushton, the Mayor and the Town Clerk, it was resolved that any police officer who was a member of the Orange Order should be dismissed.[21] How effective this measure ever was is hard to say, but allegations continued, and sectarian tensions remained within the Liverpool police service.

Liberal Reforms

The Liverpool Liberal administration of the 1830s sponsored a series of radical Acts of Parliament, which impacted on the welfare of the Irish community. These included the Liverpool Improvement Act, the Liverpool Building Act and the Liverpool Sanitary Act. These reforms brought to an end the confusing and bureaucratic system of overlapping authorities which had existed until then, vesting responsibility with the City Council, which discharged its duties through the newly established Health Committee. The Committee oversaw a programme of sewage construction, and changes to the building regulations, requiring, amongst other things, better ventilation, wider entrances to courts, and a greater distance between the facing rows of terraced dwellings.

The reforms – as is so often the case – ameliorated the problems, but did not immediately solve them. The sewage construction programme took decades. Between 1847 and 1860 there were 177,000 sewers constructed.[20] Although poor housing was condemned, many of the existing courts survived. It was in these courts built before regulation was introduced, and left to stand afterwards, that the greatest deprivation of the following decades was to be found. With the return of the Tory council on a wave of sectarian sentiment, reform was stalled. The old courts would not be demolished. Inequality in housing and education was to persist. To compound Liverpool's problems, a new wave of migration was about to engulf the city.

IN HARDSHIP AND HOPE PART TWO
1847 TO 1914

CHAPTER FOUR

THE IMPACT OF THE IRISH FAMINE ON LIVERPOOL

In December 1846, a letter from Nicholas Cummins, a Cork magistrate, was published in *The London Times*. He had visited the village of Skibbereen, in Co Cork, and had been shocked at what he found there: 'I entered some of the hovels ... and the scenes that presented themselves were such as no tongue or pen can convey the slightest idea of. In the first, six famished and ghastly skeletons, to all appearance dead were huddled in a corner on some filthy straw, their sole covering what seemed a ragged horse-cloth, and their wretched legs hanging about, naked above the knees. I approached in horror, and found by a low moaning they were alive. They were in fever – four children, a woman and what had once been a man ...'[1]

For many in Britain this was the first they learned about the human catastrophe rapidly unfolding in Ireland. It soon emerged that many thousands were starving and that there was no adequate relief system in Ireland to support them. It was also clear that these events would impact on Liverpool with devastating consequences. For those in Ireland whose only prospect was starvation, Britain was an obvious destination. There they hoped to find food and work in the towns and cities. The poor law in England gave paupers an entitlement to relief, in contrast to the law in Ireland which left the matter to the discretion of the individual poor law administrations. In practice in most areas in Ireland it was only the very young, disabled and elderly who received relief.[2]

The winter of 1846-47 was severe, and in February 1847 as the threat of fever was added to starvation, a 'headlong flight' from the worst affected areas began. For those who could afford it, North America was seen as the preferred option but for those who could not realise the fare through savings or selling what they possessed, Britain was the choice: 'The roads to the ports,' wrote Trevelyan, 'were thronged with emigrants. 'All who are able,' reported one Board of Works Officer, 'are leaving the country'. 'Crowds' were seen on the roads for Liverpool.[3]

There were daily sailings to Liverpool from Dublin, and regular weekly or twice weekly sailings from Drogheda, Youghal, Sligo, Cork, Waterford and Belfast. It is indicative of the level of concern in Liverpool that the Chief Constable sent two experienced detectives to Ireland to investigate the situation: 'During the progress of the constables ... they encountered thousands of men, women and children upon the high roads, moving towards the sea side for the purposes of embarking for England, most of them begging their way and all apparently in a state of great destitution'.[3]

It was indeed an alarming prospect. The immediate cause was the failure of the potato crop. This was significant because so many relied upon it. Colonisation in Ireland had established a system of vast country estates. Most landlords were absentee, that is they generally lived elsewhere. A large proportion of the population had been displaced, and now became tenants who could be evicted at will, and frequently were. Most had no realistic opportunity to own their own land. In the wake of the Act of Union there was little Irish industry. There was little poor law provision. Many estates were heavily in debt. Large quantities of produce were being exported for cash, often under armed guard. The system, supported by a strong British military presence, impoverished the majority, and left them vulnerable to a failure of the crop upon which they so heavily relied.[4] As the potato crop failed repeatedly, many began packing up and leaving the country. Those who lived on the margins were under threat of starvation. Many were evicted by their landlords. Some even had their passage to Liverpool paid for by their landlord, so keen were they to rid themselves of their obligation to tenants.

The arrival of these evicted families in Liverpool had a devastating impact upon the town. The citizens were shocked and appalled. Officials were overwhelmed. City services, though vigorously reorganised in recent years, were not designed to cope with an emergency on this scale. Resources fashioned to address local problems, were now being stretched to tackle what amounted to a national emergency. No support materialised from government, leaving the city to cope unaided with a disaster which was not of its own making.

In the spring of 1847 the steady stream of Irish emigrants suddenly burst into flood. Many thousands more began to arrive in Liverpool, and they were in far worse condition than any who had gone before. As with those dying of starvation, Government kept no record of the numbers of migrants. However, as early as December 1846 the Liverpool magistrate Edward Rushton was sufficiently concerned to order the police to meet the Irish steamers at the Clarence Dock, to count – and as far as possible categorise – those disembarking. He was therefore able to inform the Home Secretary on 1849 that: 'Between the 13th day of January and the 13th day of December 1847, 296,231 persons landed in this port from Ireland; that of this vast number, almost 130,000 emigrated to the U.S., that some 50,000 were passengers on business, and that the remainder were paupers, half-naked and starving, landed for the most part during the winter, and becoming immediately on landing applicants for parochial relief.'[5]

On the journey to Liverpool conditions on board for the poorest passengers were extremely harsh. They were often exposed on the open deck, frequently in freezing conditions.

'If there were no horses on board they were allowed to occupy the stables but if there are horses, people are put out.' On most vessels there was no shelter on deck, even during storm conditions in winter: '... every article of clothing being soaked through, and in that condition they were exposed on deck all night.'

Many died on route. John Besard gave evidence to the Select Committee on Emigrant Ships: 'I have gone to Liverpool expressly to wait the arrival of Irish steamers and no language can describe the scenes I witnessed there; people were positively prostrated and scarcely able to walk after they got out of the steamers, and they were seized hold of by those unprincipled runners so well known in Liverpool. In fact I consider the manner in which these passengers are carried from Irish to English ports is disgraceful, dangerous and inhuman'.[6]

Tragedies did occur. 72 died of suffocation through over-crowding on board the *Londonderry* in 1848. They were on their way from Sligo to Liverpool. During bad weather the crew had forced them into a room below deck, in a space eighteen feet by twelve feet. Amongst those dead was an eight year old girl.[7]

About one in six of those arriving could be identified as 'normal' traffic – people on business, those visiting relatives etc. About half, whilst in distress, had the means to acquire decent accommodation in Liverpool, move on to other parts of Britain, or cross to the United States and Canada. But the remaining migrants were utterly destitute. Many of them did not last long. Police found people falling dead in the street. Post mortems revealed some who had had nothing more than crust to eat for days before death. Many were discovered in dark corners of cellars and court dwellings. Their plight is documented by Neal: 'Blanket references to the hardships does little to convey the appalling reality of their experience on arrival in England, yet that experience was to colour the outlook of the immigrant Irish for generations.'[9]

The host of new permanent residents, and the even greater numbers passing through, presented Liverpool with difficulties on all sides; feeding and clothing, housing, health and sanitation, public order and crime.

Liverpool's Response

The Select Vestry – the body responsible for Poor Law administration – was under no legal obligation to provide relief. They levied additional rates from householders and property owners, and organised the administration of assistance for the poor. Although their provision was meagre, they never considered leaving people to die. Rushton stated that: 'Though the pecuniary cost to the town was enormous, the loss of lives was yet much more to be deplored.'

City administrators attempted to do their best under the circumstances. Their policy was to make a minimum provision for all who asked for relief. By December 1846 over 13,000 persons were receiving handouts of six ounces of bread per day. In Neal's words: 'Even by Victorian standards this was a Spartan handout.'[10] This ration soon had to be increased to include soup. Irish writer John Denvir referred to Liverpool as: 'a flinty hearted stepmother to the Irish.' The cost to Liverpool was considerable.

'We had to lay two additional rates of 1s in the pound, and the cost to the parish without reckoning the enormous outlay for fever hospitals, amounted to £70,000'.[11] The city was also bearing the cost of appointing more relieving officers, distributing food and accommodating increased numbers in the prison and the workhouse. As city rates rose there was anger amongst rate payers, some of whom were suffering hardship themselves. Rathbone took up their case, pointing out to city administrators that many could not afford to pay the increase.

The system of relief itself was unsatisfactory firstly because the city could not continue indefinitely distributing food to so many, and secondly because there were no checks on exactly who was receiving assistance. Officials were overwhelmed. Food was distributed from a shed in Fenwick Street near the Town Hall. Thousands thronged around this area each day.

In January 1847, a new Commissioner – Austin – was appointed. He reformed the whole system. Police officers were recruited as relieving officers, checks were made at home addresses, and food could only be obtained upon presentation of a ticket. The number of applicants quickly dropped from 22,000 to just under 5,000.

The *Liverpool Mercury*, 15 January 1847 stated: 'The fact is that in the cold and gloom of a severe winter, thousands of hungry and half naked wretches are wandering about, not knowing how to obtain a sufficiency of the commonest food nor shelter from the piercing cold. The numbers of starving Irish men women and children daily landing on our quays is appalling; and the parish of Liverpool has at present the painful and most costly task to encounter of keeping them alive, if possible …'

The Select Vestry and the Liverpool magistrates were vigorous in their efforts to obtain assistance from Government, but there was little sympathy and no effective response. Tents were offered to accommodate the homeless, but requests for financial assistance were turned down flat.

Liverpool then asked that steps be taken to prevent Irish paupers coming to England. This was also refused. It was then suggested that the law be amended to give paupers the right to relief in Ireland, just as those in England had. The expectation was that if adequate relief was provided in Ireland, the flight to Liverpool would be ended. However, impoverished Irish parishes did not have the resources to make sufficient provision, and besides landlords continued to evict and to demolish homes with brutal efficiency. The law was amended in June 1847, but emigrant numbers did not decrease.

Finally Liverpool asked that they be given wider powers to remove the poor back to their home parish. Under the existing system persons claiming relief who did not have permanent settlement in Liverpool – recently arrived

Irish for example – could be forcibly returned to their parish of origin. The new law made removal much easier. A relieving officer could bring claimants before a magistrate for immediate deportation. However, this was difficult to enforce, as they had to be brought before the magistrates before action was taken. Such were the numbers involved and the difficulty of entering the courts and alleys of Liverpool to find and bring to court those summoned, that few were effectively pursued in this way. The upshot was not the mass deportations the authorities expected. (Rushton, the stipendiary magistrate expected to deport about 40,000 in the first year.) Yet eventually considerable numbers were forcibly returned to Ireland. Bridgit Farrell, aged thirty, recounted that having lived in Liverpool for twelve years, one of her children took sick, that she made application for medical relief, that herself and her children were taken into the workhouse, and next morning sent to Dublin against her will, leaving her husband and two more children in their residence in Liverpool.'[12] William Holland, aged 87, who had lived in Liverpool for 36 years was sent home to Belfast. Between December 1849 and December 1853, 62,881 paupers were shipped back to Ireland.[13] As this legislation came into force, fear of deportation led to a further dramatic drop in the numbers claiming civic assistance.

Of those people who now stopped claiming, most went hungry. Some may have left the town, rather than risk claiming relief. Begging was common, and there was little the magistrates could do to stop it. 'The poor Irish population forced upon us in a state of wretchedness which cannot be described, would within twelve hours after they landed be found amongst one of three classes, viz ; paupers, vagrants or thieves. Few became claimants for parochial relief, for in that case they soon discovered they might at once be sent back to Ireland. Many of these forlorn creatures become beggars, many thieves.'[14] Prosecution was not a solution. The prison was full. In any case, to imprison a woman for begging meant accommodating her children in the workhouse, a further charge on the rate-payers. The Vagrancy Act, in the view of the magistrate Rushton was 'a dead letter in the whole place. We are choked out'.

The *Liverpool Mercury* reported him as saying that: 'There were now in the gaol 688 prisoners, and it ought never to have more than 450, and if we were to punish the vagrants of Liverpool it would be necessary to have a gaol for 1,000 people.'[15] It was the view of the chairman of the Select Vestry 'that in 1847 the pauperism of Ireland was relieved at the expense of Liverpool to a very enormous extent, by the emigration of destitute men women and children in overwhelming numbers'.[15]

Many of those arriving in Liverpool were in a weakened condition through poor nourishment over a long period of time, rendering them susceptible to disease. Many were already infected, and therefore brought disease with them. Overcrowding on the ships transporting migrants to Liverpool, in the hostels and in the local housing increased the incidence of infection. There was just not enough accommodation for such large numbers.

'In different parts of Liverpool 50 or 60 of these destitute people were found in houses containing three or four small rooms, about 12 feet by ten.'[16] In addition many of the 3,000 cellars which had been closed under the 1842 Health Act, were broken open again and re-occupied. To take just one example, when Sarah Burns, a mother of seven, died in December 1846 the coroner visited the cellar where she lived and reported that 'a person could not stand upright in it, the floor was composed of mud; and in that hovel there were seventeen human beings crowded together without even so much as a bail of straw to lie down on.'[17] These were the conditions in which many arriving from rural Ireland were to end their lives.

The diseases from which they suffered were mainly diarrhoea, typhus and typhoid fever. The advent of fever in 1847 was devastating. In that year over five thousand died from it, over two thousand from dysentery, and hundreds more from small pox, measles, flu, and scarlet fever. In the workhouse alone over a thousand died of fever. The epidemic began in the Irish areas, and in the early months 'about seven-eighths of the whole number were Irish.'[18] Make-shift hospital accommodation was opened, but as the disease progressed the medical authorities could not cope with the numbers. Government permission was sought and granted, to open hospital ships – lazarettos – on the Mersey, where fever patients were now isolated.

In 1849 cholera also broke out, and flu and scarlet fever returned to epidemic proportions. The diseases impacted disproportionately on the poorer districts of the town.

'The case of Lace Street demonstrated the situation in Vauxhall. Its population was almost entirely Irish and it contained many cheap lodging houses, prime breeding grounds for disease. Between 1 January and 1 March 1847, inclusive, 181 people perished in this street, not counting residents who died in hospital. This was out of a population of 1,400 (living in 109 houses). This number of deaths exceeded the combined totals for the Abercromby and Rodney wards, which together had a population of over 20,000. 'The mortality in Lace Street is not surprising, given that the water company turned the supply on only three times a week in a situation in which many people had no utensils for storing water.'[19]

To cope with the multiple epidemics the town opened up hospitals where they could, making use of existing buildings and adapting them, and of course the lazarettos. Even with this increase in provision, it is estimated that for every person in a hospital there were two outside who needed care but could not be given a bed. Voluntary and church organisations also did what they could to provide food and clothing, along with medical and spiritual care. But all services were overwhelmed. Even the workhouse was full.

One of the eight plaques erected by the Liverpool Great Hunger Committee, marking places in the city associated with The Famine years. Photo: G. Quiery.

In addition to the financial cost, social carers and officers paid a human price, though the exact numbers are not clear. Dr Duncan reported that in 1847 alone, ten catholic priests, ten medical practitioners, a missionary minister and several relieving officers died from infectious disease, which they had contracted administering to those in greatest need. A memorial to those Catholic clergy stands today at the front of St Patrick's church, Park Place. In that same year Duncan estimated there were 17,000 deaths in Liverpool, 5,845 from fever and 2,589 from dysentery and diarrhoea.[20] He calculated that these deaths left 1,200 widows and over 4,000 orphans. In April there were 654 paupers – those whose burial costs could not be met by relatives – buried in the workhouse graveyard. Elsewhere graveyard provision was overwhelmed, the small cemeteries around the Catholic chapels, and the city's burial plots being unable to cope with the many hundreds of dead bodies now requiring burial.

On 22 January 1847, the *Liverpool Mercury* reported: 'Death from Starvation. An inquest was held on Saturday on the body of a lad named Luke Brothers, who died in Banaster Street from actual starvation.'

The facts of the case, which were brief, were as follows: 'The father mother and three or four brothers of the deceased inhabited a wretched hole in Banaster Street, and since their arrival here from Ireland were steeped to the lips in poverty, and scarcely ever out of a sick bed. They were allowed three shillings a week from the parish, but it is doubtful whether they ever received that in full, for it was brought to them by a neighbour and there is some fear that on one week at least she only handed them one shilling instead of three ... Whenever the children were well enough to crawl out they went begging from door to door; but as it is seldom they were able to exercise their wretched calling, the proceeds of their mendacity must have been small. From the *post mortem* examination made by Mr H. Christmas it appeared that death had been caused by insufficient food. The surgeon added that the deceased was healthy, but he could not discover the least particle of food in his stomach, and he had not the slightest hesitation in swearing that the deceased had died from starvation.'

The numbers of emigrants continued at a high level into the eighteen fifties. Figures presented to the Select Committee on Poor Removal in 1854 are as follows:

Year	Deck passengers, emigrants, jobbers	Paupers	Total	Paupers as a %
1849	160,458	80,468	240,923	33
1850	173,236	77,765	251,001	31
1851	215,369	68,134	283,503	24
1852	153,909	78,422	232,231	34

Even after the 1850s the awful tide of emigration from Ireland continued steadily. Papworth estimates that altogether 2.3 million Irish emigrants arrived in Liverpool between 1849 and 1867. Of these over 1.5 million emigrated out of Britain, leaving a balance of 760,000. These were vast numbers thrown upon the resources of Liverpool. Many of the emigrants added to the permanent Irish population of the city, which, according to census returns, increased from 49,639 in 1841 to 83,813 in 1851, remaining at over 83,000 again in 1861. The overall population of the city was 286,656 in 1841, rising to 375,955 in 1851. The Irish as a percentage of the overall population therefore increased from 17.3% in 1841 to 22.3% by 1851; a 34,174 increase in the Irish born population in the city.[21] Those who arrived as a consequence of the Great Hunger comprised 41% of the Irish-born population in Liverpool in 1851. In other words, although famine emigrants came in great numbers, even at the peak of famine emigration they numbered less than half of the Irish-born population in the city. Additionally, by 1847 the Irish-born population had been in excess of 20,000 for nearly two decades. There was therefore a large Liverpool-born population with a strong Irish identity. Of those Irish paupers who did arrive, many had their life expectancy shortened by poor housing conditions, and soon perished of ill health and disease. Others made their way to nearby towns. The Irish-born population of Birkenhead increased, as did that of Bootle. Others walked to towns in Lancashire and Cheshire, the footways along the canals being one of their favoured routes.

The legacy of the Irish Famine in Liverpool was endemic poverty and deprivation. Housing conditions for the poorest were shocking. There was overcrowding, badly designed courts, and lack of sanitation. Incomes remained low. There was little opportunity for employment. It was many decades before these problems were effectively addressed. After the passing of the crisis the now enlarged Irish community, and the city itself, began the process of addressing the long term problems it had brought in its wake.

MARKING THE GREAT HUNGER

There are a number of public memorials in Liverpool associated with the Irish Famine. They are:

The Great Hunger Memorial in St Luke's gardens. This sculpture – a standing stone with bowl – was funded by public subscription, with support from British and Irish governments, each of the Merseyside local authorities and many other civil and voluntary organisations.

A memorial to the ten Catholic clergy who died ministering to the victims of typhus and other diseases in 1847, was erected in 1898, and still stands in the grounds of St Patrick's church, Park Place.

The crypt at St Anthony's Catholic Church, Scotland Road, where the remains of many of the victims are interred. The tomb of Father Nightingale – one of the clergy who died in 1847 – is close to the entrance.

Ten plaques mark locations around the city associated with the Irish Famine. These include Fenwick Street (the food distribution point), the paupers graveyard in Cambridge Street and the Clarence Dock Gates.

The memorial to the Irish Great Hunger, St Luke's Gardens, Liverpool, erected 1998. Sculptor: Eamonn O'Docherty. Photo: Simon Rahilly.

CHAPTER FIVE

ON THE LIVERPOOL WATERFRONT

It is often implied that the Irish migrants who remained in Liverpool were those who could not afford the passage to America. Whilst in some cases this was undoubtedly true, there were a variety of other circumstances which might have caused migrants to remain in the city. There were those who had arrived with sufficient funds to take them across the Atlantic, but found after a short time in Liverpool, they had lost most of what they once had, since malpractice, fraud, theft and intimidation were rampant in the unregulated environment along the waterfront. Others did not wish to go so far from home as the United States, or were fearful of the long and dangerous ocean crossing, preferring to make a living in Liverpool which was just a day's voyage from Ireland. Many who witnessed the conditions on the trans-atlantic vessels from the vantage point of the Liverpool dockside, took a decision on the spot not to submit their families to the ordeal of the crossing.

Irish migrants encountered brutal conditions at the Liverpool docks. The authorities provided little protection against exploitation, took a light touch approach to regulation and were lax in enforcing what regulations there were. There were easy pickings for those who were inclined to take advantage. Migrants arrived with their life savings in their pockets, or sewn into their clothing. They had sold all their possessions and heirlooms. Many had borrowed from friends to raise the money. They were not accustomed to handling such sums. They had no idea of appropriate prices for goods in Liverpool. Some had never before handled cash. They were mainly from small towns and rural communities where people knew each other and strangers were rare. In the words of one witness: 'they will believe anything. They are extremely credulous. They find themselves in a strange place and they are disposed to attend to everything that is said … consequently there could not be a more convenient prey to those who are disposed to defraud them'.[1] Those who exploited them were the notorious Liverpool runners, also commonly known as 'man catchers'. Many were Irish themselves, and could therefore more easily pass themselves off as trustworthy to fellow countrymen and women. The moment a vessel from Ireland docked in Liverpool the runners were on board ship, ahead of disembarkation, seeking out their victims. They would 'pull them by the collar or take them by the arms'.[2] 'Generally speaking the runners who are successful enough to lay hold of the boxes are pretty sure to carry the passengers with them; therefore the first object of the runner is to ascertain which are the boxes belonging to him (the passenger) then possess himself of those boxes then carry them off on the chance of the man following, which he generally does.'

Not only would the runners charge the migrants for their services, they also demanded commission from others. They took migrants to hostels with which they had arrangements and charged a percentage for each new customer they brought there. There were similar arrangements with shipping agents. The commission was from 7.5% to as high as 15%. Hostels and shipping agents who refused to pay a 'commission' would soon find that they had very little custom. The shipping broker Tapscott – himself a notorious fraudster – confirmed that his company paid 6.5% to agents in different parts of the country, and to men such as 'boarding and lodging house keepers, railway porters and others who bring passengers to us,' in other words middle men, who charged a percentage, even though passengers from Ireland could themselves have made the short journey to the trans-atlantic ticket offices and hostels. Runners also got commission from the stores where migrants purchased materials, often useless goods which they would never need. There was a licensing system for porters, but it was never policed, with the result that there were thousands of unscrupulous unlicensed porters along the docks.

Women were especially vulnerable. Many came with family or in large groups from the same parish all travelling together. Many others did not. 'A great many of these emigrants are young women of from 18 to 28 years of age, who come over from Ireland without any friend or male protection of any kind.'[3] At a time when two pence was adequate for a night's bed and breakfast, 'two girls were charged two and six (thirty pence in present day currency) 'for porterage of a light bag' fifteen times the going rate. The same witness went on to assert that 'there are frequent cases of women running short of money and turning to prostitution'.[4]

There were over 670 lodging houses in Liverpool in the 1840s[5] of which about 300 relied upon emigrants. There was keen competition between lodging houses for the constant stream of new customers, as existing residents left to board ship. This was where the runners found their opportunity. There were a number of specialist hostels run by reputable proprietors which provided for the needs of emigrants, such as Frederick Sabel's Emigrants' Home, established in 1850, and Marshall's or George Saul's. These purpose-built licensed establishments held large numbers – Sabel's accommodated 300 and Marshall's, at Clarence Dock, 650. They were ideal for large parties of emigrants on a low budget waiting to board ship. But they were constantly harassed by runners, who would not allow new arrivals to reach these premises without payment of a 'commission'. Sabel found that 'It is quite impossible to contend against the opposition that is made.' In one instance a group of 300 from Wexford, under the guidance of a priest, who had pre-booked places in Sabel's hostel, were unable to make it to his premises. The priest himself was harassed and bullied, and the members of the party carried off to inferior accommodation. Marshall encountered exactly the same problem. He had established his business at the suggestion of clergy in Ireland, who were appalled at what was happening in Liverpool. He did not provide food, but he did provide bed and blankets, hot and cold water and cooking facilities. Circumstances in Ireland had become so desperate that it was not uncommon for a local parish priest to arrange for a large party of parishioners to travel in a group to Liverpool, and on to America. Such a party would have directions to go to Marshall's hostel for an agreed price. He provided accommodation of such a standard that 'no emigrant who was aware of the existence of such a place would prefer going to a private lodging house.'

The runners were enraged at this arrangement. Marshall gave an account of the problems encountered by one such group, when asked if the runners sought to interfere with customers coming to him: 'Yes, with the utmost possible violence. Ten days ago I was told that 1,200 emigrants had arrived in Liverpool who desired to come to my home, but not more that 150 arrived there; the rest had been taken off … by persuasion, and all kinds of misrepresentation.'

In a separate incident a large party of 100 Welsh migrants were also attacked; they were beaten up, and their carts carried off. Only one person was charged as a result. In Marshall's words the runners will: 'come and stand at the door of the house, and howl and curse and blaspheme by the hour together; they will take off their coats and offer to fight me, and call me all manner of names'.[6]

Whilst proprietors such as Marshall and Sabel had established reputable hostels, there were many others in which people were subjected to appalling conditions. Sir George Stephen testified that 'in one case there are as many as 30 stowed away together on a paved floor, only covered with straw, without fire or light, and for that they paid 2d a night'.[7] Often a boarding house would be licensed for, say, fifty persons, but would then pack them all into just two rooms.

Another practice was that known as 'dollaring'. As one commentator put it 'emigrants are submitted to extortion in the exchange of money.'[8] They would be induced to exchange their sterling currency for the dollars they would need in New York. In one instance the victim paid a substantial sum in sterling for 40 California pieces, worth virtually nothing. Runners would also offer – for a fee – the guarantee of a better berth on board ship, something which was definitely not within their gift.

Getting On Board Ship

Fraud and double dealing in the business of ticket sales and distribution was widespread. Most passengers obtained their tickets through brokers. Brokers made their money in two ways; they would sell tickets on behalf of shipping lines, on a commission basis. They would also hire vessels from the ship owners, hire the crew and take profit from the ticket sales. They would advertise and have ticket outlets not only in Liverpool, but also as far afield as Ireland and the United States.

There were many avenues of abuse and opportunities for fraud in these hired ships. For example, passengers might purchase tickets from an office or agent in Ireland, only to find that when they got to Liverpool the tickets were of no value. In other cases passengers would purchase a ticket for a particular ship on a particular date, only to find that once they reached Liverpool they had been 'transferred' to a different vessel on a different date, forcing them to rent additional accommodation, while they waited for their new ship. Agents' figures for the tonnage of their vessels were notoriously unreliable. One of the largest firms of brokers – Tapscotts – advertised *The Garrick* as being of 2,000 tons, a substantial vessel. In reality, it was just 895 tons. Family members who had found work in America frequently purchased tickets in the United States for relatives back in Ireland. One broker handled 7,000 such transactions in a single year. Again there was opportunity for fraud in such arrangements.

There were both steam and sail ships making the Atlantic crossing. Steam travel was more reliable and comfortable, and took twenty days as opposed to about thirty-five for sail, depending on the weather. In the 1840s the majority of crossings were still by sail. Steam vessels took far fewer passengers and were a good deal more expensive. The great majority of Irish emigrants travelled in sailing ships.

In cases where brokers hired a ship for a fixed period, they had to fill the ship and sail by a given date, or they would make a loss. In such a situation they often had to resort to paying commission to boarding and lodging house owners to 'release' passengers. George Saul, who was by all accounts an honest broker, complained that 'if a lodging house keeper finds it in his interest to keep a man, he will do so, but if our inducement is greater than that he sends him away.'[9] In other words, the shipping broker is paying a bribe to the lodging house owner, to allow the emigrant to leave his hostel and board ship. Passengers were obviously under such a level of intimidation that they remained in their accommodation until released. Brokers improved on their profits by taking on board more passengers than were authorised. One way of doing this was to deem passengers to be children, who would count as half. In one typical instance the ship's steward confronted the representative of an agency called Hardens. The representative offered the ship's steward a bribe to keep quiet about a family called Bateman which was entered as four adults, when in fact there were thirteen of them.[10] The agent pocketed the passenger money and left the ship's crew the problem of meeting the needs of the additional numbers.

Following protests from the United States and Canada about the condition of passengers arriving there, regulations had been introduced, requiring shipping companies to see that passengers had a medical inspection before embarkation, primarily to ensure that those with infectious diseases were not allowed to travel in such cramped conditions. One observer remarked that 'the whole procedure is a regular farce. Monday morning is generally the busiest morning, and there are then sometimes a thousand or more emigrants gathered together at the 'doctor's shop', as it is called; they require the police to keep them in order. Now there are two doctors employed looking at the people's tongues and stamping their tickets as fast as they can. There is no inspection. They have no time to look into any serious matters.'[11] Doctors were paid one pound for every hundred persons inspected. The numbers were indeed great. In 1851 there were some sixteen ships a day taking emigrants from Liverpool to the Americas. The American merchant ships, larger than the British, could carry as many as a thousand passengers. Sabel went on to describe passengers being put on to ships in a very poor condition, remarking that there were certain landlords in Ireland who were notorious, the condition of tenants being expelled from their estates in appalling conditions being a public scandal.

Once having gained release from their lodging, obtained a ticket, been informed of the where and when of their vessel, and having passed the cursory medical inspection, the next tribulation for passengers was the process of boarding ship, which was often chaotic. Captains would take on cargo and provisions first, often keeping passengers waiting until the very last minute before boarding. Meanwhile runners would detain passengers as long as possible on the quayside, looking for any opportunity to extract additional money from them. Once boarding began, there would be a rush to get on the ship, as crowds milled up the narrow gangways. Witnesses testify to seeing passengers climbing up the side of the vessel. One witness, Vere Foster was asked: 'And then the captain proceeds to move his vessel out of the dock before the people have time to get on board?' to which he replied: 'Very often when she gets to the entrance to the dock where it is very narrow; she is detained there for a short time while other vessels are going out, and during that time the passengers are scrambling in; and I have seen 500 or 600 men women and children in a state of the greatest confusion, and their screams are fearful; on several occasions I have gone down and attempted to get on board, but found it to be quite out of the question …'[12] Other accounts confirm this bizarre practice. 'I have, in many instances, seen women and children handed up the side of the vessel after communication with the shore has been cut off,'[13] and another that 'men and women were pulled in any side or end foremost, like so many bundles.' As the ship pulled out into the estuary, there were often passengers left stranded on the quayside. They would be offered a place in a small boat which would take them across the stretch of water to their vessel.

'Sometimes after the vessel is gone they persuade them to take a boat out … but when they find the emigrant in the boat and in the middle of the river then is the time to make their terms.' In other words, an exorbitant charge for the privilege of getting to the ship before it sails – a final opportunity for Liverpool 'runners' to exploit the unfortunate traveller.

The ship would generally stop in the middle of the Mersey for a time. Here the captain took a roll call of those on board. They would search for stowaways, overturning barrels and boxes in which people who had paid a runner to get them on board cheaply, might be hiding. Often such containers were broken open with hammers, causing severe injury to anyone inside. At this point hawkers, such as Everton toffee ladies, and those selling ribbons, mirrors etc were put on board a rowing boat to take them ashore. Stowaways who might have bribed a sailor to get them on board would sometimes be 'discovered' by the very same sailor, and put back on shore. Only then, after all this was completed did the final departure from the clutches of Liverpool commence. They were now on board an emigrant ship where, 'they would be as entirely captive in their vessel as Africans in a slave ship, that the emigrant ship was scarcely less horrible than for filth, foul air and corrupt food, and that the slaver had a greater money interest in keeping his cargo alive'.[14]

Such were conditions along the dockside, and amongst those who set off for the United States and Canada. But what of those who remained in Liverpool?

The Clarence Dock gates, through which millions of Irish migrants entered Britain in the nineteenth and twentieth centuries. Photo: Simon Rahilly.

CHAPTER SIX

THE LIVERPOOL IRISH COMMUNITY FROM 1850-1914

With an Irish-born population of 22% in 1851, Liverpool stands out as the English city with the highest proportion of Irish-born residents in the nineteenth century.[1] Whilst there were a greater number of Irish-born persons in London, Liverpool was the second most popular destination. Manchester was another city with a substantial Irish population. The Irish population of Liverpool and Manchester taken together was in excess of Irish numbers in London.

In the north end of Liverpool, the established clusters of Irish settlement expanded during the late 1840s and 1850s to form one of the largest Irish Catholic settlements anywhere in the world, outside of Ireland itself. Only the main cities in Ireland – such as Dublin, Belfast, and Cork – had a larger Irish population. Thanks to J.D. Papworth,[2] we have an accurate picture of the districts which this huge settlement encompassed. Following the influx of the 1840s the existing districts of Irish concentration in the north end expanded to form a large Irish dominated area extending from the north docks to the Leeds-Liverpool canal and eventually to the main artery of Scotland Road. Bordered by the city centre business district to the south, this Irish area expanded northwards for several miles into the neighbouring town of Bootle. Irish emigrants also concentrated in the immediate south of the city centre around Park Lane and Jamaica Street.[3]

Besides converging on established areas of Irish settlement, there was also a tendency to cluster around the Catholic churches, such as St Patrick's, Park Place, St Augustine's in Great Howard Street, St Nicholas', Copperas Hill, St Francis Xavier's in Salisbury Street, and around St Joseph's chapel in Grosvenor Street.

In the areas of greatest concentration there were certain core streets, which were exclusively Irish, dominated by people born in rural Ireland, speaking the Irish language, yet living in an English urban environment. These included the courts off Lace Street in the north and Crosbie Street in the south. Apart from their distinctive Irishness these streets were also marked out by their extreme poverty, infant mortality of 30%, appalling living conditions, very high unemployment, and overcrowding. In these core streets the Irish dominated the court dwellings. Some courts tended to be exclusively Irish, whilst the dwellings on the main street had a lower proportion of Irish. Outside the core streets there was a lower concentration of Irish residents. Papworth also showed that Irish people were distributed widely throughout the city. In 1851, only two wards, Rodney and Abercromby, had less than 10% Irish. Nine had over 20% and two – Vauxhall and Exchange – had more than 40%, though no ward had more than 50% Irish-born residents.[4]

A large portion of the Irish population more permanently resident within Liverpool were transient within their area, that is, they lived in one district, but moved around a lot within it. Dwellings were rented and in poor condition. Employment was nearly all of a temporary nature. With so few possessions moving was an uncomplicated matter.

In some districts there was clustering by province of origin. There was a higher proportion of Connaught people in the Crosbie Street area. All the Irish in the St James Street area were of Ulster origin in 1851, whilst in the Mount Pleasant area 60% of the Irish population were from Leinster. In 1871, according to the census enumerator's returns, about 48% of the Irish in Liverpool were from Leinster, with 22% being from Ulster, 16% from Connaught and 12% from Munster. During the 1860s there was a tendency for the Irish-born population to move eastwards, overflowing from the densely populated dockside area towards Scotland Road.[5]

Before the influx of 1847, Liverpool already had the poorest living conditions of anywhere in England. In 1842 the authorities had only just begun to make progress in the fight to improve housing and sanitation for the poorest citizens. Over 3,000 cellars were closed under the provisions of the Health Act.[6] But with the arrival of the new emigrants – to the dismay of Dr Henry Duncan – these dwellings were broken open again. The poorest and most desperate Irish lived in them, either as squatters, or in return for rent. In many cases the occupants of the house above – often Irish themselves – would sub-let the condemned cellar below to indigent and homeless new arrivals. The problems which arose are reflected in the returns of the Health Committee. For example in 1850, 7,689 cellars were found to be occupied. Of these 5,871 required drainage and cleansing. 'Nearly all the cellars of the houses in Bebington Street were flooded with stagnant water; that all the filth created by the inhabitants were thrown into them, and that they served the double purposes of ash-pits and privvies … there was no sewer in the street.'[7]

There were 1,808 cases of 'information laid against owners of street cellars for illegal letting.' In the three years to 1850 over seven thousand cellars had been cleared with about two thousand of these being cellars re-cleared after a second occupation.[8] During the early 1840s dysentery in the summer months, and fever in the winter had sent the death rate soaring.

The influx of new emigrants had the effect of making housing conditions even worse than they had been in the 1830s. Court construction was better regulated from 1847, but nothing was subsequently done to improve housing for the poor. Builders and speculators provided housing for the middle classes. But by the 1850s, about 50% of the manual workers and their families lived in cellars, with a substantial proportion of the remainder living in courts.

Within the areas where Irish Catholics were concentrated there were numerous lodging houses. In 1850 there were over 1,100 lodging houses and hostels in the city. About half of these were unregisterd.[9] Many of the lodging houses were still situated near the old dock on the south side, but many more opened up close to the Clarence Dock north of the city centre, where the Irish migrants were disembarking daily. They accommodated the numerous migrants temporarily in Liverpool, on their way to the United States or elsewhere.

Work and Employment

For decades after the influx of the 1840s a large proportion of the Irish in Liverpool and their descendants remained in unskilled and semi-skilled casual employment. Those who had crossed the Atlantic were better able – in Canada and the United States – to improve their position, and advance to more highly paid and secure occupations. In Liverpool, by contrast, advancement was slow, if not impossible. 'All accounts testify to the unusually low levels of skill and high incidence of casual labour amongst the Irish in the workforce.' Whilst Finch[10] found that only 21% of heads of Irish households in the Vauxhall area in 1842 were employed as tradesmen, the influx of the 1840s and 50s made the situation even worse. For the majority life continued to be governed by the difficulty in obtaining employment. Work for most was intermittent and poorly paid. Skilled work was scarce, and in any case there was little opportunity to gain skills. Every member of the family group – women and children included – were enlisted to earn what they could. Street trading, taking in lodgers and domestic piecework were all common. Self-help was important in such a close knit and poverty stricken community. The sharing of resources and family duties such as child care was essential. This situation was to see little change throughout the second half of the century.

Amongst the Catholic parish population around St Augustine's, in the north docks area, 70% were in the unskilled or semi-skilled groups.[11] Large numbers were employed as, 'dock labourers, porters and artisans associated with the ships and shipping, such as riggers, shipwrights, carpenters and boiler-makers.'[12] There were disproportionately large numbers in the 15 to 44 age group in the parish population, implying that many young adults left Ireland, arriving in Britain too late to undertake the training required for skilled occupations in the urban environment.

Only about one third of general labourers had regular employment. The majority relied upon temporary work, which was often intermittent. There was little manufacturing in Liverpool. The possessors of capital had long since discovered that they could obtain a much better return on investment through trade, and often considered manufacturing to be beneath them.

Taylor, describing a working population: 'but little removed above pauperism in daily danger of sinking into it … living precariously at most times, dependent on the wind for the chance of procuring a subsistence', estimates that all married labourers and their families – and some craftsmen and their dependents – continuously lived below the poverty line.[12] Rents, often for the most appalling accommodation, absorbed about one third of income, and diet was often reduced from bread and meat to oatmeal and potatoes. Poverty dictated every aspect of life style. There were numerous pawnbrokers in Liverpool, where those desperate for immediate cash for everyday needs could obtain money in temporary exchange for whatever valuables they had left. Theft of money, and even food, was common, and alcohol was often used as an escape.

Those at work endured the most primitive conditions. Dowling reports that of the 4,000 labourers employed building docks in the late 1840s, about 2,800 were employed by sub-contractors. 'They let out work to a man who has a gang of men,' and 'the object of the work is to get it done as quickly as possible'. The work was 'piece work by the gangs. They are paid so much per square yard'.[13] The quickest method of digging the new docks was to under-cut the earth, and let it fall down ready for carrying away. 'Almost invariably every portion has fallen on the men while they are working'. Dowling – who was commissioner of police – had written to the surveyor on the job, pointing out the dangers of the lifting gear used for putting the stones in place for the dock walls, and suggesting that a less dangerous method be introduced, but to little effect. In his own words: 'I do not think anything has been done'. He said of these dock workers that 'a great many of them are Irish, and they are the most reckless violent set of people that can be imagined.'[13]

Vast numbers of individuals found work as dockers, porters and carters. They were mostly employed casually, on a daily or half day basis, depending on whether or not there was a ship on the quayside. Porters and carters were used to carry goods from railways to the markets, such as St John's, near Lime Street station. They also carried from the docks to the railway, and from markets to shops. Again, all such work was casual, often on a daily basis, and left the unskilled labourers reliant upon the patronage of a ganger or foreman who allocated the work. In such a situation, there was no ground in which trades unionism could take root. But there was fertile ground for divisions based on sectarian and national differences. The employer of casual labour would feel obliged to give work to 'one of our own'.

The Irish influx had the effect of keeping wages for casual work down. One witness commented in 1854 that: 'Many of the Irish are employed as the auxiliaries or drudges of the steam engine; and were it not for their influx which creates competition, in times of emergency wages of labourers would rise to a height which tradesmen, manufacturers and even agriculturalists could not afford to pay'.

When one employer was asked: 'With regard to Irish labour, is there not a great value in that type of labour in Liverpool? the reply was: 'It is extremely valuable … in the present state of the labour market English labour would be almost unpurchasable if it were not for the competition of Irish labour. The English labourers have unfortunately been taught their rights until they seem to have forgotten their duties, and they will not work themselves and they will not allow others to work. Question: I suppose you allude to some strikes which have taken place? Reply: Yes. Question: And to labour unions? Yes.'[14]

Most Irish women were confined and constrained, with responsibilities in the home and limited options in a male dominated society. Whilst many arrived in Liverpool with a partner, there were significant numbers coming unaccompanied, including those enduring ostracism because of pregnancy outside marriage. The deaths of men through ill health, injury at work or loss at sea resulted in a large number of women losing their husbands.

Women found themselves in a similar position to men when it came to the jobs market. They were in a strange country where many of their skills were redundant. The identification of certain occupations as being open to males only, and discrimination based on racial stereotypes and sectarian prejudice restricted their options even further. To make matters worse, there was a surplus of labour in the areas of unskilled or semi-skilled occupations where they might find an income. They were faced with the additional problems of caring for a family in an environment where ill health, over-crowding and extreme poverty were endemic.

Large numbers worked making clothing as piecework for an agent who called at home. Some were in domestic service.[15] Many of the Irish women in Liverpool worked in low skilled and poorly paid jobs associated with the docks and processing. Reverend James Nugent gave evidence to the Select Committee on Girls in 1883, testifying that many women found employment in match works, pickling factories, blue works, blacking works, bag and sack factories.[16]

Women in Liverpool had more difficulty getting remunerative employment than those in other parts of the country, with Irish Catholic women being the most disadvantaged. 'Protestant women were more highly represented in non-manual occupations, including teaching, dressmaking and manufacturing. Catholics were often found in less skilled occupations such as cleaning, petty retailing and hawking.'[17] Although factory work was often unhealthy and involved a good deal of drudgery, some women preferred the camaraderie, regular pay and escape for a while from the domestic environment. Kitty Wilkinson suffered severely when her fingers became swollen and twisted from the effects of working in a nail factory, where workers had to repeatedly pick up hot metal pieces and beat them into shape. Fumes and the rattle of machinery were other hazards. In the port city there was work for women picking cotton, that is separating the compressed cotton which arrived bailed and damp. In 1872 a thousand cotton pickers went on strike, winning shorter hours and better pay.[18] They had a reputation for being 'brawny' and 'drunken'. Even the indefatigable Father Nugent was wary of them, noting that cotton pickers kept late hours and frequented disreputable public houses in Marybone. Mrs Thorburn, of the Select Vestry, noted in 1900 that cotton pickers were 'rough and noisey … ignorant of domestic work and sewing.'[19]

Whilst for most women finding work was a necessity, family responsibilities often tied them to the domestic environment. Conventional wisdom from the clergy and the middle classes was that, if possible, women should not go out to work. The model of a good Catholic mother as in, for example Father Bernard O'Reilly's publications, was not a woman who left the family to take up work. As women spent more time in the home, they suffered more than men from the appalling housing conditions in Liverpool. Another factor was illness and absence. Mortality was high. If a husband died, the wife would assume responsibility for rearing the family. Should a wife die, it was usually another woman who took up responsibility. Men were often absent at sea, and a significant proportion did not return.

In the crowded and tightly knit communities there was mutual support, with informal welfare mechanisms in which women shared childcare duties, domestic tasks, and even domestic utensils. Women would often support each other in times of hardship and unemployment, with food and clothing. Census returns indicate that older children, new arrivals from Ireland, and unmarried relatives were all enlisted in such roles.

In contrast to much of the male employment, female occupations — such as the making of clothing, or work in domestic service – often required skill and consistency. Many women and their daughters carried out such work. Some would have a workshop at home, or work somewhere nearby for their own clients. Others undertook piecework for an agent, making such items as canvas trousers, flannel drawers and cotton shirts. They would be paid per item. In 1861 there were over 5,000 seamstresses in Liverpool working as shirt and trouser makers. Needless to say, as an increasing number of women were driven to rely on such work, the amount paid per item was reduced as one undercut the other, although women often resisted undercutting. In 1853, for example, seamstresses went on strike and 'refused to work for the miserable pittance doled out to them in view of the increasing costs of food and coal.'[20]

Market trading was another option. There were few overheads involved in setting up, and individuals could work where and when they chose – in some respects the female equivalent to casual dock work. Women sold whatever they could. There were groups of women in family concerns selling fruit, fish and vegetables. Others sold matches, flowers, fire paper and chips (wood chopped into smaller pieces for lighting a domestic fire). There were a large number of small markets around Liverpool where they could carry on their trade. At the Fontenoy/Sawney

Pope Street market in the 1850s, of 18 traders, 17 were Irish, and of those seven were widows.[21] In his evidence to the Select Committee on Intemperance in 1877, Father James Nugent referred to the great numbers of basket girls working on the streets of Liverpool, some of them as young as 13. They were often harassed by the police, with one example of 'a seventeen-year-old girl who had been committed to prison for street obstruction 32 times in three years,' making it more difficult for her to earn a living.[22] The link between basket girls – vulnerable women wandering the public streets unaccompanied – and prostitution was thought significant by a number of commentators.

Obtaining and holding on to a 'pitch' was the greatest challenge for street traders. Those not able to secure a pitch at a local market had to find a spot where they would not be moved on by police, and where they would not be given the push by other traders who already had the position as their own.

Irish women street traders, Liverpool, early twentieth century. Photo: T. Burke. Courtesy of Liverpool Record Office.

With so many on precarious incomes, pawn shops were common, with families swapping valued items – including shoes and clothing – for cash mid-week, redeeming them again when they had money at the weekend. In 1855 there were 129 pawn shops in Liverpool with over 500,000 items pawned that year. Irish women – many of them street traders – also became informal money lenders in their community, lending funds to dockers' wives at high rates of interest, often disguising it as 'payment for fish.' Pat O'Mara describes how: 'Mrs Sweeney used to charge fourpence to the shilling interest in addition to the fish purchase, but when she lay dying, Father Wilson refused to give her absolution until she paid back all that interest to her victims which she did very eagerly and, we assume, ascended into heaven.'[23]

Domestic violence was an everyday experience for many women living in the stressful conditions of poor housing and families surviving on a low income. O'Mara gives a vivid account of his father's violence, while Kanya-Forstner documents in Chapter II, some examples of the many court cases arising from attacks in the home.

Domestic service was neither an easy nor popular option for Irish women in Liverpool. Martha Kanya-Forstner's work gives a clear picture of what life was like for many in this work. Irish women and girls often did not have the skills or personal presentation required for work in wealthier households, where employers tended to be very choosy. Girls who were in institutions, including orphans and those whose parents were in the workhouse, received training to prepare them for service, including 'washing, mangling and other household work'. But adverts often stipulated that applicants, 'must be English'.[24] Others insisted that, 'only Protestants need apply', while some stated that 'no Welsh nor Irish need apply.' Again, in the *Liverpool Daily Post* in 1880 there was an advert for a nurse to care for five children, requiring that 'applicants should be experienced Protestants'.[25] Of course Catholic families would often prefer Catholics, but there were fewer of them. In these wealthy homes Irish girls would often be in the poorly paid role of kitchen maid. Middle class ladies frequently complained that they could not find servants 'of the right type'. A Liverpool magistrate stated that his wife had interviewed nine women, but each of them was, 'given to alcohol'.

Many Irish women, who often came from a poor rural environment, did not have the appropriate skills. Others did not take easily to the expectations. Servants would be required to be submissive, and to follow regulations related to their dress codes and general behaviour. Those likely to answer back, or bring male friends to the house, would soon be dismissed. As one female employer remarked: 'My usual stipulations as to dress were that they not wear flounces on their dresses or flowers outside their bonnets; that they wore white caps and were required to attend church regularly.'[26] Employers found that young women in

Liverpool were unwilling to accept many of these restrictions. They were 'thrill seeking freedom loving' girls. In one case it was remarked that: 'the love of dress amongst servants is quite a mania'. There were plenty of instances of domestic servants being taken to court. Offences included 'borrowing' my lady's hat or dress for the day and turning up wearing it in the local pub or music venue.

Not surprisingly, instances of taking items from a wealthy household and selling them on were also common. Cooks would often claim that as they prepared the food, they should be entitled to take the remainder home, especially as it might otherwise go to waste. As Kanya-Forstner remarks, servants would often be pouring from a bottle of wine at table which was worth more than a month's wages. One case was taken against three female servants who were found in the cellar having finished off some of the best wine in the place, and being in such a state that the police were called. In another case Mary Harrison appeared in court for robbing her master Mr Hensman of Pitt Street as she was leaving his service. Tea, sugar, soap and raisins were found in her possession.[27]

Pregnancy amongst domestic servants was common. In many cases the father was never identified, though often a male resident of the household, such as another servant, the employer himself or a son, were suspected. Becoming pregnant was, of course, regarded as shameful in the case of an unmarried woman, and led to dismissal. Servants often took steps to disguise pregnancy. In September 1853 Elizabeth Horne and her husband Robert, a joiner, employed Bridgit Cahill. Bridgit gave birth in secret, in the coal shed. Police found the baby's body, its head beaten with a hammer. The penalty was hanging.[28]

The case of Letitia Dordry was notorious. In 1867 she was employed by a Mrs Forest of 21 Everton Valley. After over a year in service she gave birth in the coal cellar and strangled the child. The body was later found in her bedroom. She was sentenced to death. The father was never identified. Letters to the Home Secretary pleaded for clemency. One letter in particular asserted that she had never been given fair treatment: 'As men were her judge, her jurors, and her seducer,' and that 'the all male judge and jury were unable to enter into this woman's feelings to make allowance for her sin'.[29] The letter went on to make reference to 'her seducer who escapes here without punishment' and that she was 'perhaps less guilty than the legislators who have made laws which have forced her to do this.' Despite such concern amongst women themselves, the law was not to change.

Irish Catholics were more likely to find positions in households lower down the social scale, where they assisted the woman of the house in daily domestic tasks for the family and the lodgers, receiving in many cases no more than her own lodging – that is a bed and food – for her services. A typical example was Rose Murphy who worked for Owen

McCluskey, a warehouseman. Mrs McCluskey had a three year old and two lodgers. Another was the family of Michael McCarthy, a tea dealer from Tipperary, and his wife Catherine, a poultress from Cavan. They had six Liverpool born children, five boys and a girl. They lived in Vauxhall Road. Two of the boys were employed, one as a cooper and one in a shop. There were also three Irish lodgers in the house. They had two Irish-born servants, Margaret O'Brien and Mary a widow aged 30. Another typical household was that of Michael Gorman, an Irish docker and his wife Elizabeth, who was an Irish fishmonger.[30] They had two children. Catherine Tully, a 26 year old servant, lived with them, mainly to look after the children.

In addition to their domestic duties many women supplemented family income by taking in lodgers. Census returns reveal a picture of many households in which relatives or family friends lived-in. Elderly relatives, couples without children, and single women, were common as lodgers. They would either carry out duties in the home, releasing the females in the household for paid work, or would themselves be working, paying an income to the household. One common practice was to rent a large house and either sub-let or take lodgers. Those taking greater numbers of lodgers were required to register. Abuse of the system was common. In the second half of the 19th century there were numerous daily arrivals at the docks, many of them Irish, who needed accommodation for a week or so, while they awaited their ship to America. This was a steady stream of business for those with large houses near the docks. Mary Kearns, for example, a widow, supported herself by taking in lodgers.[31] Her house was in Westmoreland Street. In addition to her lodgers she had four children, two relatives from Ireland and a serving girl – Margaret Loughrin – living in the house. The absence of a husband at sea, with his return often unpredictable, was another opportunity to take in lodgers, though in circumstances which would not always meet with clerical approval. The practice of taking in lodgers added to the existing problem of over-crowding.

Prostitution was widespread in nineteenth century Liverpool, where large numbers of seamen, many of them far from home and with money in their pockets, were discharged daily. 1877 there was evidence to the Select Committee on Intemperance that: 'Last year (1876) there were 102,759 men shipped in British registered vessels, and there were 100,190 men paid off in Liverpool. The men who are paid off receive sums varying from forty pounds to up to fifty pounds and I do not exaggerate when I say that of a sailor's money, over fifty per cent is spent in drink and prostitution.'[32]

Irish women were prominent in the practice, though there is little direct information from the prostitutes themselves. Father James Nugent was Catholic chaplain to Walton prison from 1862 to 1885. He became particularly concerned about the plight of female prisoners, and included much information about them in his reports. He found, for example, that of the 1,123 prostitutes punished for being disorderly in 1863, 497 were Irish.

In 1872, 1,056 of 3,968 women prosecuted for prostitution were Irish.[33] Frederick Lowndes, surgeon to the Liverpool Lock Hospital also asserted that a large proportion of prostitutes were Irish.[34] Shimmin wrote that there were many concert rooms, supper halls and public houses in Liverpool.[35] He gives an account of the free concert hall in Williamson Square, and the 'lewd entertainment' to be found there. At the Royal Casino he found sailors, prostitutes, pugilists, pick pockets and young girls. He also identified Lime Street as a centre of prostitution.

Many commentators believed that widespread prostitution was a natural and unavoidable consequence of the port. Bishop Goss and Chief Constable Greig both remarked on the problem but seemed to regard it as inevitable. Dr William Sanger writing in *The History of Prostitution* found a higher proportion of prostitutes in Liverpool compared to any other British city. Commentators on the subject tended to be doctors, clergy and social reformers, often with an evangelical standpoint. They tended to take the view that it was the debauchery of the working classes and their low moral standards rather than economic conditions, which fed prostitution.

Some such as James Nugent and Dr William Acton recognised that extreme poverty might drive a woman to prostitution. On the other hand, Frederick Lowndes of the Lock Hospital, is a good example of someone who believed that individual moral failings, including laziness, love of dress and a weakness for drink were the most significant factors. Under the provisions of the Contagious Diseases Act – designed to prevent the spread of sexually transmitted diseases in sea ports and garrison towns – women could be detained on the word of a single police officer, forced to undergo a humiliating body inspection, and be kept in custody in the Lock Hospital if found to be suffering from a sexually transmitted disease. Josephine Butler, who came to Liverpool in 1866, successfully campaigned for repeal of the Act, which targeted women only, often subjecting them to police harassment.[36]

James Nugent acknowledged that prostitution could be a source of substantial income for some women. Whilst he did attribute prostitution to sexual immorality, he was also aware of the social and economic circumstances in which it flourished. The Irish Catholic magistrate Shiel was also of the view that economic circumstances were largely responsible for the extent of prostitution. When giving evidence to the Select Committee on Intemperance in 1867, Nugent was asked why women turned to prostitution. He replied: 'I think that the atmosphere itself is such that it generates prostitution or makes a market for the trade, we have no factories … an immense number of women are thrown upon society who have difficulty getting anything at all.'[37] He was particularly concerned about young basket girls and street traders who were thought vulnerable. When asked if there were many juvenile prostitutes, Nugent replied: 'As prostitutes, I do not think there are so many girls on the street, but the number of girls who go with men is very great. Drink prevails in Liverpool and any woman who gives herself up to drink does not hesitate when once she is habituated to it. Unfortunately we have a great number of girls of 15 to 16 who are habituated to drink, and that is the case with street traders too'.[38]

Later in the same passage of evidence he emphasised the link between crime and economic circumstances: 'The inducements to crime are always great in a sea port town but these become more powerful where there is a large proportion of the population dependent on casual employment. Again, the kind of labour along the docks in the warehouses and the constant handling of valuable merchandise with the ready facilities of disposing of such property are strong temptations to the needy and ignorant'.[39]

Petty crime was also associated with prostitution. Sailors and others were frequently robbed. In June 1863, James O'Brien, an Irish sailor, met Mary Mathers in Lime Street. He bought her a glass of wine. They went to Elizabeth O'Callaghan's brothel in Spitalfields and they went to bed. Next morning O'Brien found that five pounds was missing from his pocket. He purchased a knife in a shop in Dale Street and fatally stabbed Elizabeth O'Callaghan.[40]

Prostitution houses, as in the example above, were often run by women, and situated in working class areas. They brought money and employment into the area. The prostitutes themselves were mainly young women for whom it was not a lifetime occupation but rather a temporary situation. Nugent noted that a prostitute's standard of living was notably higher than that of other women.

Measures to supplement income were often desperate and sometimes ingenious. Pieces of cotton and lumps of coal dropped in the street, or left unguarded, were collected and sold. Stealing food, such as bags of flour from bakeries and biscuit factories, was common. Picking pockets was also not unusual. Many of those involved were Irish, as in one example from 1851 where Margaret O'Shaughnessy, and Maria Murphy were convicted of theft. In the same court Bridgit Doran was convicted of passing off forged coins[41] and Mary Kelly was convicted of the common offence of 'child stripping', that is removing expensive clothing from a wealthy child who strayed into a poorer district. Two boys were convicted of the 'novel theft' of breaking into a dairy byre, and milking the cows.[42]

There were also convictions for standing on the street with portable gambling tables. One market stall holder was convicted of dressing chicken up to look like pheasant, making use of paint, glue and feathers in the process. The defence that such practice was common in Dublin –

his native city – did not carry weight with the court. Dowling, the Commissioner of Police, reported that amongst the Irish: 'forgery of coin is common'. Forgers followed Irish labourers, as they were likely to buy the forged coins from them. Forgery was not confined to coin. Stamps were also forged and sold in the street. [43]

The difficulty in obtaining work is reflected in the figures for those in receipt of relief from the parish. Adding together the numbers in the workhouses and prisons, (about 10,000) and those in receipt of relief, 39,000 plus those who were eligible for relief but never claimed through threat of deportation, (about 50,000), I would estimate that there were about 100,000 in extreme poverty in the city during the late 1840s and 1850s.

Bread Riots

How close people lived to starvation was illustrated in February 1855 when an easterly wind blew for several weeks, preventing shipping from reaching the Mersey. 15,000 to 20,000 dockers and carters had no work. People had no savings, and therefore no means of buying food. The weather was bitterly cold. The parish – equivalent of a modern local authority – gave relief to over 25,000 people, whilst the local charities helped many more. 78% of those getting assistance from the District Providence Society were Irish.[44] On 19 February a large crowd gathered in St Paul's Square close to Scotland Road, where it was rumoured that food would be distributed, thanks to a fund raised by merchants in the town. When no food handouts materialised the crowd went on the rampage and began attacking shops and especially bakeries. Food supplies – including bags of flour – were thrown into the street, and carried away. A mob entered a restaurant near the Clarence Dock, took food from the tables where diners sat, and carried off a roast from the kitchens. Those appearing before magistrates the following day were 'all Irish of the very lowest class,' including such names as Catherine Kelly, Mary Burke, Bridgit Murray.[45] For many families food shortage remained a fact of life. In 1865 a Dr Buchan testified that: 'multitudes of families are not getting parish relief, and their daily food consists at every meal of bread, tea, tea and bread.'[46]

Whilst an extremely high proportion of the Irish population were trapped in this hand to mouth existence, there were those who managed to find more rewarding work. Some managed to gain skilled occupations, in spite of the barriers of discrimination, patronage and education. Irish people entered the middle classes either through the professions or by providing service to the Irish community. Many Irish people, mostly men, were professionals in Liverpool. They included doctors, teachers and, in a city with up to seven newspapers, journalists. In 1851, 'some 6.5% of merchants, bankers and business men' in Liverpool were Irish.[47] Others had positions in the police and customs. Many had clerical jobs associated with the port. Others were ships' chandlers, or dealers in products associated with the port, such as tea and fruit.

Most Irish people would buy their goods from grocers, fruiterers, butchers, tailors, and hardware shops whose owners were also Irish. Many of these businesses, beginning as market stalls, grew to be a good size, providing work for sons and daughters in later years. In a community where alcohol consumption was high, the drink trade provided perhaps the best opportunity, especially for those who could remain abstemious. Pub management or even ownership, was an occupation which could lead to improved circumstances. Robert Cain, from Cork, set up his first brewery in Limekiln Lane, in the heart of the Irish community, in the 1840s. He eventually accumulated such wealth that he was able to construct the fabulously decorated pubs, the Vines on Lime Street and the Philharmonic on Hope Street. His son Charles Nall-Cain entered the House of Lords as Baron Brocket. He and the other brewers there were often referred to as 'the beerage'.

Patrick Byrne, a well-known popular figure on Scotland Road in the 1880s, was another. Upon arrival in Liverpool he started as a dock worker, went into pub management and eventually had sufficient wealth to purchase a large house and hotel in Birkenhead. Although he had little education, he went on to be a successful politican.[48] But these two were exceptional. For most, hardship remained the norm.

CHAPTER SEVEN

THE CATHOLIC CHURCH IN THE IRISH COMMUNITY

The Irish community had little access to political or economic power. It was marginalised in every respect, having little in common with the host community, and in many cases being confined to the poorest housing in the most unhealthy districts. The Catholic Church was the institution best placed to offer assistance to the beleaguered community, and to provide leadership. In many ways the Catholic Church occupied the position taken by the state today. Whilst English institutions either excluded the Irish or were alien to them, there was a strong allegiance to the Catholic Church. In the post famine period, many of the institutions and beliefs in which the Irish had put their faith, had failed. Alone amongst these the church remained strong. In the words of one commentator: 'The Irishman believes that there is nothing permanent or certain in the world but his religion ... there it occupies the only ground that has never given way beneath his feet'.[1] The community accepted the leadership of the church. Revolutionary movements and constitutional Nationalism had both failed. The church had been there with a message of consolation through the Famine years. An international institution, it was independent of the British regime and appeared immutable from one generation to the next. It was the one consistent source of strength and community cohesion within daily life. It provided a sense of purpose and of belonging for those who felt they had nowhere to turn otherwise. It was an organisation in which they could wear their membership with pride, an organisation which was a strength in a world where they had experienced only defeat, hardship and rejection.

During the 1850s a devotional revolution took place. Attendance at church increased, as did the fervour of religious observance. This owed its origins to developments on the continent, but gained impetus from the fear and disillusion which followed the Famine.

Amongst Irish Catholics their religion served as a badge of identity, closely bound up with nationality. The use of the penal laws, most of which had by now been repealed, had identified the church in the minds of many with the national struggle. To people alienated and isolated, and suffering the hardship and uncertainty of economic deprivation, illness and urban life, the church was a place of strength and stability, a representative of more enduring values and certainties. In addition the church in the minds of many, provided a link with the 'Catholic' Ireland they had left behind.

Apart from religious significance, the church provided a focal point for the community. It was a place to meet other Irish people, make acquaintances and build social networks. The majority of marriages in Liverpool Catholic parishes at this time were between couples from the same parish, and generally from adjoining streets. Klapas found that in the case of marriages at St Augustine's, Great Howard Street, over 60% of partners were from within a quarter mile radius of the church, with 97% being from a one mile radius. Similar figures were found at St Peter's, Seel Street.[2] Attendance at church also had the effect of conveying respectability upon an impoverished population, especially in a town where the image of the Irish in the press, and amongst the middle classes, had sunk so low. The church, with its emphasis on abstemiousness, and sexual morality provided a counterweight to the ethos of the taverns nearest the docks. To these parishioners the power and esteem of the church was associated with the status of their own community. It was with pride therefore that they watched the development of churches and schools, the outward physical manifestation of the strength and immutability of the church as an institution, and its centrality to the community.

The massive influx of immigrants in 1847 and the following years left the Catholic Church with huge problems. How were they to accommodate the new arrivals, many of whom were regular church attenders? There was a rapid growth in church buildings during the next decade. Many of the new buildings were of a temporary nature, or in very poor condition. In 1848 a shed was purchased in Norfolk Street, and used as a church. The following year a temporary building was opened in Holy Cross parish, because the clergy 'were absolutely unable to cope with the tens of thousands living in hovels east and north of their church in Edmund Street.' In the next twelve months three more churches, St Alban's, St Francis Xavier's and St Augustine's were opened. New parishes were set up first as 'missions', using temporary accommodation to establish a presence in an area, before construction of a church. In 1854, for example, a warehouse was purchased for the purpose of providing mass for the Irish community around Eldon Street. It was not until 1860 that the church was opened. Buildings were often in poor condition. In 1852 the crowded balcony at Holy Cross partially collapsed during a sermon.

Following the effective exclusion of Catholics from the Corporation schools, after the Tory victory in 1841, the building of education premises was the next priority. New schools were opened in Edgar Street in 1852 and in the following years at Copperas Hill, Islington Flags (St Nicholas' Poor School), Mount Pleasant, (a middle school for girls), at Holy Cross (the Oblate Fathers), and in Hope Street (Catholic Institute). About this time the Benedictines opened a school at St Anne's, Edge Hill. Wealthy Catholics – mainly of old Lancashire stock – continued to play an important role. Mr Thomas Gillow for example, who had once lived in Liverpool but now resided in Mexico, presented the school in Edgar Street to the parish.

However the church began to rely increasingly upon regular contributions from a relatively small group of middle and lower middle class Catholics, most of them Irish, and the weekly donations of the poor, for the realisation of the ambitious building programme. At the laying of the foundation stone of St Vincent De Paul's in 1856, Bishop Goss referred to the massive outlay involved in building the church, but assured the congregation that he relied 'hopefully and confidently' upon the mainly Irish congregation, 'because we are satisfied you carry with you the faith which you have inherited from your fathers. The foundation stone which is thus laid ... will be to you a great and glorious remembrance.' Afterwards the Irish ships carpenters of the parish passed in single file, each laying one day's wages on the newly blessed stone. Then followed the dock labourers with their offerings.[3] At St Alban's – one of Liverpool's poorest parishes – it was announced from the pulpit: 'the officer appointed to receive your subscription towards the dioscesean poor schools now stands at the church doors. Let no family be disgraced by not making an offering.'[4] Anglican churches, on the other hand, were often built using public funds, or through donations from the wealthy aristocracy. This dichotomy was a constant source of discontent amongst Irish Catholics.

At first the clergy were mainly English, and as such were the inheritors of the English rather than Irish tradition of ministry. In contrast to the Irish clergy who often acted as leaders of the whole community, dispensing advice on family matters, finance, and acting as legal and political spokesmen, the English clergy had been accustomed to adopting a much lower profile. Theirs was an exclusively spiritual role. Furthermore, the priests were hard pressed at first as there were not enough of them to administer to the increased numbers. The Irish expected a close relationship with their clergy, and the English clergy responded by being close to their flock in all matters spiritual. During the epidemic of 1847, eight priests, most of them English, died from typhus which they contracted through their attendance to the sick. 'To the townspeople such heroism conveyed the reason why Catholics reverenced the office of the priest; for Catholics it knit fresh bonds between them and the clergy.'[5]

The clergy were not exclusively English. In order to augment numbers and meet the increasing demand, many were brought in from Ireland. Most prominent amongst these was Father Bernard O'Reilly, who came close to death during the typhoid epidemic, but recovered and went on to become the third Catholic Bishop of Liverpool. Also amongst the ranks of the local clergy were those who were second generation Liverpool-Irish. The most famous of these was undoubtedly James Nugent. He was born in Liverpool in 1822 to an Irish father and a Liverpool mother. He was educated privately in Liverpool, and was trained in Lancashire and Rome. He was one of the first recalled to Liverpool to replace those priests who died in 1847, and was immediately involved in ministering to victims of cholera in the Lime Street area. Over a lifetime he did more than any other individual to advance the Catholic Church's social ministry to the poor of Liverpool. The numbers of Irish-born clergy remained significant throughout the century. In 1887 there were 81 Irish-born priests out of a total of 235.[6]

The position of the Catholic clergy is very well described by Raphael Samuel:[7] 'The priest, in the Irish mission, lived in close vicinity with his flock, having no society other than that of his parishioners: no rich to interfere … no invitations to ruin the clergy. Nor any round save that of the close quarters and the narrow streets. His daily transactions were conducted as those of a familiar, and yet one who at the same time enjoyed a peculiar and esoteric power, a figure at once accessible and remote … his life was intimately associated with that of the community, even though he was assigned an exalted role within it.'[8]

Mayhew also noted the role of the Catholic priest in Irish communities: 'Even as the priest walked along the street, boys running at full speed would pull up to touch their hair, and the stall women would rise from their baskets; while all noise, even a quarrel, ceased until he had passed by. Still there was no look of fear in the people. He called them all by their names and asked after their families …'[8]

Church authorities took every precaution to maintain the high clerical reputation. 'The saintly image of Liverpool's priests … was diligently guarded by Catholic leaders.'[9] Priests lived an isolated and often lonely life. There is occasional evidence of drunkenness and misbehaviour, though not on any significant scale. In 1856 parishioners reported seeing a Father Newisham in a drunken state. In 1875 Bishop O'Reilly withdrew Father Bradshaw from duties at St Anthony's for unspecified 'outrageous behaviour'.

The church became the focal point for social activity. In the words of Lowe, 'The only significant organisation of Lancashire Irishmen during 1846-71 that was established without church approval or support, was the IRB'.[10] In Liverpool such organisations included the Catholic Club, with a predominantly middle class membership, which raised funds for schools and churches, and the Catholic Defence Association, formed in response to attacks on Catholics and Catholicism in the press and from the pulpit following the formation of the Protestant Association. It was a forerunner of the pamphleteering Catholic Truth Society. Many other organisations – such as the Catholic Benevolent Association and the St Vincent De Paul Society – met gaps in welfare, and made provision for the poor.

An extremely influential association at the time was the Catholic Young Mens Society (CYMS). First formed in Limerick in Ireland after the Famine it was concerned to sustain Catholic values amongst young men during the demoralising years following that seismic social upheaval. As Burke puts it 'it served as an antidote to outside temptations, and carried on under the banner of the Church, minimising the possibility of any weakening of their faith.'[11] Primarily concerned with moral rather than physical welfare, it had educational and social functions. It was one of a number of Catholic organisations which had branches both in Ireland and in Britain. Therefore, members in a parish in Ireland upon coming to Liverpool could easily make contact with the local branch in their parish, make acquaintances and join in activities. There were branches with meeting rooms or a hall in every parish in Liverpool.[11]

Catholic association could at times be effectively utilised in politics. During the general election of 1847, the Liberals benefitted when middle class Catholics voted on block against the Tory Sir Digby Mackworth, who wanted Catholics excluded from all public office, including Parliament. Again in 1857 when the Conservative Charles Turner called for an end to the annual grant in aid of the Catholic seminary in Maynooth, Ireland, Bishop Goss made a speech advising Catholics to vote against Turner, who was subsequently defeated. But such instances were the exception. The Catholic hierarchy generally remained aloof from direct intervention in politics.

The Catholic Church in Liverpool in the second half of the 19th century was confronted with a multitude of social welfare challenges. They regarded themselves as responsible for the spiritual and temporal welfare of all Catholics. This obligation was reciprocated in community expectations. Numbers had grown from no more than a few thousand at the start of the century to, according to some estimates, over 90,000. The majority lived in extreme poverty in unsanitary housing. Disease was endemic. They were in unskilled occupations, with uncertainty in finding employment. Child mortality was high. In the poorest wards, 64 out of every 100 would die before the age of nine, from preventable diseases. Many resorted to crime and prostitution to supplement income. Many children were without parents to support and care for them. Many households were without a wage earner, or were single parent families.

In the face of such widespread deprivation the Catholic authorities had capacity issues. They feared that poorer Catholics would turn from religion. They did not have enough space in the churches. They felt obliged to build, fund and staff schools. They considered it their duty to meet the needs of the destitute, and those in workhouses and prisons. Yet they had a very narrow cohort of middle class members with disposable income who could contribute. And fresh arrivals came daily through the gates of the Clarence Dock.

The Catholic Church soon became deeply involved in social welfare, and the hugh financial and manpower commitment it entailed. With state provision at a minimum, and often unsympathetic to the spiritual needs of Catholics, the church was the only organisation with the authority, structure and resources to tackle the problems. The workhouse did not have the capacity to meet the needs of the numbers who were destitute. The relieving officers did not have the resource required to feed the hungry. The education system did not have the capacity, and where it did, it had little sympathy for Catholic belief. The Catholic response was reactive and instinctive, responding to needs as they arose, with little central planning. In many cases it was individual initiative which provided the initial stimulus. The sheer scale of the need was daunting, as the Catholic clergy living as they did, in the community, knew from first hand experience in their daily lives.

Amongst the Irish a sense of national pride was a driving force. Those in poverty were Irish people far from home and in distress. There was an obligation to 'look after our own'. The community needed to retain respectability and restore self-respect. The clergy and the hierarchy were mainly English Catholics. There was a degree of antipathy towards the Irish, with their poverty, their politics and their particular brand of Catholic ritual. But there was also a strong sense of obligation. There was a sacred duty, a task entrusted by God to the English Church, to minister to the needs of their co-religionists. There is no doubt that whatever the conflicts over politics and custom, the English clergy remained dedicated to the task of pastoral care.

The size of the Irish Catholic community in Liverpool – about 177,000[12] – was significant. Not only was there a great need, but there was a substantial Catholic population, numbers of them business people and merchants with close links in the community. In contrast to smaller towns further from the coast, where there were few Catholics, Liverpool potentially had the resource – with such great numbers in their congregations – to create the provision that would meet local needs.

A sense of rivalry with other denominations was also a factor. Forstner notes that: 'It was the willingness of the poor to turn elsewhere which encouraged Catholic leaders to provide generous and varied forms of relief for their less fortunate parishioners.'[13] There was a fear – whether real or imagined – amongst the Catholic authorities, that poor Catholics would be vulnerable to prosletisation, that is conversion to another religion. Any means or mechanism which brought Catholics into contact with other religious groups was seen as putting 'the Faith' in jeopardy. There were reports that 'mass is neglected by multitudes.'[14] In particular there was a danger that the poor and uneducated could leave the Catholic religion in large numbers if they were attending schools run by Anglicans or Presbyterians and in receipt of relief from non-Catholic organisations. But in reality conversion to Protestantism was not common, even in those who ceased to practise the Catholic faith. 'Distrust of Protestantism was, like the faith itself, inveterate, and might survive even a formal separation from the church.'[15]

These problems were all the greater as the Catholic Church still did not have the capacity to meet the basic needs required by Catholic Church practice – such as weekly Sunday mass – for the mainstream population. Churches were full to capacity with parishes forced to use temporary accommodation.

To compound these fears it was already obvious that a significant number of newly arrived Irish Catholics were not practising their religion, a phenomenon known within the church as 'leakage'. In John Belchem's view: 'Prevention of 'leakage' from the faith was the over-riding consideration, the obligation to win back the negligent and lapsed to a proper observance of their religion.'[16]

The result of all this was that – under the leadership of active clergy and leading members of the Catholic laity – the church sought to duplicate every component of welfare provision supported by other religions and philanthropic organisations. The aspiration was that there should be no need for Catholics to resort to any organisation outside the church for welfare provision, whether it be schools, refuges for children, support for the homeless, or reformatories.

Welfare came to be seen as an integral part of the church's mission. Spiritual and corporal needs were seen as of equal importance, and closely linked. If you were to save a soul you must first feed the body. Spiritual nourishment was required to overcome the hardships and temptations of life in the slums. There would be reward in heaven for those who took part in such work. Church members were urged to carry out the 'corporal works of mercy'.

Parish Welfare

The two pillars of Catholic provision were the parish and the religious orders. The number of parishes grew rapidly after the eighteen forties, from six in the first half of the century to 18 by 1870 and 24 by 1918.[17] Each parish was administered by a team of clergy, under the direction of a parish priest. There would also often be a convent from which nuns would carry out local duties. The clergy visited homes regularly, and although such visits were often resented, for others they provided consolation, and certainly gave the clergy first hand knowledge of the needs of their area, right down to the level of individual families. Not only did the clergy preside at mass each Sunday, and hear confessions, they also conducted weddings, baptisms and funerals. Even people who were no more than nominal Catholics would attend such events. The ambition for each parish, fulfilled in almost every case, was to have – in addition to its own church – its own school and parish hall. Resources at their disposal were limited. They could offer the spiritual support which many parishioners found consoling, but they had limited church funds to offer, although they could direct others within the parish network to assist those in difficulty. Parish organisations included devotional groups for men and women, a local St Vincent De Paul (SVP) Society, plus social clubs, football teams and outings. 'By 1886 there were a total of 43 different sodalities, confraternities of guilds throughout the diocese'.[18]

SVP confraternities were parish based self-help organisations which relied mostly on voluntary contributions and fund-raising activities in their local congregation to provide welfare, usually in the form of cash, to parish members in need. In contrast to many of the philanthropic organisations of the time, where wealthy middle and upper class donors dispensed aid to the poor, those distributing assistance were not all that distant in social class from the recipients. The parish became the locus of local welfare provision, addressing the daily needs in particular of families resident there. Each parish SVP group enjoyed autonomy, recruiting new members locally, managing their own funds and formulating their own policies for support of those in need. Recipients were almost exclusively Catholic. Those who were not regular church attenders were often encouraged to resume religious practice as a condition of relief. In addition to help in the form of cash for basic foodstuffs, groups assisted in other ways, including, in some instances, paying the cost of a licence for street trading, or a union subscription to allow a man to obtain a union card, essential if he was to find dock work. William Denison, in 1870, was given assistance so that his wife could set up a stall in 'the Paddy Market'.[19] Catherine Grant was given money to set herself up as a street trader and to stock her basket. Paying fares back to Ireland for those who wished to return was also common.

Local SVP groups grappled with the contemporary issues which preoccupied so many philanthropists of the Victorian era, that of the deserving and the undeserving poor. Usually applicants for support had to be 'sober and willing to work.' Many were widows with young families, or whose husbands were absent at sea. The undeserving were perceived as being those who led chaotic lives, were persistent in alcohol abuse, 'feckless' with their cash, and were lazy and unclean. An indication of the attitudes of the time can be found in a report of the Liverpool Society for Prevention of Cruelty to Children, which recorded that in one year 568 children came into their care, having suffered neglect. The estimate was that only 50 of these admissions were as a result of poverty. The immorality and cruelty of parents was considered a more important cause.[20]

Measures were adopted in order to address the needs of persistent recipients, such as distributing tokens which could only be exchanged for food stuffs, so as to prevent the expenditure of cash on alcohol and tobacco. Women – being the ones who managed the purchase of food in most families – were the most frequent receivers of help.

SVP members monitored the drinking habits of recipients. As Father Nugent had said, 'If an ignorant girl once takes to drink ... she soon casts off all sense of shame, becomes bold and defiant in vice, and abandons herself to every form of crime.'[21] In 1870, in a typical instance, the stipendiary magistrate, Mr Raffles, wrote to the local SVP asking them to relieve the Murphy family. SVP members – known as Brothers – visited and found that Mr and Mrs Murphy were 'addicted to drink'. Brothers considered that appropriate action was to refer the case to Father Pozzie (sic) for spiritual guidance, rather than offer cash assistance.[22]

In the face of the extreme hardships of the time, there were also robust informal networks of support within the poorer districts. Margaret Simey refers to the Dock Labourers' Relief Fund, founded in 1885. She observed that: 'two committee men sit during the whole evening, never exchanging a word, keenly scrutinizing each applicant who comes in, and the imposter would indeed be clever who could deceive their long experience … On the desk lies a string of tallies, each of which represents two shillings in food, payable by a neighbouring provision dealer.'

She makes the point that this is the poor assisting the poor: 'These men, who work the charity themselves, for their fellows, we may even say for their fellow sufferers, for they are poor enough themselves, have no intention of being imposed upon.'[23]

During the 1860s and the decades following, there were attempts to co-ordinate the efforts of the growing numbers of persons and organisations providing relief to the poor, prompted by concerns that recipients were claiming relief from more than one organisation. In 1863 the Liverpool Central Relief Society was founded, to co-ordinate voluntary social work efforts across the city. However, the Catholic bishops and Catholic charitable organisations did not agree to take part, maintaining that they had the resource to meet the needs of their own congregations within their separate network.

Catholic Religious Orders

The most striking aspect of Catholic provision was that established by religious orders. These were international organisations, in which individuals were committed to a lifetime of service. Members remained single, swore obedience to the order and took a vow of poverty. Each order had a specialism, such as education, or ministering to the sick. A large number of these organisations came to Liverpool, usually at the suggestion of local clergy, during the second half of the century. To add to the positives from the Catholic Church's point of view, religious organisations were self-governing. They trained their own staff, provided for their upkeep, and usually undertook their own fundraising, both through vigorous local activity and soliciting donations from wealthy Catholic benefactors wherever they were to be found. Perhaps most important of all, they had the organisation, commitment and sense of mission to take up what seemed like insurmountable challenges. Their most substantial and significant interventions were in education.

At a time when there was no teacher training establishment in England for Catholic lay teachers, religious orders were brought in to carry on the work of education. The Oblates, Benedictines, Notre Dame sisters, Redemptorists, Jesuits and Christian Brothers were among those who came to Liverpool. Many of these arrivals were at the instigation of Father Nugent, or the zeal of some other local priest. They invariably had to overcome the doubts of the bishop who would always have misgivings about allowing autonomous religious orders to intrude upon his domain. Some were more welcome than others. The Jesuits had been excluded from Liverpool in the previous century, and were only gradually re-introduced, with strict conditions agreed in advance. The introduction of nuns excited the Anglican fundamentalist Hugh McNeile, who suggested that all convents should be subject to inspection.

Amongst the most successful of the new arrivals were the Sisters of Notre Dame, originally from Belgium. They were invited to come to Liverpool by James Nugent and arrived in March 1851.[24] He had already established schools for boys, and came to the conclusion that the effective way to set up similar provision for girls was through a teaching order of nuns. There was a strong current of opinion that the whole thing was a waste of time, as the nuns would take one look at the situation in Liverpool and return to their convents in Lancashire and Belgium. They, after all, had little personal experience of such harsh conditions and meagre resources as obtained in the city. There was such fear that they would not stay that even the parish priest himself was involved in cleaning the residence prepared for the nuns at Islington Flags, the night before their arrival. They took over the chaotic St Nicholas Poor School on Copperas Hill, where there were 600 pupils divided into class groups in one long room. By the nuns' own account 'We found great disorder prevailing throughout.'[24] The school was immediately restored to order, with the result that it received a glowing inspection report within a year of the arrival of the sisters. Nugent had given them the target of opening a secondary school for girls, some time in the coming years. It was opened within weeks. Later in the same year they took charge of the Falkner Street Girls' Orphanage. They went on to establish a girls' school and teacher training college on Mount Pleasant, in premises purchased for the order by the wealthy family of one of their members. This institution provided opportunities for local born lower middle-class girls of Irish descent to enter teaching, whilst also stocking local Catholic schools with trained staff. These imposing buildings are now part of Liverpool John Moores University.

More controversial were the Christian Brothers who came from Ireland. They relied upon funding from their own resources – primarily collected from the local community – and staff who worked for very little.

They were fiercely independent and refused to submit to government inspection, even though this meant they were ineligible for the state funding now available to other Catholic schools. Their commitment to Catholicism, and Irish nationalism, won them an important place amongst the Catholic community, though their strict discipline and harsh physical punishments did not always endear them to their pupils. They came to manage St Patrick's School, Park Place in 1837, eventually running five schools in Liverpool incuding Seel Street, and St Nicholas'.[25] When the parish priest at St Mary's decided to dispense with their services in 1852, he was immediately 'severely censored by the Irish portion of his flock'[26] who were anxious that the Brothers stayed in the parish. Father Sheridan had wished to have the parish schools open to inspection, thus qualifying for government grants. The Irish parishioners offered to pay annually the amount of such grants into the parish coffers. But Father Sheridan refused and the Brothers, rather than submit to inspection, left.

Such tension between the Christian Brothers and local clergy was common. One issue was how Irish history was to be taught to these children, born and reared in England, but from an Irish background. The English church never encouraged exploration of Irish history and politics, and was especially wary of Irish nationalism. In practice, the particular cultural values and political beliefs expressed through teaching, or from the pulpit, depended very much upon the views of the individual priest or teacher on the spot. The church generally ensured that schools were not teaching Irish nationalism. In many cases the children of Irish parents learned nothing of Ireland at all.

'I was a boy of about nine years attending Copperas Hill schools. Mr Connolly, who was in charge, was a very good master, but there was nothing very Irish in his teaching. Some idea of this may be found when I mention that – though there were not a dozen boys in the school who were not of Irish extraction – the first map of Ireland I ever saw was on the back of one of O'Connell's Repeal cards. It was not until the Christian Brothers came, a few years afterwards, that this was changed. I shall always be grateful to that noble body of men, not only for the religious but for the national training they gave.'[27]

In later years, after the Brothers had left Seel Street, another Liverpool Irish writer, Pat O'Mara observed: 'St Peter's school in Seel Street was in a way a new vista in my life. Here was an English school filled, mainly, with Irish-Catholic boys. But the tutors in this school, although all of them were Catholics, had been trained in England, and all their teaching smacked of this English training. The Empire, and the sacredness of its preservation, ran through every text book. Our navy, and the necessity of keeping Britannia ruling the waves, is another indelible mark left on my memory, though the reason for this was never satisfactorily explained. The British always won wars – not the English but the British – giving the impression that we were all more or less brothers under the skin – the Irish, the English, the Scots and the Welsh.'[28]

The Oblate Fathers, Benedictines and Jesuits all had houses and teaching and welfare establishments in Liverpool. And there were many other initiatives. The Faithful Companions of Jesus, for example, opened a boarding school in 1844. They supervised St Patrick's girls school and opened a 'night school' for girls with over 200 attending.[29] The Sisters of Charity opened and ran a school for the blind.

It was the commitment, organisation and fund raising capacity of these religious organisations which allowed them to carry forward the task of providing education for Irish Catholic children on Merseyside, so essential if the community was ever to escape the low paid casual employment in which so many were trapped. There were large numbers in primary provision, and increased capacity at secondary level, though still restricted to a minority in both the academic and technical sectors.

There remained the problem of a large number of children from the very poorest families, who still were not in attendance at school. In an effort to meet the needs of such children, many of them living on the streets, the Church of England began establishing 'Ragged Schools' in the 1840s. There were 32 of these – run by a variety of individuals and societies – in Liverpool by 1853. The first initiative by the social activist Father Nugent, upon his arrival in Liverpool in 1849, was to found a Catholic ragged school, which was situated at Spitalfields. Provision in such schools was very basic by any standard. Whilst they were educational in intent, the first priority in many cases became to supply food and clothing, and sometimes shelter, to those children who attended.

Where Catholic children were attending non-Catholic ragged schools, such schools were perceived as a threat by the church. In 1847 clergy organised a meeting outside the Ragged School in Hodgson Street, not far from Holy Cross church. It was feared that local Catholic children were being attracted to the school by the free meals distributed there, 'selling their souls for bacon rolls and flitches of hairy bacon.' Two clergymen, 'forced their way into the building and bore away in triumph a number of Catholic children.'[30] The clergy at the same time asked local parishioners to have patience, as a local Catholic school for such children would be established as soon as possible.

The passing of the Education Act of 1870 (Foster's Act) put further pressure on Catholic authorities. It established School Boards in areas such as Liverpool, where there was a shortfall in education provision. The Board could raise funds through taxation to establish and support the schools required. This opened up the possibility that in areas where there were not sufficient places in Catholic schools, the children of Catholic families might begin attending Board schools. In order to maintain an influential role in the new system, church authorities and Catholic politicians quickly became expert in the electoral systems established for the School Boards. The campaign to have Catholic members elected to the School Board was successful. As a result there was a board decision to make use of Section 25 of the Act, which allowed the Board to pay the school fees of pupils attending denominational schools, a significant victory for Catholic authorities and another setback for both secular and inter-denominational education.

By the end of the nineteenth century there was a patchwork but effective network of Catholic schools catering for the needs of the Liverpool Irish population. It was a church based system, with each parish having its own schools administered either by the diocese, or, more usually, by an autonomous religious organisation operating with the permission of the diocese, under the watchful eye of a parish priest.

In addition to mainstream schools, there was specialist provision, including Catholic reformatories, orphanages and schools for the blind organised on a diocese wide basis. Much of the Catholic provision relied on regular parish collections and the fundraising acumen of religious orders.

Most of the teachers were not members of religious orders. Pay was low. In Bootle in 1890 a bricklayer might earn £100 per annum, a teacher £50 to £70. The schools were registered within the state system and in most cases submitted to inspection. They were required to meet minimum standards of accommodation. One school inspector remarked that 'only those fired by religious zeal would take on the very difficult task of educating the type of child (chiefly noisey unwashed young Hibernians) to be found in Catholic schools'.[31]

Some Catholic schools, on a minimum budget, were in extremely poor condition. School discipline generally in the nineteenth century was harsh, and Catholic schools were no exception. George Garrett in his fictional story Apostate describes a priest who 'viciously slashed out at boys' bare legs with a thick cane,' a punishment for not attending Sunday Mass. 'When one broke another was produced,'[32] leaving many in tears.

Church and state provision soon became dependent on each other. Church organisations would have found it extremely difficult to fund the whole system to the existing standard, out of their own resources in the long term. On the other hand, state provision would have had to increase local taxation or provide substantial government assistance through the tax payer if the church was to stop funding such a large number of schools in what was now deemed to be an essential public service.

Catholic Social Welfare
There were large numbers of destitute children in Liverpool in the 1840s. The dispersal of communities and displacement of population during the famine years was one cause. The high death rate from disease, injury at work and loss at sea were others. When James Nugent began making

provision for destitute children in the late 1840s, there was little impetus for action either within the Town Council, or the Select Vestry, who administered the poor law and workhouses. He did find an ally in the chief magistrate, Edward Rushton, whose colleagues saw at first hand the consequences of deprivation daily in the law courts. Together they persuaded the mayor to launch the 'Save the child' campaign. The campaign was remarkable, in that it brought together on the one platform the Protestant fundamentalist McNeile, the Catholic bishop of Liverpool, and the Unitarian ministers. Following the opening of the Ragged School in Spitalfields, Nugent opened a boys' refuge in Soho Street, which soon had such demand that he had great difficulty raising sufficient funds to support the service. With the help of the political activist, author and journalist John Denvir an appeal was launched at St George's Hall. Nugent personally approached the members of the Catholic Club, made up of wealthy Catholic lay people who, amongst other activities, provided funding for welfare initiatives. It was with their help that the Spitalfields School and the refuge for destitute children in Soho Street were able to continue. The promise of food was crucial. It was said of these schools that 'education was but a means to moral uplift; and the primary object was to get the boys to Mass on Sundays. They were marched from the schools to church by one of the Sisters of Charity,' returning after Mass to the Ragged School for breakfast.[33]

During the following fifteen years a network of provision for the destitute was established through the work of church organisations. Orders of nuns, each with their own specialism, such as the Sisters of Charity (care for the blind), the Sisters of Mercy (care of the poor), the Poor Servants of the Mother of God (homeless women) and the Little Sisters of the Poor (care of the elderly) were invited to establish themselves in Liverpool. In 1858, for example, the Good Shepherd Sisters – who cared for homeless young women – came to Liverpool and established a home on Netherfield Road. Later they moved to Mason Street, then Edge Hill, and eventually to Ford. Nugent helped them to raise funds to expand their work. In his evidence to the Parliamentary Committee for the Protection of Young Girls, Nugent stated that: 'in Ireland if a girl falls, she cannot remain in a parish or district to which her parents belong; public opinion is so strong against anything of that kind, and then the girl is forced out into the world; she comes to Liverpool; sometimes her seducer may give her a pound or two, and she comes to a strange country, nameless and friendless, and burdened with a child.'[34] The women admitted into the Good Shepherd provision – referred to as 'unfortunates' – were given lectures on the value of humility, obedience, modesty and industry. They worked in the laundry, often in silence. Discipline was harsh. Many were later given free passage to Canada, where they would often be found menial occupations in vulnerable situations.

Many women played a leadership role in welfare provision. Frances

Taylor, a convert to Catholicism and colleague of Florence Nightingale, took the name Mother Magdalene Taylor when she founded the Poor Servants of the Mother of God. This order came to Liverpool at Nugent's request and established the womens' sheltering home at Bevington Bush. She once defied Nugent when he wanted to make use of the personal details of her residents in a fundraising campaign. She considered client confidentiality to be of greater importance. Hannah May Thom was a Unitarian who provided nursing services and nurse training around Holy Cross parish with such dedication that a statue funded by local subscription was erected in her memory. Amy Elizabeth Imrie, also a convert, was heiress to the White Star Line fortune. As Sister Mary Clare she established the Fox Street priory, once known as the 'Vatican of the North' because of its elaborate décor. Each worked in the Irish community around Scotland Road, north of Liverpool city centre.

The restored statue of Hannah May Thom, which stands in the grounds of Mazenod Court, a residential home in Addison Street, Liverpool. Photo: Simon Rahilly.

While Nugent was the most active and best known of the Catholic clergy, there were others who felt the need to utilise their position in the community to take action on social issues. Father Fisher established the Beacon Lane orphanage in 1861. Father Gibson initiated the Working Boys Home in 1865. James Nugent remained the most active, initiating a second crusade for destitute children in 1865. The launch was in a prestigious venue, St George's Hall. At a second event the following year every member of the council, Conservatives included, attended the meeting. The money raised supported the Soho Street refuge which now catered for 400 children.

Father John Berry, who was based in St Philip Neri's parish, opened a Home for Street Trading Boys in 1892. It was based at premises in Catharine Street and Marble Street. The boys admitted were identified as belonging roughly to one of two classes – either having no parents or no home, or having parents leading 'drunken and dissolute lives'.

'Rescued from vicious surroundings they are taught the practice of their religion, and trained in habits of cleanliness, regularity, and thrift.'[35] The St Vincent De Paul Society home was also put under Father Berry's control. As well as residential facilities it had: 'a gymnasium and a recreation-room, fitted with billiards, bagatelle, and other games. Under the management of Mr T.J. Maguire, evening classes had been carried on during the winter months, and the boys readily availed themselves of the opportunities thus afforded them of improving themselves.'[35] Children, mainly boys, would be given supper and a bed. Large numbers took advantage of the facility.

Perhaps the most novel of all initiatives was that by Bishop Goss in 1863, to establish a training ship on the Mersey, for the purposes of 'rescue work'. Father Nugent was the first president. Concerned that boys of the Catholic faith might not receive appropriate religious instruction in state institutions, the Catholic Church had established their own reformatories, which accommodated boys who had been convicted of petty offences in the magistrates' courts. Goss's proposal was for a ship on the Mersey, which would at once be secure and disciplined, and prepare boys for work at sea, which was plentiful. The training ship *Akbar* was already in place. The Catholic equivalent, *The Clarence*, was donated by the admiralty. It was administered by the Catholic Reformatory Association, was moored out on the Mersey estuary, and survived under a regime of severe discipline until set alight by six boys in 1884.[36]

Sending Children to Canada

In the late nineteenth century the practice of sending children who were orphaned or from disadvantaged backgrounds, to 'white commonwealth' countries became common. It was thought that there they would have better opportunities in life, and escape the degradation found in British urban settings. The Liverpool Sheltering Home, sponsored by wealthy shipowners, was opened in 1873, with the stated purpose of rescuing destitute and neglected children, and preparing them for reception into families in Canada. Predictably, Catholic authorities were concerned that there was no equivalent Catholic organisation, opening the possibility that Catholic children might be taken up by the Sheltering Home and as a consequence lose their Catholic belief. In 1881 the Liverpool Catholic Children's Protection Society was formed at the initiative of Bishop O'Reilly and Father Nugent.[40] They provided for over 500 children in Liverpool, with premises at 99 Shaw Street and other locations. They had facilities in both Montreal and Ottawa in Canada, to which children from Liverpool were sent to begin a new life. The first party of 50 children – aged between four and sixteen – went to Canada in 1883.

There were many criticisms of the system. It was alleged that children were abandoned, were too young to make such momentous decisions, lacked support, or were used as cheap labour. It is certainly true that there was no effective system to monitor how they were being treated where they eventually were settled. The Annual Report of 1894[40] finally admitted the legitimacy of such arguments, stating that 'where possible it is better to provide for the children in England.'

Funding Catholic Welfare

Bishop Goss, who was renowned for his energy in continuing the work of consolidating welfare provision under Catholic control, was able to say in 1914, that there were 'over thirty institutions founded for the work of alleviating all manner of human misery and poverty, comprising seven industrial schools, three reformatories, four poor-law schools, one blind asylum, three refuges for the aged poor, seven institutions for looking after waifs and strays, and other places, including the group of Homes at Everton Crescent.'[37]

Meeting the cost of Catholic social services was a substantial commitment. Every Catholic with any means, from the casual docker to the wealthy business man was expected to make a contribution. To support parish expenses and church and school building funds clergy would regularly call at homes of parishioners to collect money. There were also weekly parish collections at Sunday mass. In some cases the names of those contributing and the amount paid was read out in public. Parishes and voluntary organisations held regular fund raising events. For example, the largest single amount donated to Father Berry's Homes annually was from the ladies' sale of work.[38]

Religious orders had to seek permission to collect at parish masses. Others had their own wealthy donors. Middle class Catholics were frequently approached to commit to regular donations or give an annual sum. They would be invited to attend Father Nugent's fund-raising events and be expected to contribute. In addition, organisations such as refuges and residential provision relied on donations in kind, including bread, vegetables and other goods from Catholic businesses. Staff in religious orders were expected to work for a minimum, having taken a vow of poverty.

Undoubtedly the provision of Catholic welfare services saved the public purse much expense, though this was seldom acknowledged. Councillor Doughan, addressing councillors in 1894, recommended that charitable donors, Catholic and non-Catholic alike, support a struggling charity funding Father Berry's Homes, with the following argument: 'There was a more practical reason why such homes should appeal to the charitable people of Liverpool, and that was because they directly saved the pockets of the ratepayers. He thought he was justified in making that statement, because, if they looked closely into the fact, they must come to the conclusion that if those boys were not cared for in such institutions as Father Berry's Homes, they would almost certainly drift into the workhouse or the jail.'[39]

All of this provision had been founded in response to immediate need, often in a crisis situation, on the initiative of an individual, in situations where state provision was minimal. On other occasions provision was established because there was no 'Catholic' equivalent to existing Anglican or local authority provision. The church was anxious to maintain its dominant position in the community, and to reduce the numbers who might leave the Catholic faith. Catholic provision undoubtedly achieved great things, especially in the field of education, and the provision of emergency relief. Although many thousands benefitted, there was no overall plan. The provision relied on the skill and lifelong commitment of both religious and lay staff, who often received little acknowledgement.

The caring methodology was very much left to those staffing the provision. Many of the institutions maintained a harsh discipline. There were rigid rules on the daily timetable for meals, getting up and going to bed, mode of dress, and acceptable behaviour. Religious observance was rigidly enforced, and contemporary Catholic teaching was usually the foundation of the institutional ethos. The emphasis was on sin, guilt, prayer, punishment in hell and repentance, set within prevailing Victorian values of hard work, discipline and social class hierarchies. The institutions were largely autonomous, with management leaving key decisions on behaviour, discipline and staffing to the head of the organisation, usually a nun or clergyman.

In some women's refuges, for example, those offered shelter and protection were also required to repent for their sins. The Magdalen laundries were a notorious example, where women deemed to be sinners were condemned to long hours scrubbing stains from white linen laundry.

Conditions were often harsh. Provision – reliant on voluntary contributions – was basic. Some of the consequences of provision, born out of necessity, were not ideal. The confinement of hundreds of boys who had committed minor offences to a ship on the Mersey was a misconceived policy when judged by present day criteria. Sending young people and children to Canada was another which appeared at first to be a good idea, allowing escape from extreme urban poverty. It was only later that questions were asked about how their labour was used in Canada, their loneliness, their separation from relatives and other issues around what we would today call child protection.

In the early years of the twentieth century such provision was more difficult to maintain. The initial wave of pioneering founders were no longer involved. The momentum and commitment needed to maintain such provision was weakened. State provision became more systematic, while gradual improvements in public health removed many of the problems. Standards were increasingly raised through new legislation, making it more difficult to maintain voluntary provision.

In time much of the provision became more closely linked to the state, relying on public funding for a substantial part of their services. Other provision closed down or adapted by reducing their services or restructuring. The legacy of this pioneering welfare work remains to this day, with many schools still being managed and partly maintained by religious organisations. In social welfare the Nugent Care Society is the inheritor of James Nugent's many initiatives. Other religious groups, such as the Sisters of Mercy or the Poor Servants of the Mother of God, continue their work in Liverpool and the surrounding areas. However, they no longer have the resources which were available to their predecessors, and survive largely on the periphery of the much larger state provision.

One of the consequences of so much Catholic welfare provision was that the Irish community was slow to integrate.[41] With parish life, and its social setting of clubs and societies, Catholic schools and welfare organisations, the community looked inwards on itself, becoming self-reliant, and taking pride in doing so. Church authorities, anxious to preserve their own numbers, encouraged this position.

Of course, commentators point out that there were many institutions and influential individuals in the host community who were unsympathetic, not to say hostile, towards the Irish, which also had the effect of cementing their relative isolation. Stereotyped as dirty, feckless, lazy, violent and quick tempered, not to be trusted, their pathway to integration was not a smooth one. Integration into the local Liverpool community was to be a gradual process, taking generations.

CHAPTER EIGHT

THE IRISH NATIONALIST PARTY

The Irish Nationalist Party entered Liverpool politics in October 1875, when Lawrence Connolly, a business man, fruit merchant and popular local figure, was persuaded to oppose William Williams in Scotland Ward. Williams was a Liberal with a 'spotless' personal and political record, who was supportive of Home Rule for Ireland. He was exactly the sort of candidate Irish voters had been supporting for years. With the franchise restricted to business people and property owners, political leadership at this time was exclusively middle class. There was little opportunity for Irish people, however wealthy, to enter the Conservative ranks, where local connections, loyalty to the crown and commitment to the Church of England were of such importance. The Liberal Party, on the other hand, was sympathetic to reform, and contained many non-conformists opposed to the established Church. The Liberals supported Catholic rights, and were natural opponents of the Tories.

The Catholic Club – founded by Richard Sheil in 1844 – was a rallying point for wealthy Catholics who supported the Liberals.[1] Its forerunner was the Protector Society, founded in 1839 to register Catholic voters. It was intended as a counterweight to Hugh McNeile's Protestant Association. Here middle class Irish Catholics with an interest in local politics had found a home. C.J. Corbally and Richard Sheil, both Irish and Catholic, were club members who had been successful local politicians within the Liberal Party. Both had been active in the struggle to establish Catholic rights in local administration.

In 1873 the Catholic Club could boast of five Liberal councillors in their ranks. The Wexford born James Whitty was a successful Liverpool merchant, who had held seats in the Council, the School Board and the Select Vestry over a period of thirty years. C.J. Corbally was a magistrate and a councillor and driving force behind the Catholic Benevolent Society. Others were John Yates, James Fairhurst, P.S. Bidwell and John McArdle. Catholic clergy knew that they could be relied upon at all times to consistently put forward the Catholic point of view, and to resist proposals which might have an adverse effect on Catholic church interests. This was the establishment which was threatened by the new wave of nationalism.[2]

By the early 1870s the long standing alliance between the Liberals and the Irish Catholics was beginning to come apart. In the first place the numbers of Irish-born voters had grown steadily since the 1830s. The widening of the franchise in 1867 further increased their number. Many felt that this increased presence could be converted to a more vocally Irish Nationalist political movement if a suitable cause were to be found.

In 1870 the Liberal government introduced an Education Bill, which proposed universal primary schooling. The Catholic Church was vocal in its opposition, fearing that Catholic parishes could not afford to support sufficient schools for all Catholic children of primary age. They found unlikely allies in the Anglicans who had similar fears. In 1873 Bishop O'Reilly – Liverpool's first Irish-born Bishop – declared 'all Catholics were prepared to throw every Party to the winds and remain simply Catholic.'[3] The new legislation was passed that same year. It established local School Boards whose members were to be elected. Women were allowed a vote in the process. As the Board was the body which made key decisions about the financing of local schools, it was a significant election for the Catholic Church. Priests took an active part, arranging meetings for voters and instructing Catholics how to vote. All five Catholic candidates were elected. This victory confirmed the growing strength of the Irish in local politics, and resulted in more intense competition for their votes. Liberals now needed candidates who would support Irish Home Rule if they wanted to ensure election. In January 1873 ex-Fenian John Denvir and Alfred Crilly were the moving forces behind the establishment of the nationalist Home Government Association branch in Liverpool.[4] Though small to begin with, it rapidly grew in strength during the following two years, being the first constitutional organisation in many years prioritising the Irish Nationalist cause.

In October 1875 this group decided to enter the political arena. Denvir and his colleagues selected Connolly as a popular local figure. Connolly, an Irishman, put himself forward as a Catholic candidate. Boys from Father Nugent's Soho Street Refuge distributed leaflets.[5] Opposing him was the Liberal Williams, a Welsh Protestant. Only at the last minute did Connolly declare himself to be the Home Rule candidate. How would this go down with the voters? He defeated the Liberal by 928 votes, thus heralding the arrival of Irish Nationalism in Liverpool politics.

The uneasy alliance between the Irish and the Liberals now became even more fraught. One commentator summed-up the situation as follows: 'The Tory is regarded as an open enemy; the Whig as a treacherous friend.'

In marginal wards, such as St Anne's and Pitt Street, Liberals ensured that their candidates supported Home Rule, in order to secure the Irish vote. When Charles McArdle's cousin, John McArdle – a Catholic Irishman, a Liberal, and the sitting councillor – was defeated by Home Ruler Dr Alexander Bligh in a bitter contest in Scotland Ward, feelings were running very high. Home Rulers packed Liberal meetings with their supporters, heckled and generally caused disruption. Charles McArdle received a letter of expulsion from the Liberal Catholic Club for his nationalist views. Nationalists urged on by John Denvir, resigned. With the loss of the great majority of Catholic support, the Club was now impotent in local politics, and never contested another election.

Most of the new Nationalist councillors had formerly been members of the Catholic Club. They were middle class, well educated – with one barrister and one doctor in their ranks – fairly well off, and, of course, Catholic. The more radical Nationalists, under Denvir's leadership, had fresh inspiration from a new arrival at Westminster – Charles Stewart Parnell. Young, handsome and charismatic, he made his Fenian sympathies clear when he stated in Parliament that he did not believe the Manchester Martyrs – convicted of shooting a prison officer in a Fenian jail break – were guilty. He also began holding meetings with Fenian revolutionaries in France and the United States. In the same year, his radical approach was supported at the Home Rule Association conference in Liverpool when the following motion was carried.

'That members of this branch consider that the past policy of the Home Rule Party would not be sufficiently rigorous for the exigencies of the present situation and in our opinion a more independent policy should be adopted in future.'[6]

With calls for 'a more active and vigorous policy on the part of their parliamentary representatives' Parnell was elected President of the Home Rule Association at the Liverpool meeting. It was soon afterwards that J.L. Finegan, MP made the suggestion, on St Patrick's Day 1878, that the Irish in Liverpool: 'must send a Irishman of its own to Parliament.'[7] Another inspiration for the radicals was Parliamentarian Michael Davitt – a radical with libertarian and socialist beliefs – who had been brought up in Lancashire, and was active in the Land League, which resisted the increasing evictions in Ireland. Parnell's visit to Liverpool in 1879 was organised by Denvir, in the teeth of resistance from the moderates. The strength of the radical wing of the Party was confirmed when Parnell, escorted by the newly formed Irish National Foresters in full regalia, addressed a crowd of 20,000 from the steps of St George's Hall.[8] The Nationalist councillors must have felt that they had been catapulted from the quiet backwaters of the Liberal Party into the eye of a hurricane.

The Tory leader, Arthur Forwood, regarded the arrival of an openly nationalist Irish party in Liverpool as a significant turning point. Up until then, in his view, parties may have had their differences, but all 'believed in the unity of the Empire for Liverpool purposes' – the Liverpool purposes being prosperity through trade. Prominent Tory Edward Whitley suggested a Tory/Liberal alliance, to ensure that the city was governed by 'respectable people'. However, the Tories had little need to enter an alliance. In many districts, the Irish Home Rule agitation worked strongly in their favour. As E.F. Rathbone put it, 'Hughes of Everton, known as Hughes, beat Vining by 15. Hughes, Home Rule candidate, after Everton knew it, was beaten by 1,500'.[9]

The Liverpool Nationalists could rely on a wide spectrum of support within the Irish community. The elected representatives were cautious middle-class councillors, whilst party leadership and membership was much more radical. The party was held together by the common commitment to the aspirations of Irish Nationalism, and their perceived common identity. The party was not divided by class interests. Nor did they have a social policy, although their strongholds were in working class areas.

The Catholic hierarchy remained suspicious of nationalism and where it might lead. It was not only an alternative power base in the community, but it might foster hostility towards Catholicism in Tory ranks, and lead congregations into subversive activity. On the other hand, the elected Irish Nationalist representatives in Liverpool – unlike those in Ireland – were exclusively Catholic and in most instances would take the church 'line' on issues which might come up, including education. In the council chamber the Irish councillors could be relied upon to fiercely defend the Catholic position. They needed to keep on the right side of the Catholic clergy who were extremely influential amongst the people, and were generally conservative in social attitudes and outlook. In contrast to the church hierarchy, the political attitudes of parish clergy towards the Empire and towards Nationalism varied greatly from one individual to the next. Pat O'Mara remembers Father Twomey, at St Vincent's, as follows.

'He hated the English more bitterly than any Irishman I have ever known and was always a source of irritation to the more prudent and diplomatic Father Ryan. The Twomey sermons from the pulpit were always looked forward to with intense glee from the congregation, and with equally intense dissatisfaction by Father Ryan.'[10]

Such divisions amongst parish clergy on the issue of Irish politics were not unusual, leaving parishioners free to make up their own mind as to which brand of nationalism they should follow.

The newly elected Nationalists on the council allied with the Liberals in the council chamber. The Nationalists could not be defeated in certain core wards, including Vauxhall and Scotland, with three seats in each. They could also make recommendations to Irish voters, which was a powerful tool in marginal seats. Where Liberals selected candidates with the Irish vote in mind, they ran the risk of alienating other sections of the electorate. In time relations with the Nationalists became more formalised, and included permission to attend Liberal executive committee meetings, admission to shadow Council posts and Council committee positions.

When the Liberals came into power at Westminster under Gladstone relations with the Nationalists became more complicated. Though committed to land reform, Gladstone did not introduce a Home Rule bill as the radicals had wanted. Rather he passed a Coercion Act, with the result that Parnell was imprisoned in Ireland for his activities in support of tenant rights.

The moderate Nationalists, who continued to support the Liberals in spite of these measures, were labelled as unpatriotic. In 1883 the militants managed to take over the Central Council of the Liverpool Land and Labour League.[11] The moderates were expelled. But this move, orchestrated by John Denvir, did not resolve the difficulties. Dr Commins and Lawrence Connolly, although both expelled, held elected positions locally, were popular with voters and were friends of Parnell. In November 1883 the militants ran four candidates – including 'Dandy' Pat Byrne and John Denvir – against the moderates. Both Denvir and Byrne went down to heavy defeats, a tough lesson for the hard liners.[12]

Byrne came back again the following year, challenging the moderate Charles McArdle in Vauxhall. Denvir's newspaper the *Nationalist and Irish Programme* attacked McArdle as both a traitor and a hypocrite 'for he had on his address that he was a follower of Charles Stewart Parnell, whereas he had publicly and notoriously disobeyed him.'[13] This time Byrne was successful. There was now civil war within the local party, and open conflict between Commins and Byrne. To Commins and other established councillors, Byrne was not an appropriate addition to the council chamber. They were appalled at the prospect of sitting in the chamber with an uneducated former dock labourer. Commins, a barrister, and now a member of parliament, distanced himself from Byrne by openly insulting him in the council chamber, suggesting that he return to primary school, to learn how to read and to acquire some manners – a blatant attack on Byrne's working-class background. That Byrne was now just as wealthy as any establishment figure seems to have enraged his opponents even further.

A secton of the Dandy Pat memorial which stands in the grounds of St Anthony's Church, Scotland Road, Liverpool. Photo: Simon Rahilly.

Besides advocating a more radical direction in Nationalist policies, Byrne was also conscious of the need for an articulated social programme. Established nationalist councillors, though they represented some of the most deprived districts in the city, never came forward with any programme for social improvement. Byrne, having himself been a dock worker, and being in close daily contact with local people through his business, was more aware of the need for action. Commins was dismissive of Byrne's social conscience as 'ridiculous philanthropy'. Byrne campaigned for better wages for those who collected sewage waste from the courts – the 'scavengers'. He was insulted as 'the scavenger's friend', a badge he wore with pride in the local area.

Holding on to a local council seat was important for aspiring middle-class candidates, since a common career path for Liverpool Nationalist councillors was to advance to take a parliamentary seat. Parnell was in a position to promote those he thought worthy, as candidates for seats in Ireland. Commins was successful in South Roscommon as was Lawrence Connolly in South Longford.

But by 1885 the character of elected representatives was changing. The patrician figures, converts to Nationalism, who had formerly been Liberals, had lost influence, retired or moved on to other things. Those who replaced them were more grounded locally, business people in service to the Irish community, such as butchers, shopkeepers and publicans.

The Election of T.P. O'Connor

Reforms introduced by Gladstone's Liberal administration in 1885 included the widening of the franchise, an increase in representation for the cities, and the introduction of single member constituencies. Liverpool was now to have representation increased from three seats to nine, the largest number of any city outside of London. The creation of these seats caused great excitement amongst Liverpool nationalists. They calculated that there was the possibility of a successful Nationalist candidate, certainly in the Scotland seat, but also possibly in Exchange.[14] Some optimists added Kirkdale as a possibility, far fetched though it might seem.

The boundaries of the new constituencies would be crucial, and there was heated debate over the decisions being taken. In Exchange, where the core council wards of Exchange and Vauxhall were solidly Nationalist, the decision on which adjoining areas would be included with them was crucial. The addition of Lime Street – which nationalists insisted should have been positioned in Abercromby – ensured that the seat would be marginal for the Nationalists, with their best chance now being the Scotland constituency.

Parnell began the electioneering process by intervening to impose discipline and unity on the local factions. He came to Liverpool personally to persuade Dandy Pat Byrne of the need to end divisions.[15] The Irish National League (INL) of Great Britain was now the title of the Nationalist organisation. Branches in Liverpool expanded from three to fourteen in just two years. A National Conference was held in Liverpool to decide strategy for the election. Parnell's grip on party discipline was tightened. The branches were established to provide – amongst other things – electoral support, organising voters and canvassing, rather than debating and shaping policy. Parnell and his election co-ordinator T.P. O'Connor made Liverpool their headquarters for the election campaign, staying at the North Western Hotel.

There was popular support for the idea that Parnell himself should stand in Liverpool. There was also strong support for the local favourite 'Dandy' Pat Byrne, the choice of the radical Nationalists. Parnell decided that Galway man T.P. O'Connor – who was not well known in Liverpool – should be nominated for the Scotland seat, where Irish support was strongest. The local party had little choice but to bow to this decision. There was also a strong possibility that a Home Rule candidate might have success in Exchange. The journalist Justin Carthy was nominated. However, the politics in Exchange were to become extremely contorted during the campaign. The Liberals nominated T.E. Stevens, a local councillor. Later Parnell put himself forward as a candidate, presumably with the idea that such a strong candidate might actually have the political weight to carry this marginal seat. John Redmond, a future Party leader, stood in Kirkdale. The extent of Catholic clerical support for Parnell can be seen from the names of those who appeared on the platform at an election meeting in the League Hall, St Anne Street – a venue which held some two thousand – during the campaign. Those attending included Fathers Roche, Gaughan, Dowling, Dooley, Hikey, Doyle and Rigby. The long list of local dignitaries at the meeting did not include Patrick Byrne.[16]

Parnell's overall strategy was to gain enough seats to hold the balance of power at Westminster, so as to be in a position to bargain with both the Liberals and the Tories for the introduction of a Home Rule Bill. There was intense excitement at this prospect within the Irish community.

The Liberal leadership – following a meeting in Liverpool – nominated Captain O'Shea for Exchange. Nationalist canvassers had a difficult task. They advised voters to vote for Parnell if he stayed on the ballot. If he did not stand, then the advice was to vote Tory, as an additional Tory seat would reduce the Liberal total, making the hung parliament they wanted more likely.

At this time Parnell was having an affair with O'Shea's wife, Catherine, a matter which was not public knowledge. Parnell wanted O'Shea to agree to a divorce, thus allowing Catherine (Kitty) the freedom to marry. O'Shea was refusing, as he was expecting a generous payment when Kitty inherited from her aunt, who was so far refusing to die. Were negotiations on these matters taking place behind the scenes? Did O'Shea undertake to allow the divorce if he gained the seat? We can only speculate. In a surprise move two days before polling Parnell withdrew his candidature. Not only that, but rather than follow the current party line until then, that Nationalists should support the Tory, Parnell recommended support for the Liberal O'Shea, who was, after all, an Irish man and a Catholic. This move, which was contrary to the manifesto, astounded his colleagues. The local Liberal candidate, Stevens, also withdrew, but not early enough to stop his name going on the ballot. As the *Daily Post* commented: 'Captain O'Shea came into the field at the eleventh hour, and might therefore naturally be supposed to labour under a great disadvantage.'

The atmosphere ahead of the election was feverish. In one incident an Irishman challenged some of those holding the local business vote, in the registration court. He was dramatically forced to flee the court when his action failed and costs were awarded against him.[17] When votes were counted, O'Shea lost by just 55 votes. The 36 cast for the withdrawn Stevens would have reduced that margin to just 19. In other words, had the campaign been less chaotic on Parnell's part, the seat might well have been won by an Irish candidate.

O'Connor, as predicted, was elected for the Liverpool Scotland constituency, thus becoming the first, and only, Irish nationalist parliamentary representative in Britain. He had a comfortable victory, defeating the independent Woodward by 2,728 to 1,492. He was also elected for Galway. However, Parnell, in a further twist, persuaded him to step aside in Galway and allow Captain O'Shea to take the seat. Elsewhere in Liverpool the remaining seven seats went to the Conservatives. In parliament the Liberals had an advantage over the Tories by 86 seats, which also happened to be the exact number of seats Parnell had won. He had achieved his goal of holding the balance of power. He supported the Tories at first, but when they could not come up with a workable proposal on Ireland, he sided with the Liberals. The resulting rebellion in the Liberal ranks led to the downfall of the Liberal government and another election. This time in Liverpool, with their support strengthened by Liberal identification with Home Rule, the Tory vote increased. They again took every seat in the city, with the exception of Scotland. The Tory organiser, Forwood, refused to put a candidate against O'Connor, remarking that the constituency 'was as Irish as County Tipperary.'

Nationalists in Liverpool Council

The Liverpool Nationalists were now part of an efficient electoral machine, tightly controlled by Parnell. The character of the leadership had changed. John Denvir had left Liverpool to work nationally for the INL. Patrick Byrne died (1890) and Lawrence Connolly and others retired. Younger men, such as the Galway born solicitor Jeremy Lynskey (28) and Tom Kelly (26) came into leadership positions.

A significant addition to the nationalist group at this time was J.G. Taggart (27) first elected to the Corporation in 1888. Often described as, 'Liverpool's first working class councillor' (a title Dandy Pat Byrne might well have claimed for himself) he was extremely capable. He had come to England as a boy of five, and had worked in coal mines and as a labourer in the Tate and Lyle sugar works. He was an accomplished musician, and a teetotaller. He attended evening classes, winning Queen's prizes in many subjects including chemistry, maths, mechanics and physiology. He was described as, 'the ablest of the Nationalists, who knows more about municipal administration, perhaps, than even the town clerk.'[18] He was an early manifestation of the Nationalist/Labour stance which was to become popular in later decades. He was anti-imperialist and frequently outspoken in the Nationalist cause, often baiting the Conservatives. In 1900 he was expelled – at the initiative of the Conservative leader Salvidge – from the Corporation Estate Committee and the Lancashire Asylums Board, because of his support for the Boers (who were fighting the British) in the Boer War. On the labour side he worked with the Liverpool Trades Council to campaign for a Fair Wages Clause in council contracts.

'The nationalist party was now a close-knit thoroughly organised electorally influential body of men who effectively maintained the local Irish organisation as an efficient locally powerful cog in a national electioneering machine.'[19] In other words an organisation whose main function was not to contribute to the democratic formation of policy, but which was merely an electioneering machine.[20]

On 24 December 1889, Captain O'Shea filed for divorce, citing Parnell as co-respondent, although the case did not come for trial until 15 November 1890. This news was a scandalous bombshell in Victorian society and amongst Irish Catholics. Opponents of Nationalism saw it as an opportunity to bring Parnell down and to seriously wound the Nationalist cause. Support for Parnell remained strong for some months. However, Catholic clerical disapproval began to undermine him, especially in rural areas. Once the divorce was granted the Irish party split, with a radical minority continuing to support Parnell. In Liverpool three party branches remained loyal to him. Shortly before the Party's leadership election in 1890, the Central Branch, under Denvir's control, turned against Parnell, passing a motion – by sixty-one votes to three – declaring: 'that we appreciate deeply the services of Mr Parnell to Ireland, but we regret that on the ground of high moral principle, and in the best interests of our country, we cannot join in the wishes which have been expressed for his continuing at the present time to retain the position he has held.'[21] Although Parnell survived a leadership election, he was eventually rejected when Gladstone declared that the next general election – and therefore the Home Rule cause – would be lost if Parnell continued in his position.

In Liverpool three local branches – St Anne's, South Toxteth and Exchange – formed the Liverpool Parnell Leadership Committee the following March. These branches were more leftwing in their politics and fought 'on the basis that they represented the working classes, and would effect social reforms within the Irish community … sympathising with the Labour cause'.[22] Although Parnell died the following year, divisions between the Parnellite and anti-Parnell factions persisted for years.

In November 1892 the Liberals, with the support of the Irish Nationalists, were able to take control of Liverpool city council, for the first time in 51 years. Their success was short lived. The Tories were to return to local dominance in 1895. Nationalists held public office on the Council for the first time when five of their number were given posts as deputy-chairmen of committees.

Arthur Forwood, Conservative leader and electioneering tactician, made good use of the Irish link to attack the new administration. Addressing the Working Men's Christian Association, he put the question: 'Was Liverpool to be governed by the Irish Nationalists?' With the predictable cries of 'No' in response. 'Welshmen and Scotsmen,' he noted, 'became good citizens, leaving their national fads outside the council chamber,' but 'it was different with the body of Irishmen (a voice 'Papists')'.[23]

The short lived administration achieved little. The Nationalist movement was engaged in the Home Rule issue at a national level. Locally housing and deprivation in the inner-city districts were pressing questions, but little progress was made. The coalition came under attack from both the left and right.

The Nationalists were now led by Jeremy Lynskey, a Galway-born Irish Catholic and a Liverpool solicitor. He was put in charge of drawing up local boundary changes, with the result that Nationalists stood to gain a number of seats. When accused of unfair practice he declared '200,000 Irishmen had a right to fair representation,'[24] implying that they had been under-represented in the previous distribution. There were now twenty two wards in place of sixteen. With close to a hundred thousand voters, Liverpool was the largest municipal constituency, by population, in Britain.

In the subsequent election, in spite of Lynskey's juggling, Conservative seats increased from twenty nine to sixty four. The Liberal-Nationalist group declined from thirty three to thirty two, thus cementing Conservative domination of municipal politics for the foreseeable future.[25] Forwood's methods – known as Tory democracy – having been developed in Liverpool, were now applied more generally across the country, to such an extent that Forwood claimed credit for the Tory general election victory that same year.[26]

The Liberals blamed their municipal set-backs on the Irish, claiming that it was Irish aggressiveness which drove voters into the arms of the Tories, with the argument that electors in Liverpool did not want to see the world's greatest port dominated by Irish Nationalists.

Defeat in the municipal elections left the Nationalist party leadership vulnerable. Lynskey, one of four Irish Nationalist councillors who worked in the office of Irish-born Liverpool lawyer W. Madden in Church Street, continued the tradition of strict party discipline established under Parnell. But he was not associated with the radical wing of the Party. He was closely associated with the Liberal leaders, and like the Catholic clubbers of years gone by enjoyed the receptions and dinners associated with municipal office. While keeping his distance from the more radical Nationalists who were making preparations for commemorating the centenary of the 1798 Rising, Lynskey attended Queen Victoria's Jubilee celebrations at the Adelphi Hotel, thus earning for himself the nick-name 'Jubilee Jeremy' also known as the 'mutton eater' as lamb had been on the menu. He was also widely criticised for neglect of the poor social conditions which still persisted in the Irish wards, and was eventually forced to resign.

Harford Challenges O'Connor

Liverpool born Irish Nationalists now became increasingly important in the party. Local man Frank Harford stood against Lynskey in 1898. Lynskey – a lawyer – had him disqualified on a technicality. When this decision was eventually over-ruled, both Frank Harford and his brother Austin won council seats. The brothers now established their own organisation, the Irish Nationalist Association based in South Scotland ward.[27] They were influenced by the ideas of Arthur Griffith and William O'Brien, Irish politicians who advocated social reform alongside nationalism. The new party included reformers such as John O'Shea, who had been elected to the School Board. With the support of the newspaper the *Liverpool Catholic Herald* – which welcomed 'the opportunity to join a Party founded on democratic lines' – the new party was to be more focused on poverty and deprivation. The old party had not been opposed to the working poor. Lynskey was sympathetic – he had represented the dockers during strikes – but they had never done anything effective to address the obvious needs of the poorest in the city. Lynskey and his group were nationalists first and foremost. Austin Harford – though nationalist – stood as 'champion of the poor' and as a representative of 'the suffering poor of the city'.[28]

The *Liverpool Mercury*'s view was that Harford's aim was to: 'better the Irish cause in the city, and that betterment to be in the hands of the people, and to let them have the working out of their own destiny.' Harford's message struck a chord with the most deprived. The Basket Women and Street Traders Association gave him their active support.[29] The Harfords, in contrast to Lynskey, were vocal in their support for the

1798 and Manchester Martyrs Commemorations. They put on concerts featuring popular Irish songs, recitations and dancing. 'Frank was in great demand for his poignant rendition of Irish ballads.'

1898 was a significant point in the party's history. For the first time Liverpool born Nationalists, such as the Harfords, were in the majority amongst the Nationalist city councillors. This factor alone does much to explain the growing emphasis on local issues.

The Harfords were resentful that their breakaway organisation – the Irish Nationalist Association (INA) – which was now so successful at the polls, was not gaining recognition from the powerful parliamentary party. Austin Harford spoke out publicly against mainstream Nationalists, and eventually took the bold step of proposing to stand against O'Connor for the parliamentary seat. The prospect was now a three-cornered fight, as the Conservative Rutherford – courting the left in the form of the Liverpool Trades Council – advocated improved housing. He was a strong candidate who made references to his Irish ancestry in his election material, and took to dressing his horses – which drew his coach around the constituency – in khaki, to remind people of his support for the Boer war. To attract nationalists he reminded them that the Boers – whom many Nationalist politicians, including Taggart, supported – had oppressed Catholics. Should Harford split the Irish vote, Rutherford was in with a chance.

O'Connor presented an easy target. He had been in the seat for thirteen years, but had largely neglected it. When parliament was not sitting he preferred to head for Paris rather than Liverpool. He was known for throwing lavish parties and enjoying a good glass of wine. He concentrated his attention on the affairs of the party nationally, and stood above local issues, which proved to be his Achilles Heel. Harford, with his local popularity, his activism and his social policy, was in a strong position. O'Connor, enraged that 'the torch of discord was introduced for the first time into Scotland Division' was forced to come to Liverpool and spend time and money electioneering. O'Connor and Harford lambasted each other. O'Connor raged against 'the rival gang', characterising Harford as 'coming from the miserable opposition, a hole in the corner place', while Harford referred to 'the dilettante purveyor of small talk and boudoir gossip.'[30] John Redmond, the leader of the newly re-united national party stepped in, sending a telegram to Harford with the message, 'My urgent advice is to retire for the sake of Ireland.' Harford obeyed. O'Connor's opponent Rutherford continued to attack his lifestyle, stating that he 'keeps a carriage and a footman, and moves in the most swaggering society of modern Babylon.'[31] O'Connor polled 2,044 against Rutherford's 1,484, his narrowest margin to date.

His victory was tempered by the continued success of Harford's INA in local politics. In November John O'Shea took the third of three seats in the heartland of South Scotland ward.[32] He was from Kerry in Ireland, a tea dealer on a small scale locally, who was part of Harford's group. He was a well-established party figure with a long-standing commitment in the Scotland Road area. He had canvassed for Lawrence Connolly back in 1875. He was 64 when he took the seat, and, in accordance with the group's social commitment, went on to become active in the Corporation Slum Clearance Committee, a sub-committee of the Housing Committee. He held the seat until his death in 1922.[33]

It was clear that the progressive agenda of Harford and his colleagues remained popular and that they were not going to go away. Their politics were a combination of two streams. The first was a commitment to a resolution of the Irish situation through Home Rule, alongside a strong cultural and sentimental attachment to that country. The other, and now more important plank in the platform was action on the local issues of housing, safety at work, health, sanitation and related issues. Conditions in the area were such that it was clear that these questions now had to take priority. Such objectives were so close to those of the emerging Labour Party, that Harford's position is often described as 'Nat-Labism'.

Following his victory in 1900, O'Connor remained circumspect. In spite of his robust rhetoric against Harford during the campaign, he seemed uncertain as to his standing in the constituency. At the same time he was preoccupied with difficulties elsewhere in his life. His marriage was breaking down. At one point he seemed to be considering a withdrawal from politics. His mood soon changed, however, as he accepted the need to become more active if he was to hold on to his seat. He began making frequent appearances in Liverpool. His cultivation of the constituency in 1901 included touring the area, addressing public meetings, and attending an executive meeting of the National Union of Dock Labourers (NUDL), where there was a strong Irish contingent. The General Secretary, James Sexton, was of Irish stock and an ex-Fenian. O'Connor agreed to promote their proposed amendments to the Factory and Workshops Bill then before Parliament. He was successful in this, and was applauded by the dockers upon his return in October. 'For the first time in our history, we have effective control over the plant and machinery, gear, gangways and ladders.'[34]

However, Harford's INA remained a worrying presence. It was democratic, the officers were local, and members were actively involved in shaping policy. O'Connor remarked that Liverpool was now the only place where Nationalists were divided, and continued to make pointed references to this in his speeches. 'When there is unity throughout the world, there should be unity in Liverpool. Liverpool should hold the vanguard in the fight to right Ireland's wrongs.'[35] O'Connor soon came up with a settlement proposal, which Harford accepted. Harford's INA would join the Irish National League and take control of the local branch.

Harford was to be the chairman. Fellow party members – including the old guard, such as Dr Commins, the former Liberal – would now be fellow party members. It was a bitter pill to swallow, but Harford accepted the need for compromise. He even agreed to withdraw his own progressive candidate, Daly, in favour of the old enemy, Lynskey. Others in the Lynskey circle – such as his brother-in-law Kearney, 'a man concerned almost solely with literature and gardening,' – continued to be advanced, while in the council chamber Harford continued to play second fiddle to the established councillors, including Taggart and Commins.[36]

Reconciliation with Harford gave a powerful impetus to O'Connor's re-incarnation as a local man of the people. Harford organised mass meetings for O'Connor to address, and accompanied him to sports meetings and concerts. Harford and his brother Frank were popular speakers, who were active in putting on 'Irish' entertainment. In addition they had the powerful support of Diamond's *Liverpool Catholic Herald*. At the same time Harford and O'Shea were dedicated to making progress on housing reform. O'Connor found his place in this context, taking up social issues where parliamentary action was required, and using his natural charm at Irish entertainments, sports events and parish occasions. He played the role of patrician politician to a tee; well dressed, courteous, aloof from the grubby dealings of local politics, golden tongued and magnanimous. Having no difficulty relating to others of an Irish background, O'Connor soon became very popular amongst constituents.

He seemed to be just as surprised by this as everyone else, and derived great enjoyment from his new position. He became the unofficial civic leader of what was almost a small nation of its own, centred on the Vauxhall Road and Scotland Road arteries. It was a compact self-sufficient community with close extended family ties and networks of churches, parish halls, clubs, pubs and entertainment venues. Employment was found nearby in the docks and allied processing and carting occupations. The party had three pillars. Its suppporters were Irish, Catholic and primarily working class. O'Connor and Harford between them were well equipped to thrive in this environment and to protect the party's position within it. They frequently appeared together at events such as St Patrick's Day celebrations in March or the Irish Athletic Festival in August. Harford remained the driving force locally, personally attending branch meetings to keep in touch with local members. He took the lead at key events in the nationalist calendar, including the annual commemoration of the Manchester Martyrs and a torchlight procession to St George's Hall in 1903, to mark the centenary of Robert Emmet's rising.

These days were perhaps the high point for Nationalism in Liverpool. The continued drama of the possibility that a Home Rule Bill might again be introduced, supported by O'Connor and his colleagues at Westminster, was the life blood of the movement. The re-invigorated local leadership was addressing housing issues. Nationalist meetings were well attended and branches were thriving.

The continued attacks from Protestant demagoguery and Conservative politicians served only to cement the party further, engendering a feeling of solidarity amongst Irish Catholics in the face of local hostility, not just to their politics, but to their identity and their presence in the city. The Nationalist party functioned as a voice and vehicle for their resolve and defiance. But in the words of James Larkin 'Home Rule never put a loaf of bread in any workingman's pocket.'

Which Way for Nationalism – Irish, Catholic or Labour?

Whilst attacks from the Protestant side served only to strengthen the party, criticism from Catholic sources and the growing strength of Labour both presented real challenges. On the one hand Labour's social programme was attractive to the core Nationalist working class vote, whilst on the other there was growing support for the idea of a specifically Catholic party.

Labour in the first decade of the twentieth century did not have the strength to challenge the Nationalists. Up until then the Labour movement had been greatly squeezed in Liverpool. The Tory electoral machine, promoting 'Tory democracy' as the way to protect the bible, the crown and the constitution from godless socialists and subversive Irish, with the support of the Conservative Working Men's Associations (CWMA), struck a resonant chord with Liverpool Protestants. Many heads were still filled with the fears of Catholic aggression promoted by the preacher George Wise and his colleagues. At the same time Irish Nationalists were fiercely protective of their own vote, emphasising traditional Catholic and Irish values at election times.

When the Independent Labour Party – forerunner of the present day Labour Party – contested Great George ward in 1892, their candidate – Rouse – faced a Liberal on one side and a Conservative on the other. As the Liberal was a Home Rule supporter, the Irish vote went to him. The Tory Democracy platform, with policies on pensions and wages designed to appeal to the working man attracted most of the remaining votes, leaving Rouse with just 20.[37] Lynskey's advice to his voters at the time was to 'remember that they are Irishmen first and Liverpudlians after.' In the same year the United Irish League (UIL) branch in Toxteth refused to support the Labour candidate. That he was not Catholic was a significant factor in their decision.

Where Labour put up candidates with strong Irish and Catholic connections, they had a better chance of success. In 1905, harried by sectarianism from both sides, they managed to win two seats in the council. In both cases the candidates had Catholic and Nationalist credentials. James Sexton stood in St Anne's. He was a dockers' leader and trade unionist, but he was also Catholic with an Irish heritage and a record of Nationalist sympathies. Although some UIL members resigned following the decision to support him, Sexton won the seat. The other victor was John Morrissey. His Irish credentials were clearly displayed in his full name, John Wolfe Tone Morrissey (Wolfe Tone being the leader of the Irish rebellion in 1798). With a brother in the priesthood his Catholic credentials were impeccable. He became the first socialist elected to public office in Liverpool when he won the contest for city auditor in 1901. His prospects were greatly enhanced when he proved to be diligent and efficient in the post, exposing malpractice and corruption. He won the Kensington seat in a three cornered fight with a Liberal and a Conservative. This left the Conservatives with a narrow majority on the council, with 69 members against 47 Liberals, 13 Nationalists, five Protestants and two Labour. Conservatives had lost ground, some said because they did not raise the sectarian issue. 'When the party defended its municipal record without effective sectarian incitement, it palpably failed.'[38]

The Irish vote was again enlisted in support of Labour in Toxteth in the 1906 parliamentary election, when Sexton stood against the Conservative Houston. Sexton's agent was James Larkin, another with an Irish Catholic background, and an active trade unionist. Sexton knew Larkin's strengths. He was a local, he was strong, popular, a gifted speaker, and fiercely combative; ideal qualifications for an election agent in Liverpool during that era. Although there was no Nationalist standing, the contest was relentlessly sectarian. Houston had strong support from the Orange Order who regarded the seat as theirs as of right. Tories were surprised at the audacity of Labour putting up a candidate. It had been ten years since Houston had been challenged. The contest proved to be bitter. Sexton recalled that Larkin 'displayed an energy that was almost superhuman. The division was one of the storm centres of religious strife, and a stronghold of the Orange Order, through whom Mr Houston held the seat. My being a Roman Catholic naturally made the situation still more lively. But nothing could frighten Jim. He plunged recklessly into the fray where the fighting was most furious, organised gigantic processions against Chinese labour on the Rand, faced hostile mobs saturated with religious bigotry who were howling for our blood'.[39] In Sexton's words: 'The Dingle boys beat the Protestant drum until the skin nearly burst.' A Tory leaflet was distributed to all voters explaining, 'What socialism really means', stating that, 'Socialism would destroy family life, 'no man would rise' as everything would be state planned, state-run and state-crushed'.[40]

Sexton later remarked: 'I am convinced that it was largely owing to Larkin's overwhelming labours that we reduced a Tory majority from four thousand to five hundred, but I would rather not give my opinion on some of the methods he adopted to achieve that highly commendable result'.[41] Sexton lost by 781 votes.

Labour candidates continued to be denounced as godless socialists by both Catholic and Protestant opponents. They were branded a threat to religious and family values. Such statements, whether from clergy or politicians of any shade, helped to sustain the Nationalist vote. The emerging new political geography was well illustrated in the Kirkdale parliamentary by-election of 1907, when the Labour candidate, John Hill, stood against the conservative, McArthur. Hill was a religious man, involved in bible teaching, a teetotaller who was critical of secular education. Salvidge launched a vicious campaign, making use of his army of canvassers in the CWMA to deliver scurrilous pamphlets door to door. For many voters, their first introduction to socialist ideas was through Salvidge's pamphlets. The newspaper *The Protestant Standard* chorused that Socialism would generate 'absolute infidelity' 'the grossest immoralities' and 'rivers of blood'.[42] As Waller points out, the argument had shifted from Protestant against Catholic to religion against atheism, referred to in the Labour Clarion as 'a Holy War ... with an over-population of drummers.' Ramsay MacDonald remarked that 'Socialism will never advance in Liverpool until Orangeism is broken.' In what many would today describe as a 'natural' Labour district, the Conservative McArthur won the election comfortably. A Labour breakthrough against Nationalism or Orangeism was still a distance away.

The impetus for a Catholic party in Liverpool came for those unhappy with both Nationalism and Labour. The idea was in the air – from organsations such as the Catholic Federation and the Catholic Labour League – that only a dedicated Catholic party could properly protect Catholic interests. But such a move would mean dumping the Home Rule agenda. The *Liverpool Catholic Herald* was outspoken. 'Any attempt to form a Catholic Party at this moment is in our opinion not calculated to serve Catholic interests, but to harm them.'

The education issue pushed the question of establishing a parliament in Dublin down to second place on the Liverpool Irish Catholic agenda. The Irish vote in Liverpool now took Catholicism as its central priority. Nationalist Councillor Burke – author of *The Catholic History of Liverpool* – said in council that the Conservative and Liberal parties did not represent the views of conservative and liberal Catholics, whereas the Nationalists did represent all Catholics. In the press, references began to be made to the 'Catholic' vote, rather than the 'Nationalist' vote.

Catholics continued to be concerned about Liberal education proposals. In the 1890s Bishop Whiteside, who was from an English aristocratic family and was a natural conservative and Unionist, had an uneasy relationship with the Nationalists. However, both Nationalists and the Catholic hierarchy were united against Birrell's Education Bill, brought forward by the Liberal government in 1906. Whiteside personally headed a rally opposing the proposed expansion of school provision.[43] For Catholics this raised the issue of how the Catholic diocese could afford to provide the new school places and teachers' salaries. It was suggested that Irish Catholic voters should support the Tories because of the education issue. T.P. O'Connor was quick to attack the idea in time honoured style. 'Every Irishman base enough to support a Tory candidate sells his country, his faith and his manhood.'[44] Nevertheless, the Conservatives benefitted in Liverpool, gaining five council seats that year, and raising the question of just how strong a Catholic vote might be.

The council debate on education in April 1905 was typical, with councillors Kelly and O'Shea defending Catholic schools, the standard of teaching and the condition of premises, and councillor George Wise of the Protestant Party opposing them. The proposal was to increase the education budget to meet the rising cost of teachers' salaries, mainly in the denominational schools. There were at the time '45 council schools, educating 54,000 children and 113 Voluntary schools educating 77,000.' Catholics, it was pointed out, had for years paid their rates to meet the cost of teaching salaries in Board schools – which would permit only Anglican teaching – whilst at the same time funding Catholic schools. Councillor Kelly pointed out that 'the Catholic section of the community for thirty-three years paid for keeping up the religion taught in Board schools and did not whine about it, but at the same time kept their own schools going.'[45] With Nationalist councillors so consistently supporting the Catholic cause, it was a small step to suppose that they might form a Catholic party.

The widespread sectarian rioting in Liverpool – dealt with in Chapter Ten – centred on the Scotland Road district in 1909, brought the focus back to local issues, local rivalries and local deprivation. Then in 1911, the Nationalist question returned to centre stage, when the Liberal government brought forward the Home Rule Bill. The strong Orange presence in Liverpool supported Unionists in Ulster, who threatened civil war if they were to be forced into a United Ireland. As Tory politicians lined up to support them, sectarian tensions once again increased.

CHAPTER NINE

IRISH REVOLUTIONARIES IN LIVERPOOL

During the nineteenth century, amongst Irish Nationalists, the issue of Irish independence – which most took to mean the establishment of a parliament in Dublin – was seen as the key to effectively addressing issues of social inequality and self-determination. It remained the main item on the political agenda.

Whilst we now know that it was the revolutionary option which eventually led to independence, for much of the nineteenth century the constitutional path to reform was preferred. However, frustration at the repeated rejection of Irish aspirations led to regular upsurges of revolutionary activity, where physical force – which had been so effective in the United States and France – was seen as the only realistic option. These two strands – constitutional and revolutionary – each with their own political philosophy, strategies and modes of organisation, existed alongside each other within Irish Nationalist politics throughout the nineteenth century. There were times when constitutional politicians kept well clear of those with rebellious ideas, and others – such as Parnell's 'plan of campaign' years – when parliamentarians flirted with the revolutionary movement. Boundaries between the two were never set in stone. Individuals would veer from one side to the other, depending on events at the time.

There were shifting currents of opinion within Irish political and cultural circles. A number of leaders in the constitutional movement were, or had formerly been, involved in revolutionary activity. Their ranks included Michael Davitt, and in Liverpool John Denvir and James Sexton. In many cases solidly constitutional politicians were not embarrassed by associating with commemorations and anniversaries sacred to the revolutionary calendar. Austin Harford in Liverpool – a consistent constitutionalist – is a good example. He was enthusiastic in his celebration of the 1798 centenary, and took the lead in commemorations of the Manchester Martyrs. For some a commitment to the revolutionary tradition was mere sentimentality, taking its place alongside Celtic mythology in bar room discussions. For many constitutional politicians, homage to the martyrs of the past was an essential ingredient in the formula for getting the vote out. For others the reality, or at least the threat, of physical force, was the only avenue through which independence could be achieved. Even for those politicians who eschewed any subscription to such ideas, the revolutionary culture – with its songs and heroes – remained the backdrop to their political environment and a significant aspect of the context within which they operated.

In each of the Irish revolutionary episodes between the eighteen forties and the nineteen twenties, Liverpool played a significant role. It had a large Irish population, with a wealthy Irish middle class, well placed to provide funding and contribute to leadership. It was the most important British sea port for traffic to and from Ireland, with such a volume of goods and passengers that illicit activity was difficult for the authorities to monitor.

There were two significant revolutionary episodes during the nineteenth century, the Confederate activities of 1847, and the Fenian movement of the 1870s. These were followed by the Easter Rising and the War of Independence in the twentieth century.

Confederates in Liverpool – 1840s
Whilst the Confederate movement achieved little in Liverpool, it was a widespread and popular movement, which played an important role in the Irish community at the time. The Young Ireland movement of the 1840s included Francis Meagher, Michael Doheny and John Mitchell in its ranks. They were concerned not just with the failure of O'Connell's agitation for Home Rule, but also with the horrendous social conditions in Ireland during the Famine years. The social reformer James Fintan Lalor was the inspiration for the radical and Confederate activist John Mitchell, whose newspaper *The United Irishman* advocated passive resistance to landlords – who were evicting the starving – and even the use of physical force if necessary.

O'Connell's Repeal Association was strong in Liverpool. The 'repeal rent' collected outside churches on Sundays and forwarded to Dublin, was as large in Liverpool as in any Irish city.[1] The majority of the Irish clergy were supportive of O'Connell's campaign, especially since he played a central role in restoring Catholic rights. English priests did not always take the same attitude.

As resort to physical force began to be more openly discussed, O'Connell – who was always strongly opposed to violence – took a firm line. George Archdeacon was a leading member of O'Connell's organisation in Liverpool. When he made a speech in which he declared that Irish men 'were prepared, even with their physical strength if necessary, to defend their principles,' O'Connell expelled him from the movement.[2] Following this and other similar incidents, the Young Ireland movement broke from the Repeal Association.

One of the leading figures in Irish Liverpool at the time was the wealthy businessman Terence Bellew McManus, a merchant with warehousing along the Liverpool docks and an office in North John Street. He was extremely well-known in Ireland through his trading activities, and was a popular figure in Liverpool. He was one of the first in Liverpool to leave the Repeal Association. Shortly afterwards, in

January 1847 – at the height of the Famine – he travelled to Dublin to attend the foundation meeting of the revolutionary Irish Confederation, and took up a position on its Council. Upon his return to Liverpool he was instrumental in establishing the first Confederate Club. He was assisted in this by George Smyth, another Ulsterman, who had a hat manufacturing business and shop in Paradise Street. Smyth was a 'gifted organiser and fund raiser'. In addition to these two businessmen, others in the leadership group included the Birkenhead architect Martin McDermott, and the Liverpool doctors Patrick Murphy, Francis O'Donnell and Lawrence Reynolds.

The Irish middle class in Liverpool at this time had three channels through which to direct their activities, should they wish to become involved in politics; the rebellious Confederates, the constitutional agitation of the Repeal Association, or the recently founded Catholic Club, allied to the Liberal establishment. The Confederates, when looking for partner organisations in England, looked to the Chartists who also had a radical agenda, a national organisation based on local clubs and societies, prepared to use physical force if necessary to achieve their goals. In addition, they had a prominent Irishman – Fergus O'Connor – amongst their leaders. Yet whilst Chartism was strong in Manchester, in neighbouring Liverpool there was not the same level of activity. Instead, the Confederates developed their own network on Merseyside. In the following months the Confederate leadership established a number of local clubs,[4] linked to existing semi-secret largely pub based ribbon networks, such as the Hibernian Friendly Society, the Third Mechanical Hibernian Society and the Ancient Order of Hibernians.

The rebellion in France in February 1848 had a huge impact on the Confederates. Up until then, whilst the debate between the constitutionalists and those who had favoured outright rebellion continued, both the Repealers and the Confederates remained largely peaceful organisations. But when the regime in Paris was overthrown by force, Liverpool Confederates soon became keen to follow their example. The Chartists – who wanted radical change in England – would be their allies. The policy was to maintain a broad based unified and popular organisation in public, whilst preparing in secret for revolutionary activity.

The death of Daniel O'Connell in May 1847 severely weakened the Repeal Association. Without his authority injunctions against alliance with revolutionary groups were more difficult to enforce. Confederate meetings in Liverpool were packed with enthusiastic supporters as those who for years had been frustrated by O'Connell's lack of effective action felt energised. Posters supporting the French were distributed. Activity on Liverpool streets became more frenetic. Unemployed porters – many of them Irish – were actively agitating against recent de-regulation. Police used baton charges and water cannon against them. The Liverpool magistrates cancelled the annual St Patrick's Day parade. Magistrates placed troops on the alert, enrolled 5,000 special constables, and introduced restrictions on the movement of certain goods.

The edginess of the Liverpool authorities was understandable. From March 1847 onwards there was scarcely a country in Europe which had not experienced a revolutionary upheaval. Everywhere governments were falling or negotiating with rebels. The authorities in Dublin began bringing charges against the leadership of the Confederates. The outspoken John Mitchell was sentenced to 14 years transportation under the Felons Act. Terence McManus now became firmly committed to revolution. His plan was to 'seize a couple of largest Irish steamers at Liverpool, load them with arms and ammunition taken from Chester Castle and proceed to Ireland. As regards diversionary activity, he intended to cripple the port by setting a blaze at low tide to quayside cotton warehouses.'[5]

The Confederates continued forming clubs in imitation of the system which had been used in Paris. There were at least 23 clubs in Liverpool and several more in Birkenhead.[7] As the club meetings were generally public it was an easy matter for the police to keep a watch on them. Each club was to have its own commanding officer and command structure. One example, from the account of a police informer, was the Bagenal Harvey Club, which was set up at Bevington Bush with Dr O'Donnell as its commanding officer. The informant had registered as member 111. 'The club met every weekday evening, to read the Irish newspapers'[6] and also appears to have had a training programme of sorts, as members 'receive instructions how to construct barricades, with floats, carts etc etc, which no cavalry can get over.' Dr Reynolds, who had now set up a workshop in Liverpool for the production of pikes for use in battle, had agents attending meetings to advertise his produce. At the first meeting of the Bermuda Club – so called because Bermuda was where John Mitchell was now detained – in Great Howard Street reporters were ordered to leave. Behind barred doors Reynolds – now nick-named 'The Ironmonger' – demonstrated how to use a pike sixteen inches long, attached to a long pole.[7]

It was a comparatively simple matter for the police, rather than trying to infiltrate meetings, to turn an existing member into a police informer by offering rewards in what was a poor community. The chief magistrate, Horsfall, established a special committee to monitor the situation. McManus made efforts to tighten security at meetings in Liverpool by introducing membership cards and monitoring attendance. The Confederates organised para-military practice on Liverpool's north shore, with pikes and guns. Police raids discovered weapons, including cutlasses and gunpowder. The most obvious target was Dr Reynolds' warehouse, where pikes were found. Raids also found documents giving accounts of meetings and membership lists. Additional troops were sent to Liverpool. Most significantly for the Confederates, the government began arresting the leadership.

The date for the rising was brought forward, only to collapse drastically at a farm in Tipperary, where members of the remaining leadership – including McManus – were arrested. It may well be that McManus issued orders for Liverpool activists to come to Dublin, in anticipation of the rebellion taking place there, as police reports confirm that 400 from the Liverpool Felon Club arrived in Dublin around that time, but took no active part.

McManus had been called to Dublin on 24 July, and was injured taking part in the rebellion the following week. According to accounts of events there he proved himself 'the boldest fellow amongst the entire body of insurgents.'[8] Trouble in Liverpool was expected. Troops were now in a large camp at Everton, the local police force had been increased from 800 to 1,300, and armed marines were on the Mersey.

In the aftermath of the failed rebellion Lawrence Reynolds managed to escape to America, where he later served as a doctor in the 63rd Regiment, New York Volunteers (Irish Brigade) in the civil war. Dr Murphy spent sixteen years in France before returning to continue to practise medicine in Liverpool. Terence McManus was convicted and transported to Tasmania. In time he managed to escape from there and lived the remainder of his life in San Francisco. He never managed to re-establish himself in business and died in poverty.

Fenianism in Liverpool
In the years following the events of 1848 the revolutionary leadership was scattered. Some had fled to that centre of revolutionary activity, Paris. Others were in the United States, whilst some were still living in Ireland. In time veterans of '48 began forming new organisations and making plans. The Irish Republican Brotherhood (IRB) was founded in Dublin in 1858, and allied organisations including Clan Na Gael and the Fenian Brotherhood grew up in the United States. Given Liverpool's close connections with Dublin, it was not long before the IRB organisation spread to Merseyside.

The organisation was largely working class in character. The intention of the leadership was that the new organisation would be based on a cell structure. Members would retain anonymity by being referred to as letters in the alphabet, the leader being A, the deputies B etc. The idea was that if one cell was discovered, this might not necessarily lead to others being found.

The IRB – also frequently referred to as the Fenians (the terms became interchangeable) – was never intended to be a forum for policy discussion or conventional political activity. The sole objective of the organisation throughout its existence was to bring about Irish independence through military means. As with the Confederates before them, the Fenians relied on existing local networks. Meetings usually took place in pubs, because of the shortage of any other available places with confidential rooms. Domestic premises would have been too small, especially since the organisation was composed largely of working class men. Church premises could not be used, as the church openly condemned the organisation.

Pubs did have the advantage that men had good reason to be there in any case, making it more difficult to monitor who was going to a meeting. Another advantage was that sympathetic landlords could be relied upon to keep the matter quiet. The obvious disadvantage was that business was being conducted as drink was being taken. It is likely that only a small minority of members were genuinely committed to armed revolution, with the determination and intent such a course required.

The movement in Liverpool was given added impetus in 1861 by events around the death, in San Francisco, of Terence Bellew McManus. The National Brotherhood of St Patrick was formed to quickly raise funds for the funeral, which attracted large crowds.[9]

Though at first a separate organisation without the intense secrecy and oaths of the IRB, the new Brotherhood soon became a front for the IRB and was subsumed into its organisation. Another veteran of the '40s who became actively involved was George Archdeacon, who had been expelled from O'Connell's Repeal organisation. He became 'Head Centre' of the IRB in Liverpool.

The Royal Irish Constabulary (RIC) appear to have been more aware of the Fenian threat than the local police,[10] and posted officers in Liverpool to keep a watch on characters who were known to them. They followed George Archdeacon and in 1865 arrested him under a warrant from Dublin for High Treason.[10]

The end of the American Civil War in 1864 brought a fresh wave of recruits to the Fenian movement. Many Irish men had been involved in that conflict, gaining experience in the use of arms and military action in fierce fighting. A large group of former soldiers, including some senior officers, had long been involved with Fenianism, and felt that they now had the capacity to challenge British dominance in Ireland. Many of these men passed through Liverpool on their way to Dublin, or when returning to the States. Some became involved in Liverpool Fenian circles.

In spite of the measures taken to maintain secrecy, the police were able to place informers at the heart of the Fenian movement. One of these in Liverpool was Peter Oakes, a former US army lieutenant. After the Civil War he had been recruited to the Fenians by John O'Mahony and sent to Liverpool. However things there did not work out as planned. Oakes became dissatisfied with his position. He was not being paid as promised by the IRB, and was running short of money. He was recruited by Clear, an RIC officer resident in Liverpool. In return for his fare to Canada, Oakes gave detailed testimony to the police.

Another was John Joseph Corydon, who was recruited to the Fenians whilst still a medical officer in the US army. He came to Dublin and worked directly with James Stevens, the leader of the Fenian organisation. He then arrived in Liverpool where he seems to have been happy to pass information to the police. One aspect of his evidence concerned the extent to which Fenian membership existed amongst the large numbers of Irish men who were in the British Army. Corydon reported to Constable Ride in 1866 that about three-quarters of the men in the 64th Lance Rifles Volunteers were Fenians, and had the idea of seizing stockpiles of military weapons when the time came.

Another senior RIC officer permanently resident in Liverpool – McHale – confirmed this information in one of his reports. 'I find that the great majority of Irish labourers in this town ... if not actually enrolled members of the brotherhood, are strongly impressed with the spirit of Fenianism. There are also numerous young Irish men who are Fenians. Many of them joined volunteer corps in order to gain a knowledge of drill and military movements for the express purpose of using it in the Fenian cause ...'[11]

Chief Constable Greig continued to maintain that there was no reason for concern. However, he soon was forced to change his view when, in 1866 *The Times* reported as follows: 'It has been suspected for some time that there were Fenian movements going on in Liverpool, but hitherto there have been no revelations of moment. A few days ago, however, the authorities at Dublin sent two officers over to Liverpool, and they at once placed themselves in communication with the local force. The result was that on Thursday morning a body of police went to 84 Salisbury Street.'[12]

The police had been looking for three men, all members of the Irish Volunteers Brigade, and an American who had joined them. In a padlocked locker at the premises they found explosives. Two weeks later police intercepted a cart of guns and explosives, including 800 sticks of phosphorus and rifles. Greig now had to admit that there was a real threat in Liverpool. The Liverpool police began mounting pressure on the leadership, by increasing searches and making arrests, forcing some to leave Liverpool to avoid detention.

During January the following year – 1867 – Lancashire Fenians were extremely quiet. It looked as if the arrest and dispersal of the leadership had crippled the organisation. One paper even announced: 'the death and burial of Fenianism'. But on 10 February the informer Corydon told his police contact Superintendent Ride that there was to be a raid on Chester Castle on the twelfth.[13] Five hundred troops were rushed from London and additional local constables were sworn in. During the morning of the twelfth Fenians began arriving in Chester in small groups from most of the main Lancashire towns, including Liverpool. There were about 1,300 of them altogether, but with such a strong and visible presence of troops and police, they were soon dispersed, some leaving behind hand guns and ammunition in their hurry to get away. The plan had been similar to that of McManus in the eighteen forties – to raid the Castle, take arms and ammunition, put it on a train and transport it to Ireland via Holyhead. The failure of the raid was a blow to Fenian plans. There were risings in Kerry later that February, and in other parts of Ireland during March, but the effectiveness of the British informer network led to them being neutralised fairly quickly.

Later that year the Fenians reorganised. The new leader – Thomas Kelly – was soon arrested in Manchester, along with Timothy Deasey. Seven days later they were sprung from a prison van in Hyde Road, Manchester. During the raid a police officer – Sergeant Brett – was looking through the keyhole of the van in which they were detained when a shot was fired with the intention of opening the lock. He died from his wound.[14] There were thirty arrests later in chases and raids. The public were shocked at such an act of Fenian violence against a police officer. Liverpool police carried out thorough searches, even opening coffins. Five men were eventually tried and convicted for the killing of Brett – Condon, Maguire, Allen, Larkin and O'Brien. Maguire was later acquitted, and Condon's sentence was commuted to imprisonment. The others were condemned to death. Public opinion was divided as to whether they should be executed. With feelings running high in the Irish community, police remained vigilant and drafted in additional constables.

Allen, Larkin and O'Brien were hanged on Saturday 23 November 1867. The violent reaction which the police had expected never materialised. In the words of Frank Neal: 'the hanging caused great anger and bitterness among the Irish in Britain and in many towns funeral processions were planned.'[15] Posters calling for a 'Monstre (sic) funeral procession' were issued in Liverpool in December. The Catholic bishops were aware that feelings in the Irish community were running high, and that there was the distinct possibility of a strong reaction to the procession. Bishop Goss, who had little sympathy with Irish Nationalism, issued a public statement – also distributed in poster form – urging 'our beloved flock' not to take part in the procession, which might 'excite and arouse feelings of rancour and hatred.' At the same time, an Orange Order delegation met with the Liverpool Mayor, Edward Whitley, a 'Conservative and Orange sympathiser', telling him that if the procession took place they would be organising a counter-demonstration. The following day a notice appeared in the local press, calling the procession off. On the appointed day itself, a large police presence prevented any crowd forming. However, in the following years processions and events commemorating the Manchester Martyrs became well established in both Liverpool and Manchester.

For the remainder of the century the return to constitutional politics – nurtured by the widening franchise, the introduction of the secret ballot, and the rise of Parnell – eclipsed Fenian activity. The Irish Republican Brotherhood continued as an international organisation committed to establishing an Irish Republic. Parnell had meetings with the leadership in both Paris and the United States in the 1870s. A breakaway group carried out assassinations in Dublin in the 1880s. In 1881 there was a dynamite attack on Liverpool Town Hall and on Hatton Garden police station.[16] By the early years of the 20th century the organisation was more or less moribund. However, continued frustration with the failure of the constitutional movement to make any significant progress on the issue of reform would eventually lead to the revival of the IRB.

CHAPTER TEN

PERSISTING SECTARIANISM

Throughout the nineteenth century, sectarian prejudice was common throughout Liverpool society. Sectarian attitudes persisted in the press and in politics and were encouraged in organisations such as the Orange Order and the Working Men's Conservative Association, and from both Catholic and Protestant pulpits. Institutional sectarianism was also rife. There is no shortage of examples. In 1856 the West Derby Union passed a resolution to exclude Catholic nuns from the premises.[1] In 1859 a lay visitor, Miss Gillow, was dismissed, following an accusation that she had 'tampered with the religion' of a girl. This was a girl who had been registered as a Catholic in the Kirkdale Schools, but was registered as Protestant when taken into the workhouse. The Gillows a wealthy Catholic family, raised objections, but the dismissal was confirmed.[2] Catholic mass was eventually permitted in the workhouse in 1859, following an inquiry by a Mr Cropper. The concession was granted, not so much through religious tolerance, but to ensure inmates remained within the walls of the institution. Unlike their Anglican colleagues doing the same job, Catholic clergy attending were not paid. In 1878 at a meeting of the Board of the Toxteth Workhouse, when certain more narrow minded members were absent, it was agreed that Catholic services be allowed. The resolution was quickly reversed at the next, more fully attended, meeting.[3]

On the Irish Catholic side the sectarian divide bolstered both nationalism and the position of the Catholic Church. Loyalty to the national cause and the church became extremely important in the context of outside hostility. Being Catholic and nationalist became a core part of an individual's personal identity. To deny either could lead to splits from family and community. Advancement in Irish politics and business often depended upon demonstrative support for these core values.

The Garibaldi Riots
Sectarian tension increased in 1862, when Garibaldi began taking over papal estates in Italy. The profile of these events was raised when Garibaldi's party opened a recruiting office in Liverpool. When the vicar of Holy Trinity Anglican church in Birkenhead announced that there was to be a debate on the motion, 'Sympathy with Garibaldi and Italy', an Irish crowd of some three thousand surrounded the church building where the debate was scheduled to take place, throwing stones and breaking windows. The following week some 2,000 special constables were enlisted to control the crowd. 'The mob assembled in thousands,

men women and children, a great number of them surrounded the Reverend Dr Bayliss's church.'[4] Sixty mounted police, armed with cutlasses, charged the crowd. Women with their aprons filled with stones kept the mob supplied with missiles. 'It was not until two or three in the morning that order was completely restored.'

The *Liverpool Mercury* was particularly concerned that a detachment of soldiers in the Monk's Ferry Hotel were left, 'snugly in their quarters, smoking their pipes and drinking their beer,'[4] but not called upon to keep order.

The increase in Fenian activity in the late 1860s exacerbated sectarian tensions. In April 1868 the retiring Catholic member of the Select Vestry, Thomas Martin, was challenged by Joseph Ball in an openly sectarian campaign. Ball stated that 'no Catholic of any nationality or political belief should be allowed a seat on any public body.'[5] In those times, polling stations were open for a number of days, to allow all those who were entitled to, to vote. Many were persons with businesses or property in the town, who did not necessarily live there. Some, through property qualification, had more than one vote. 'A tremendous struggle, unequalled in the history of the town, was the result, and for ten days practically all business was suspended.' Although Ball took a clear lead in the opening days, there was pressure from the Liberals and Catholics, to keep polls open. Finally, after an extended polling period, Martin was the clear winner. Ball, identified in the *Liverpool Mercury* as 'the Orange candidate' was defeated.

The *Liverpool Mercury* reported that: 'Yesterday the inhabitants of Fontenoy Street, Marylebone, Vauxhall Road and several of the neighbouring streets, in their exuberance of joy at the success of Mr Martin, displayed flags and banners, mostly green, some of which were inscribed with the words, 'Long Live Martin'.[6]

Whilst most of those celebrating the victory did not have a vote, they saw the success of their candidate as evidence that Irish and Catholic influence was increasing in local politics. The whole episode is indicative of the way in which local affairs were contaminated by sectarian attitudes.

Throughout the nineteenth century and into the twentieth, the Conservatives in Liverpool excelled at networking. Tory politicians who led the way were Edward Whitley, Sir Arthur Forwood, Sir Archibald Salvidge and Sir Thomas White. They were politicians with 'the common touch', who, despite the differences of class, were happy to congregate with working men, and address them in language they would understand. Much of this network was built on common values – Church, crown, bible, Empire – and common self-interest – employment and trade. They joined every association there was, including the Freemasons, the Buffaloes and the Oddfellows. Most importantly the Conservatives maintained close links with the Orange Order. They even attended Trade

Union balls and mixed with the crowd. In Waller's words 'They were practised in stooping to conquer'. [7]

The Conservative party saw itself as the natural home of the Protestant working class voter. The party founded the Liverpool Working Men's Conservative Association (LWMCA) in 1867, the year in which the 'Manchester Martyrs' were hanged, an event which brought about an upsurge in Irish Nationalist activity. The LWMCA was exclusively Protestant, and became the core of an extremely efficient Tory Party machine in Liverpool over the following decades[8] providing regular subscriptions and support for campaigns, including leafleting, canvassing and transport at election times. Here working men could associate with those in the higher social ranks, Tory aristocrats, such as Lord Sandon, and big business men, such as shipping magnate Sir Arthur Forwood. It provided an opportunity to associate with 'your betters' and to perhaps gain advancement through being in the right network. In turn the aristocrats and business grandees were not averse to associating with the skilled working class in such an environment if that was what had to be done to hold on to municipal power and secure parliamentary seats.

John Houlding, was a good example of a Liverpool Tory. He started out as a daily wage earner, but founded a brewery in 1870 and soon became wealthy. He was chairman of the Everton Conservative Association, a councillor, a Freemason, an Orangeman, and regular churchgoer. He was a benefactor of non-conformist bodies, and played a key role in the foundation of both Liverpool and Everton football clubs. He frequently reminded voters that he had 'intimate acquaintance, through personal experience, with the condition and requirements of the working classes …'[8]

Sir Arthur Forwood – a merchant ship owner – was for years the man responsible for getting the Tory vote out. He designated his methods 'Tory democracy'. He was the architect of a system which kept the Tories in power locally and was even influential in Tory strategy nationally. Sectarianism was an important ingredient, which could be utilised at appropriate moments, to increase electoral support. It gave those in the networks a feeling of separateness and superiority. Them and us attitudes were reinforced.

Forwood was Secretary of the Liverpool Conservative Association from 1868. He promoted his idea of 'Tory Democracy' as a populist and pragmatic policy, which constantly came up with ideas designed to appeal to the working man and cut the ground from under the Liberals. Support for church education, for the Empire's adventures abroad, a widening of the franchise, and an increase in employment were among the popular policies he promoted; and of course, opposition to Irish Nationalism. He once described the Irish as: 'the lowest strata of society … too idle to work, too much of an inebriate to find employment, and too impecunious to find a permanent home.'[9] His view was that: 'The presence of a large Irish population, enables us to get a hold of a large number of workingmen, who hate the Irish for coming to this country and lowering the rate of wages. In addition, there is the question of religion. People are still afraid of popery ... We get in Liverpool what our party receives in no other town in the kingdom – the non-conformist vote.'

Forwood would use the Irish issue in times when his party was at a disadvantage. During the brief interlude when the Liberal/Nationalist alliance gained control of the Corporation from 1892 to 95, he stepped up the anti-Irish rhetoric. This campaign coincided with the proposal for Irish Home Rule, which appeared a real possibility at the time.

Forwood attacked the Nationalists in the council as: 'men who regarded the English as foreigners in Ireland.' Going on to say that: 'the influx of the Irish into Liverpool brought poverty, disease, dirt and misery, drunkenness and crime, in addition to a disturbance in the labour market and the cost to the ratepayers of an enormous sum of money.'[10]

Forwood's style – he said it was his habit to 'call a spade a spade' – in later years became so abrasive that he began losing support within his own Tory ranks, in spite of his vote-winning track record.

When Forwood died in 1898 Archibald Salvidge took over the role of Tory boss. He was managing director of Bent's Brewery, and was vice-chairman and later Chairman (1892) of the LWMCA, making it his power base. It was the strongest such association in the country, with around six thousand members in eighteen branches, paying annual subscriptions to the branch, with a contribution to the Central Committee. The Associations maintained a busy round of activities, such as dances, lectures and concerts, though they were not drinking clubs. Only one had a bar.

There were other working class networks in the city, with sectarian overtones, which often worked to the advantage of the Conservatives. Pastor George Wise had his own church congregation and bible classes. He had a combative presence on the streets, and organised meetings with a distinctly anti-Catholic tone. In one typical instance he brought Miss N F Cusack on to the stage at Hope Hall. She was a former nun, who lectured about 'the iniquity, treachery and cruelty of that abominable system'.[11] 'The rule of obedience symbolised Rome's slavery, the vow of poverty supplied Rome's avarice and stories of sexual transgressions made a Briton's blood boil with righteous indignation.'

Whilst the LWMCA could be relied upon to follow Tory policy to the letter, the Orange Order, which was consistently and vociferously sectarian, would frequently take issue with Conservative policy on a number of issues, such as the grant to Maynooth – the Catholic clerical college in Ireland – and grants to Catholic schools. The disestablishment of the Church of Ireland in 1869 also aroused indignation. Tories often held important positions in the Order, including that of Lodge Grand Master.

But the Orange Order would never be under direct Conservative control. It was a loose cannon, and there were occasions, when sectarian tensions were running high, that association with the Order was a disadvantage at the ballot box, and could be embarrassing to the Party establishment.

But for Orangemen there was a hierarchy of dislike. Whatever they thought of the Conservatives, they detested the Liberals, not only for disestablishing the Anglican church, but for their support of Home Rule. The Home Rule campaign of 1886, which saw O'Connor elected as an Irish Nationalist, brought the Order out on to the streets of Liverpool in force, with attacks on St Patrick's Church, and street fighting both in Toxteth and the Scotland Road district. At this time the practice of Orange bands organising ad hoc parades became increasingly popular. These 'wildcat' processions made policing in the city extremely difficult. Catholics responded by attacking marches, and burning effigies of King Billy[12] – the victor at the Battle of the Boyne whose image was often paraded at Orange events. These activities created a rift in the working class, which benefitted both the Conservative Party and the Irish Nationalists. Those who lost out were the Liberals and the emerging Labour Party, who could not unite voters so divided on sectarian lines. In 1895, for example, in a sectarian atmosphere fired up by the Conservatives, the Liberals were roundly defeated both in local and parliamentary elections. Labour did not fare any better. In the strongly working class Domingo and Netherfield wards, all six councillors were Tory and each of them was an Orangeman.

It was eventually through George Wise that sectarian animosity came to a crisis. Wise was a Protestant evangelical who played a leading role in exacerbating sectarian animosity. He came to Liverpool in 1888. He did not begin speaking out against Catholicism until around 1897. He first became well known when he took a leading role in the anti-ritualist campaign. This was a movement to oppose those Church of England clergy who were thought to be adopting practices – such as elaborate vestments, and excessive use of ceremonial accoutrements including candles – which were too close to those of the Catholic Church. He formed an alliance with Salvidge to push a bill through parliament which would make it easier to prosecute such clergy. Local Tory MPs were pressurised to state that they supported this rather arcane and extreme bill, and most of them did so. Wise's sermons and demonstrations, including a march to St Catherine's church, Grove Street in 1901, brought him a wider audience. He also came to the attention of the police with greater frequency. They dispersed his supporters when they tried to form ad hoc processions, or heckle outside churches.[13] Inevitably he began transferring his attentions to Catholicism itself, partly in response to certain Catholic clergy who spoke out on occasions against the errors of Protestantism.

Later that same year he organised meetings at Islington Square, not far from St Francis Xavier's Church, an area where there were large numbers of Irish Catholics. His style was to be insulting and controversial, mocking Catholic beliefs with remarks designed to elicit an angry response. Amongst his favourite themes was 'The Jesuits and the Coronation oath', an obscure topic which he used to arouse fear of Catholicism as a threat to the constitution. In addition to gratuitous insults he emphasised the Britishness of Liverpool Protestants in contrast to the alien Irish.[14] When police took him to court for incitement his suspicion of the establishment was confirmed. He asserted that there was a co-ordinated campaign to compromise the right to free speech by silencing him. His conspiracy theories were reinforced when he discovered that the magistrate who convicted him himself attended a 'ritualist' church. Wise set himself up as a sort of folk hero, who defied authority in defence of the Protestant cause, an approach which greatly extended his public support.

In 1902 things were stepped up when two more preachers, the London based Kensits – father and son – began campaigning in Liverpool. They also latched on to the ritualist issue, and were vehemently anti-Catholic. The banner at the head of their procession that August read: 'We protest against the idolatrous Mass and the God dishonoured in our schools.'[15] Their meetings at venues such as Islington Square and St George's Hall attracted large crowds, and were frequently attacked by Catholics, often armed with stones, sticks and other weapons. There was widespread public concern that the meetings – with their inflammatory speeches and unruly crowds – were allowed to continue. Police brought the younger Kensit before a magistrate, presenting evidence of his incendiary language. He was bound over to keep the peace, but opted to go to prison instead, thus up-staging Wise as a latter-day Protestant martyr.[16] Kensit senior immediately came to Liverpool to continue his son's campaign. Both he and Wise were now running rival organisations, outbidding each other in their anti-Catholic rhetoric. Matters came to a head one evening when Kensit senior slipped from his police escort after addressing a meeting in Birkenhead. He was on the ferry landing stage, waiting to cross to the Liverpool side when he was struck by an iron file thrown from the crowd and fatally wounded. The death of Kensit, which was followed by the trial and acquittal of John McKeever, raised tensions even further.[17]

The following year Wise was again before magistrates, and once more bound over to keep the peace. In evidence the police presented statements officers had recorded from recent meetings at St Domingo Pit and other venues. The lurid rhetoric included the assertion that Catholic clergy, 'waste their lives with harlots', and that, 'they rob the poor to feed their own children', and that, 'the monks in monasteries were living lives of devils.'[18] Such gratuitous insults were calculated to anger Catholics and exacerbate tensions in an increasingly unsettled city. Wise refused to be bound over and was sent to jail. A vigorous campaign for his release began at once. Free speech was being denied. The right to hold open air meetings was compromised. The Tory establishment could not avoid becoming involved. Charles McArthur, MP presented a petition for the release of Wise – with 50,000 names on it – to the Home Secretary.[19] Wise served out his sentence, and upon release immediately addressed a meeting of some 2,000 at Birkenhead.

The situation had now become chaotic. Rivals to Wise began establishing their own territory in the city. Albert Stones had been an employee of the Kensits. He had taken over Wise's 'crusade' when Wise had been in prison. He was unhappy when his pay was reduced as Wise took over again after his release. Questions began to be raised about the movement's finances. Stones failed to account for certain of his collections,[20] and Wise denied that collections at open air meetings lined his own pockets. Stones soon attracted his own following in the south end, where he set up a rival organisation. Another preacher brought in by the Kensits was Louis Ewart, who now established his own congregation in Garston. Each of these populist preachers measured their success by the numbers attracted to church meetings, bible classes, Sunday schools, and outdoor rallies. There was a strong social element to these congregations, including children's activities, women's bible classes and Sunday outings. George Wise's cycling club was the largest in Liverpool.[21]

The situation became increasingly competitive, with each organisation keen to maintain their position in relation to the others by holding on to members. Anger, fear and protest were promoted with increasing frequency. There was growing animosity between Wise and Chief Constable Dunning, and between Stones and Superintendent Breeze in Toxteth. The Tory authorities were also a target, for not taking up the Protestant cause with sufficient vigour, for not defending the established church and for allowing Catholic education. Irish Catholics remained the most significant target. Catholic activities were constantly presented as a threat. The presence of Catholic emblems on the street was one such concern, and it was from this issue that the crisis in Liverpool was to unfold.

Had these fundamentalist groups been the only organisations promoting sectarian feeling, the situation might have been recovered. But there were other powerful engines of sectarian tension in the city. Orange 'scratch bands' became increasingly popular, and there was plenty of activity for such marching groups.[22] Meetings organised by Wise and others usually involved a march headed by a band. Orange Lodge meetings and commemorations also involved bands. Military drilling was very popular at this time in any case, with numerous drill halls around the city. And of course Irish meetings also often involved a band. Scratch bands would appear in local areas with little advance notice, creating particular difficulties for the police. They were organised by local musicians, beyond the control of preachers or Orange Order officials. These Protestant parades attracted Catholic youths. There was much public disorder, and fierce street fighting, in which innocent people were often injured, homes attacked and property damaged. There were over 600 such incidents in 1904 alone. In a typical outbreak in Window Street, Garston, that year, Catholic youths attacked a Protestant procession. When the police arrived both sides then turned on them.[23]

The 1909 Sectarian Disturbances

The Catholic hierarchy had organised a Eucharist Conference in London in 1908. There were rumours that there was to be a procession as part of this conference, in which the host was to be carried through the streets. The 1829 Catholic Emancipation Act had included provisions that Catholic clergy should not exercise any of their functions in any place other than a Catholic church. Wise maintained that this meant that this procession would be illegal. Although the proposed procession never actually took place, the idea that Catholic processions were illegal and should be opposed entered into public discourse. In the following year – 1909 – the parish of Holy Cross, in Liverpool, was celebrating its 60th anniversary. There was to be a procession around the streets adjoining the church. Protestant organisations quickly took up the issue. Alexander Colter – Liverpool Grand Secretary of the Orange Institution – wrote to the Chief Constable.[24] The executive of the George Wise Crusade also wrote, as did the president of the Protestant Labour Club. They were all assured that the procession would be legal. There was a great deal of tension over the issue, as the significance of the procession in the public mind was magnified by those opposed to it. Opposition was vocally expressed in public meetings, press reports and political lobbying. The procession was cast in a sinister light by the statement from the Wise Crusade that they had been advised that 'an attempt will be made to carry the host', and that Catholic modes of clerical dress forbidden under the 1829 Act were to be worn. At the actual procession there were many who wore cassocks and other religious garments, but there was a misunderstanding of the law on the Protestant side, as such practices were not those forbidden by the Act. A very large crowd of several thousand attended the procession, probably as a result of the publicity which had been generated by the controversy. The small number of Protestant protestors were soon dispersed by police.[25]

Some weeks later, on 20 June, a similar procession was planned in the nearby St Joseph's parish. There was pressure from the Protestant side for a counter demonstration. George Wise opposed the idea and refused to take part. But the Orange Order did arrange a march. About 1,000

Orangemen took part, arriving in Juvenal Street earlier than planned, right at the point where the Catholic parish procession was to begin. As Chief Constable Dunning was on holiday in Ireland, his deputy H P Lane was in charge of the police presence.[26] When disturbances broke out the mounted police charged the Orange march. A fierce fight broke out with weapons including knives, swords and iron pipes being used. The mounted police used considerable force to drive the marchers back. There was severe and prolonged fighting between police and marchers in Prince Edwin Street.[27] A curtailed and hurried church procession did eventually take place, but the matter was not to end there.

The Protestant districts along Netherfield Road were in uproar at the activity of the police and disorder continued well into the night. Many Protestants were shocked that the police had taken such action against the Orangemen, rather than coming down on the Catholic procession. Over the following days the most severe sectarian rioting in Liverpool's history took place. In the words of Frank Neal: 'it was as if all the frustration arising from poverty, overcrowding and unemployment broke the surface and found an outlet in sectarian violence as the readiest 'legitimate' excuse'.[28] The anger, animosity and fear which had been stoked up over the previous decade, particularly by street preachers, now found expression. During the following week sectarian brawls broke out across the city, often in or around pubs. There were clashes between gangs of school children which in turn led to mothers becoming involved. On the Tuesday afternoon fighting broke out between children from St Polycarp's Church of England school, and St Anthony's Catholic school in the Scotland Road area. Soon mothers became involved in fighting so fierce that police reinforcements had to be drawn from other parts of the city. There followed attacks on businesses, homes and schools across the north end of the city. Roscommon Street and Collingwood Street schools were attacked. Classrooms were invaded, teachers were assaulted. There were rumours of schools being vandalised and even burnt down.[29] The atmosphere became hysterical. The situation on Tuesday had become so unpredictable that the School Management Sub-committee met amid rumours that women had invaded classrooms brandishing Orange swords, and that in one instance an armed man had turned up 'to defend the school'. They took the decision to close seventeen schools.[30]

Many people were attacked in their homes, with Protestants being evicted from Catholic areas, and Catholics from Protestant districts. Witnesses to the inquiry which followed presented evidence of the level of mutual intimidation. The two areas most affected were those between Scotland Road and the docks, and the Netherfield Road area. The Reverend Sherwood Jones was vicar of St Martin's-in-the-Field, Sylvester Street. He estimated that 110 Protestant families had to leave his parish because of intimidation.[31]

The Catholic community in the Netherfield Road area also suffered. There Father John Fitzgerald was an impressive witness to the Inquiry. He felt so strongly about the situation that he submitted his own report to the city council. He calculated that about 3,200 Catholics had been forced out of the area following the intimidation at this time. He also recorded the frequent street incidents not only during the disturbances, but in the months leading up to them, including attacks on homes, schools, convents, churches and businesses belonging to Catholics.[32] In addition, clergy and nuns were frequently subjected to insults on the street.

Many people of both religions were attacked at work, and on their journey to and from work. Protestants were chased out of the Palatine Oil Cake Mills. William Daniels was one. He was Grand Master of Kirkdale Orange Lodge and had been foolish enough to take his ceremonial sword to his workplace 'to have it sharpened'. He was driven from his workplace, as was his brother.[33] Although he had an escort of six police officers on his way home he was attacked and injured by a group of women carrying tongs. Travel to work was a particular problem for the large numbers of Protestant men from Everton who had to make their way through the strongly Catholic Vauxhall Road district to get to their work along the docks. Many of the carters whose horses were stabled near the docks each evening were subjected to attacks. On Monday 21 June, in the most serious incident of all, Andrew Cathcart and two others – Protestants returning from work – were attacked in Hopwood Street. Cathcart was so severely beaten that he later died from his injuries.[34] As the widespread unrest continued into mid-week, the police became exhausted. Many incidents received no police response, and crimes went unreported.

Provocative Orange Order activity continued unabated. The Ashton Inquiry,[35] later set up to investigate the matter, found that: 'Orange bands were another cause of the disturbances. These bands constantly paraded the streets at night during the summer of 1909. They attended the meetings at George Wise's favoured outdoor venue – 'the Pit', a small outdoor arena in the St Domingo district of Everton – far more frequently than they had done before. When they marched away from a meeting they followed routes which frequently passed Roman Catholic institutions and buildings. The crowds which followed them did constant damage with stones and other missiles. Buildings, including houses and shops known to belong to Roman Catholics, were the targets. Out of a total of 55 cases of riotous damage reported in E division after 1 June, 31 were cases of persons following Orange bands, of which 19 were cases of persons going to and from the Pit.'[36] Ashton identified the well-recognised problems created by 'scratch bands', which at this time formed points of attraction around which crowds gathered, as one witness said, 'out for any kind of devilment', they, 'proved an intolerable nuisance'.[37]

However appalling these events were, they did not cause George

Wise to change his plans. He was determined to press ahead with a march planned for the 27th, just seven days after the rioting had first broken out. Chief Constable Dunning had him arrested. He was sentenced to four months in prison. However, Wise in prison seemed to be just as great a problem as Wise free. A campaign for his release was started, with frequent clashes between police and his supporters, and more attacks on Catholic premises. The Wiseite campaign made frequent personal attacks on Dunning – calling for him to be sacked – and on the magistrates. Conservative politicians, including ardent Unionist Charles McArthur MP and active Orangeman W.W. Rutherford, MP for West Derby, joined the campaign to lobby the Home Secretary for Wise's release. The Home Secretary called for a report from the Chief Constable, who informed him of the continued unrest and communal violence which persisted whilst Wise remained in jail.

The Home Secretary's dilemma was how to intervene to relieve the situation, without being seen to over-ride the local magistrates and police officers. He eventually found an opportunity in the Protestant campaign against the police, which alleged that the police had been biased and heavy-handed in their treatment of Protestants during the events in June. Although the request 'seems ludicrous' in view of police behaviour towards Catholic Irish at the time, the city council requested such an investigation. The Home Secretary granted their request by passing the Police (Liverpool Inquiry) Act. A commissioner – Arthur Ashton – was appointed to take evidence primarily from five interest groups; the City Council, the police, the Orange Order, the George Wise Protestant Crusade and Catholic representatives. The establishment of the inquiry permitted the authorities to release Wise, to allow him to take part in the proceedings. Although he gave undertakings to the Home Secretary not to conduct meetings, he immediately organised an outdoor meeting at St Domingo Pit, which included his customary rhetoric, thus breaking the terms of the agreement under which he had been set free.[38]

In the formal forum of the Inquiry it soon became evident that most of the allegations brought by Wise and others, both about police behaviour and the illegality of the Catholic processions, had little basis in law or fact. Most of the allegations were soon withdrawn. Counsel for Wise stated that: 'The facts as disclosed during the Inquiry have led my clients and me to believe Mr Dunning, in the steps and measures he took against Mr Wise, was actuated in the direction of the peace of the city, and not against Mr Wise personally'.[39]

The Inquiry report established that: 'when the petitioners had fully and frankly agreed that the Head Constable had no sinister or improper motive in acting as he did … the charge as a charge was gone'.[40] Furthermore, under examination, Wise was forced to agree that he had, in fact, had a fair trial before magistrates. Finally, Ashton found that: 'All charges of 'preferential treatment' by the police of Roman Catholics as against Protestants were withdrawn.' This conclusion came as a disappointment to a number of Conservative councillors who had supported the calls for an Inquiry, in the hope that it would find against the Head Constable and his attitudes to Orangemen and the Wise Crusade.

The Irish / Catholic side fared better in the Inquiry, with Ashton forming a favourable opinion of the Nationalist councillor Austin Harford, whose call for a thorough examination of the root causes of the disturbances was favourably received and adopted by the commissioner. When questioned about the causes the Head Constable in his evidence stated that: 'After Mr Wise commenced his work at St Domingo Pit, we have had troubles more or less, and I attribute the causes entirely to the meetings at St Domingo Pit and the violent language that is used there, not just against the Catholics but against the powers generally.'[41]

Catholic evidence supported this view, stating that, in Ashton's words: 'the real cause of the disturbances in 1909 was to be found in the active onslaughts upon the Roman Catholic faith made by the speakers at the Pit.'[42] Catholic evidence asserted that Catholics were content to live in harmony with their Protestant fellow citizens, but not with the insults from Wise and his supporters. Ashton admitted to being puzzled by the 'strange enigma' of Wise himself, concluding that: 'I think Mr Wise is responsible to a far greater extent than he himself appreciates for the disturbance which happened last year.' He went on to add: 'I report that the manner in which Pastor George Wise has in the past conducted his propaganda against Roman Catholicism was one of the causes which led to the disturbances'.

The Inquiry recommendations were that there should be new controls on outdoor meetings, marches and parades, and that there should be a conciliation conference in Liverpool. The Conservative controlled council did little or nothing to implement the proposals, even though they themselves had requested the Inquiry. During the following summer Protestant sectarian meetings and associated violence continued unabated. Catholic churchmen continued to be concerned at the unrest and the role of Catholic church processions within it. A deputation led by Bishop Whiteside met the Mayor to request that meetings by Wise supporters at the Pit be banned. At the same time they undertook that no Catholic processions would be allowed for the following year. It would take a further upsurge of public disorder in 1911, bringing Liverpool to the brink of outright revolution, which would finally bring about the conciliation conference proposed by Ashton.

T.P. O'Connor was one of the government appointees, charged with mediating in the 1911 disputes. Once the issues related to labour disputes had been addressed – with varying degrees of success – O'Connor extended his remit to focus on sectarianism, and establish at last, the Conciliation Conference recommended by Ashton's Inquiry two years before. Lord Derby was appointed chairman, with the delegates being local figures of importance, including George Wise and the Anglican and Catholic bishops. The strength of the Conference was that Wise and others were involved in the process, rather than being on the outside. Many of the recommendations concerning processions and their regulation, control of outdoor meetings, emblems, parades and weapons were included in the Liverpool Corporation Act of 1911. It was a step in the right direction.

Sectarian violence in Liverpool was to continue for decades, but never again on the same scale as in 1909. In the following years labour disputes assumed greater importance. They pointed up the common hardships endured by both sides. The advent of war was another factor, taking young men off the streets. The death of the leading agitator, George Wise, was also significant, as was the conciliatory attitude of the Catholic hierarchy. Lastly, the establishment of a parliament in Dublin in the 1920s, resulted in a decline in the fervour of Liverpool Nationalists. Sectarian violence and animosity remained a factor in Liverpool everyday life and politics, but the levels of communal hatred seen in 1909 were never to be repeated. This decline can be contrasted with the situations in Glasgow and Belfast, which both had similar patterns at this time, and where animosity has persisted, albeit in different circumstances.

When two strikers – both Catholics – were shot dead by the military on Vauxhall Road during the 1911 Liverpool General Strike, people from both sides of the sectarian divide took part in the funerals. Unions – some of which had a predominance of workers from either one side or the other in their ranks – worked together for the common objectives of the strike.

Another significant factor was the large numbers from both Wise's bible groups and from the Nationalist Irish Volunteers who joined up at the outbreak of War. This had the effect not only of reducing street clashes, but of providing a common experience of conflict, harrowing though it was. As time went by, individuals began to see that social issues such as health and housing were of greater importance than ritualism and related arcane issues presented by preachers such as Wise.

CHAPTER ELEVEN

THE IRISH ON THE LIVERPOOL DOCKS

Many Irish men played a leading role in the struggle for better conditions for casual dock workers and recognition of trade unions. Their leadership was a significant factor on the Mersey waterfront during the closing decades of the nineteenth century, and in the events leading up to 1911. The challenge faced by Irish migrants coming to Liverpool in the nineteenth century is difficult for us to imagine today. Irish Catholics tended to be locked out of much of the better paid work. They lacked qualifications, and were not part of the paternalistic, religious and political networks which gave access to many trades and workplaces. They were discriminated against on the basis of nationality and religion. The casual unskilled or semi-skilled work along the docks was a magnet for them. There was a huge variety of occupations on the waterfront, with thousands of jobs, but there was always a surplus of labour because of the densely packed population locally.

For the adventurous or the desperate in Liverpool there was the option of life at sea. When unemployment rose steeply in the early 1890s, the young James Larkin – who lived in Combermere Street near the waterfront – took the short walk to the docks and secretly boarded a steamer bound for Montevideo. When he was discovered, he was soon put to work in the bowels of the ship, shovelling and heaving coal from the storage bunkers to the engine room – the most strenuous work on the ship, down in the dark and under oppressive heat. He jumped ship at Santa Lucia, where he lived for a time as a beach comber. He seems to have found it easy to get another ship, perhaps because he was willing to do the dirty work other crew members hated, but maybe also because of his Liverpool identity. At that time a large proportion of ships across the world were either coming from or going to Liverpool, and were manned by Liverpool sailors who presumably would have been happy to give a job to one of their own. Whatever the circumstance, he sailed to Rio De Janeiro, later returned to Galveston on the Texas coast, then sailed to Valparaiso, Chile, Buenos Aires, Galveston again and eventually Newport News, Virginia. There he again found a Liverpool ship, and worked his passage aross the Atlantic, arriving home in time for his eighteenth birthday.[1] His story is not unique, and illustrates the sort of opportunity which was available on the Liverpool waterfront in those days. There were positions at all levels, from captain, through to highly skilled workers such as navigators and engineers, to unskilled men.

The work had certain characteristics. First and foremost, life at sea was hard; the discomfort of the boats, the nature of the work, the weather and the food all added to this. Secondly the work was dangerous, and it was still not uncommon for men to be lost at sea. The work was often temporary and casual. Whilst many ships had regular crew, there are many accounts of people being recruited on the spot, for long voyages, often in highly irregular fashion. And of course, when sailors returned from a voyage they would receive pay which had accumulated over many weeks. With money in their pockets and not having had decent food, drink or female company for many weeks, these daily arrivals had a great impact upon life on the Liverpool waterfront. The sea faring culture was also disruptive of a settled family life, taking men away for long stretches at a time, leaving families without an income or social support until their return.

For those who stayed on land, much of the work available in Liverpool also lacked continuity. Dock work continued to be casual. An individual could just turn up any given morning or early afternoon and look for a job. Some had regular semi-skilled positions. The rest stood in pens and were hired for the day or half day, by a foreman. The system was abusive and degrading, and persisted even though there were many jobs where specialist skills were required.[2] It is estimated that between 1861 and 1869, the numbers available for work along the docks increased from 12,000 to 24,000, yet no more than about 13,000 were regularly needed.[3]

Casual workers did not have the protection of a union organisation. There was no incentive for employers to train workers in the skills required, or to pay attention to health and safety. There was little opportunity to increase earning power by acquiring qualifications and skills. Pay remained static for very long periods. From 1870 to 1915 (after the outbreak of the Great War) wages did not increase, whilst employers continued to accumulate vast fortunes.[4]

Yet much of the work along the docks was in fact either skilled or semi-skilled. Operating lifting equipment was not something which could be left to casual workers. And shipowners needed efficient skilled workers if cargo such as grain was to be unloaded quickly, or if fruit and vegetables were to be transported without being damaged.

The first accident statistics for the docks became available in 1899, following the Factory Acts.[5] In that year it was recorded that there were over 41,000 accidents, and 89 fatalities, a staggering total by modern standards. Accidents involving cranes and lifting tackle accounted for about a third of these. Equipment was poorly maintained, and workers poorly trained. With heavy items such as barrels, crates and bails being hooked or slung to a crane then lifted down into a hold or raised from below to the dock – with men below the load either down in the hold or on the quayside – the scope for accidents is obvious. Carrying goods from ship to quayside was another hazardous occupation. The narrow wooden walkways were often steep, shifting and slippery. Men would hurry along carrying loads of timber or other goods.

141

Certain dockers had the skill or 'knack' for particular jobs. Those accustomed to carrying heavy wood such as deal, for example, would develop a characteristic hardened skin on their right shoulder, allowing them to be especially efficient in this work. Grain was unloaded in sacks. 'Bushellers' were specialists who filled sacks and quickly stitched them across the mouth with string. Others then carried the sacks – each weighing one hundred kilos – along narrow gang planks, often without protective railings, to the quay. Again, there was plenty of opportunity for accidents to occur. Accidents actually aboard ship were not included in the official figures, as they were deemed to be outside the scope of the Factory Acts.[5]

The casual nature of the work meant that men who were known to complain about conditions did not get hired. One of these was James Sexton, who was branded as an agitator. He was born in Newcastle-upon-Tyne into an Irish emigrant family. He was raised in St Helens. He worked at first for Pilkington's Glass in St Helens then found work at sea, on one of the few remaining rigged and masted ships. He was active for a time in the revolutionary Fenian movement. Later he worked on the Liverpool docks, where he suffered a serious injury when his eye was permanently damaged and his cheek bone smashed by the boom of a collapsing crane. He was taken to hospital for treatment and returned to work some weeks later. It was found that as a result of his injury he was not able to do the same work as others. He was therefore put on a boy's wage. To make matters worse, in his first pay packet upon his return there was a deduction to cover the cost of the fare for the taxi which had taken him to hospital following his accident. He was later to become a firm believer in the need for trade unions for all dock workers.[6]

Casualism also served to reinforce sectarianism. The north end docks tended to be the territory of Irish Catholics, whilst the south end was Protestant dominated.[7] The divisions between dockers inhibited labour solidarity and the growth of a united labour movement.

In addition to casual work, there were also those who had a permanent post with an employer, including foremen, supervisors, and clerks to manage the mountain of paperwork required. But generally employers had few full time employees towards whom they felt they had any obligation.

In 1904 Eleanor Rathbone, on her own initiative, published her Report of an *Inquiry into the Conditions of Dock Labour at the Liverpool Docks*, which brought to light the iniquities of the casual system. She found, for example, that the weekly income of dockers fluctuated wildly, with men on average finding work for about three days per week. She found that it was common practice amongst dock workers for the husband to keep a fixed amount for himself, with the remainder going to the family. In a week when his wage was low, the impact was on his wife and children, who would get less.[8]

The casual system had a profound impact on Liverpool culture. In many other towns employment was regular. The working day was governed by the clock, with set starting and finishing times, and predictable regular wages, allowing families to plan and budget. Workers in mass employment such as mills and factories were more likely to form unions and act collectively. In Liverpool workers were often set against each other in competition for work, as there was never enough work to go around. Many set off each morning intent on finding work but were not successful. They had the rest of the day to themselves, with little to do. Pubs thrived in Liverpool. The uncertainty of the working hours, and the variations in the pay packet meant that long term planning and saving were not on the agenda for many workers, whether seamen, dockers or casual porters.[9]

When the severe depression of the late 1870s led employers on the Liverpool waterfront to introduce a reduction in wages, a massive industrial dispute broke out on the Mersey, involving many Irish workers.[10] In January 1879 the Birkenhead dockers were the first to strike against the wage cut, with those in north Liverpool following shortly afterwards. Seamen also came out on strike. A week later the south end dockers joined. Carters – who transported goods by horse drawn carts to and from the docks and were largely Protestant – also joined the dispute. There were mass meetings at the Pier Head and later at Huskisson Dock. A dock strike in Liverpool was a threat to the very life blood of the city. Employers brought in strike breakers from all parts of the country. Some strikers stayed out for three weeks, causing great hardship to families. In Liverpool, it was the north end dockers who held out the longest, with those in Birkenhead the last to yield. In both districts there was a strong Irish contingent.

In Liverpool the Catholic clergy intervened to bring the strike to an end. Bishop O'Reilly, who had worked amongst the poorest in Liverpool during the epidemics of the Famine years, was well respected in the Catholic community. His letter urging an end to the strike and a return to work, was read out in all Catholic churches.[11] Following the conclusion of the strikes, it was not long before dockers' unions – such as the Liverpool Union of Stevedores – were formed. Further strikes and the threat of increasing actions led to agreements through arbitration which reversed the pay cuts, a considerable achievement for the workforce. Although these strikes persisted longest in the areas where Irish dockers predominated, as yet leaders had not emerged from the Irish community. Some of the unions formed at this time, such as the Stevedores, and the Clarence Dock Club, remained strong, but mostly membership declined, since union members were often refused work.[12]

Nearly ten years later – in 1889 – the momentous Great London Dock Strike took place.[13] In June that year Liverpool tramway workers began a dispute which was to last several months.[14] The seamen then struck in June and July. In this restless atmosphere a new union appeared along the docks. The Glasgow based National Union of Dock Labourers began recruiting vigorously in Liverpool in 1890. There was a strong Irish presence in the leadership. The General Secretary Edward McHugh and the president Richard McGhee were both Irish and both active in the Irish Land League. When this Union began recruiting members in Liverpool, matters soon came to a head. The strikers were motivated by a number of issues of immediate concern, including the threat of mechanisation. For union leadership, the solution to casualisation was the formation of a strong union, including all dock workers, with the muscle to resist employers, to agitate for the ending of casual practice, and improved health and safety. The dockers strike was a bitter dispute, lasting a month. The employers brought in 13,000 strike breakers – referred to in those days as 'knobsticks'. The Liverpool Trades Council – a representative body to which local unions affiliated – denounced the Poor Law Guardians for allowing employers to recruit 'knobstick' labour from those in the workhouse. Magistrates imposed heavy sentences on strikers who sought to intimidate strike-breakers taking up work.[15]

In a major breakthrough union leaders managed to get the agreement of some employers that union members would be preferred when hiring. On some quays this led to an immediate increase in the numbers of union members. Disputes followed on the waterfront, between union and non-union men, with many refusing to work alongside those who had not taken out union membership. The rapid growth in union numbers, and the growing strength of the strikers – by March 1890, 20,000 were out – brought the Glasgow based union leader McHugh to Liverpool.[16]

He found the situation extremely difficult to manage. By the third week the strike was causing increasing hardship to families. The seamen had settled, and other parties were urging the dockers union to do likewise. In the end the strikers came to a settlement, through the services of Irish Nationalist MP Michael Davitt, who acted as arbitrator. Davitt, who had been brought up in Lancashire, was an Irishman and a prominent leader of the Land League and Home Rule movements. The Employers Labour Association (ELA) had thirty ship-owning companies in its membership. Between them they employed the majority of Liverpool dockers. During arbitration talks employers agreed to some of the demands, especially over working hours, but the union – against the wishes of members – agreed that in some cases union men would work alongside those not in unions. The employers offered weekly contracts, which the union would have agreed to, but the proposal was turned down by the men who believed that 'any alternative would be designed primarily for the benefit of employers.'[17]

Though some union leaders claimed that Davitt's settlement had been a victory for the workers, the real test was how long the settlement would last, and whether there would be union recognition. The issue of recognition became central to dock disputes in the following years. The ELA was intent on banning union membership, and was in a position to do so by simply not hiring those men who wore the union badge or 'button'. As those wearing the union button found it more difficult to get work, union membership fell from 15,000 to 6,000. The remaining members were mostly on the south docks where some companies – Holt's and Houston's – honoured earlier agreements to allow membership. It was not long after the Davitt settlement that things returned to the status quo ante for the majority – dangerous work, irregular hours and no unionisation.

Liverpool dockers leaving the stand. Photo by Thomas Burke, courtesy of Liverpool Record Office Archive.

In 1893 the influence of Irish dockers in union affairs was well illustrated in the contest for secretary of the NUDL. The existing secretary Edward McHugh, and president Richard McGhee both resigned, finding that they were widely considered to be out of touch. McHugh was replaced by James Sexton, who had first joined the union in 1890. Sexton was 'clubbable', in that he enjoyed a pint and was popular with the men. He was to hold the post for a generation. His inclination was to negotiate and avoid controversy, rather than utilise strike action. Under his leadership union membership increased steadily.

James Larkin and the Harrison Dispute
James Larkin emerged as a union leader during the Harrison's dispute in 1905. One of the points agreed with employers at T & J Harrison's was that all foremen should be union members. In June 1905, the union demanded that the seven foremen who had let their union membership

lapse should either re-join the union or be dismissed. When the demand was not met, 800 men took unofficial action (that is, a strike not sanctioned by the union leadership). Sexton's arbitration and negotiation mechanisms had been ignored. Most of the recalcitrant foremen re-joined the union, but the employers took advantage of the walk-out to begin action to break the closed shop. They repudiated their long standing agreement with the Union, and on the day following the walk-out brought in outside labour to do the work, demonstrating that they had been making preparations for breaking the strike for some time.[18] This move was a serious blow to job security, and to the Union, whose authority was dependent on high membership numbers, giving them negotiating clout. Sexton intervened in the dispute but soon found himself enduring hostility from both sides. The men rejected his advice to go back to work while he negotiated on their behalf. Sexton attempted to have the strike breakers' accommodation in a warehouse on site condemned on public health grounds, but the local Medical Officer of Health refused to take action. Sexton appealed to the City Council's Health Committee who also – by a margin of just two votes – refused to condemn the arrangement.

As a dock foreman himself and a union member involved in the dispute, James Larkin was in a much stronger position than Sexton to influence the men. With his charismatic platform style, the strength of his oratory, and his defiance of the company, he quickly became popular with the workers and immediately rose to a leadership position. He was elected to the strike committee soon after the dispute began. Strike leaders were confident they could hold out a long time. At St George's Plateau in the second week Sexton and Larkin both addressed a mass meeting. Larkin said that 'this struggle was an attempt to break the Union, but he believed that the men who had ceased work at Harrison's sheds would die in the streets before they gave in'.[19] In a later speech he asserted that the workers would 'chew the grass in Sefton Park', rather than submit. In addition to union funds, there was a public collection for the strikers, with contributions from Liberals, Irish Nationalists and even some Conservatives.

After some weeks, with strike pay funds running low, the men returned to work without their demands being met. Sexton's fears about the loss of Union recognition across the south docks did not materialise, but the lessons he took from the dispute were very different from those of Larkin. In Sexton's view the dispute 'might have been avoided with a little more tact, had the men employed in the firm listened to reason.'[20] He went on to say that there was 'an urgent necessity of more central control than at present exists.' As a Union officer Sexton was also concerned at the cost of the dispute. He was of the view that those like Larkin, who advocate a continuation of strike action, should be more aware of the financial cost of such actions both to the Union funds and to the men and their families. Larkin, on the other hand, was convinced that if more workers in allied trades, and in other workplaces had joined the dispute, the employers could have been defeated.

Having taken such an active role in leading the dispute Larkin was now not going to be re-employed in his position as a foreman at Harrison's. If fact no employer along the docks would offer work to the person who had spearheaded the dispute. The NUDL appointed Larkin as a national organiser. Since Larkin and Sexton had clashed repeatedly on the appropriate tactic to use during the strike, appointing Larkin to the national position had the effect of removing him from Liverpool, which remained Sexton's fiefdom. Animosity between the two persisted.[21] Sexton remained distrustful of Larkin thereafter, referring to him on occasion as 'the devil' whose 'cloven hoof' would occasionally re-appear, though he always recognised Larkin's exceptional ability to recruit new membership to the union.

In spite of their differences, the two subsequently worked together not just in Union matters, but also on local politics, when Larkin was chosen by Sexton to be his election agent the following year, during his unsuccessful bid to win the parliamentary seat of Toxteth.[22] Larkin went on to re-invigorate the Union in the Scottish ports, and was then posted to Ireland, where he played a central role in national politics and in the Dublin Lock-out of 1913.

The 1911 Liverpool General Transport Strike

The widespread sectarian unrest in Liverpool in 1909, was followed two years later by the Liverpool general strike. Both took place within a context of extreme poverty, over-crowding, unemployment, low wages, and poor public health standards. There were extreme levels of social inequality, both between the working class and those in the middle class, and – even more marked – between both of these and the most wealthy. Eleanor Rathbone found that whilst a dock labourer might expect to take home about £60 per annum, a lower middle-class clerk had an income of around £300. In spite of the thriving economy and ostentatious wealth of the most powerful, wages of dock workers had not improved since the 1870s. There was a sense of frustration, hopelessness and hardship. This was undoubtedly so in the close-knit Irish communities.

An important figure in the strike leadership was George Milligan. Born in 1869, he began his working life as a quay porter on the north docks. He then became a regular with White Star line, working as a checker. He joined the NUDL in 1908, at a time when union membership was proscribed by employers. Those thought to be members of the union would be dismissed, and were blacklisted by all employers.

Milligan organised the No12 branch of the Union. It was an uphill task. Membership was low, with most men being unwilling to sign up, as this might put them in danger of losing their livelihood. Milligan founded the Mersey Magazine, which consisted of articles, poems and letters. It was designed to appeal to the north end dockers and their families. It was strongly Catholic in tone. Milligan himself was a devout Catholic but also advocated support for the Labour Party – whose role would be to introduce legislation to protect working people – and the benefits of unionisation. Milligan became well-known and respected, with the result that when the strike broke out he was immediately elected to the strike committee, where he worked alongside Sexton.[23]

Initially there was tension between the two as Milligan was a working docker who took a stronger line than the office based union organiser Sexton. Sexton was committed to negotiation where possible rather than strike action. Milligan was aware of the conflict there had been between Sexton and Larkin during the Harrison dispute some years before. Milligan's intense work in the north end may well have been an influential factor in the response of the workforce. Once the strike began men were willing to come out in the open as union members. Milligan was enrolling hundreds of new recruits each day. The balance of power on the quayside was shifting, as it became apparent that those who were not in the Union may soon find it more difficult to obtain work, reversing the previous status quo.

In June 1911 the Seamen's Union, which had been negotiating for months with little success for a bargaining structure with employers, announced that they were to call a strike. Rank and file seamen were so committed to the action that they began coming out on strike before the date agreed, forcing the Union to bring the action forward. As soon as the seamen struck, there were a number of unofficial sympathy strikes as groups of dock workers refused to touch ships which were using strike breaking labour. One docker was reported as saying that 'no riverside worker will knowingly help a 'scab' firm, not for their sake but for his own. The carters and the dockers may even officially declare against the strike, but they cannot prevent their members taking sides with the strikers.'[24]

It was a feature of the strike that 'the dockers and carters were working in unison, a remarkable fact since the dockers were largely Roman Catholic and the carters largely Protestant'.[24] Once the strikes gained momentum – 'In five weeks the strength of the dockers union had swelled from 8,000 to 26,000'[25] – the widespread militancy and solidarity of the workforce unsettled employers and continued to surprise and discomfort union leaders who had difficulty controlling events both in Liverpool and in Birkenhead. By the end of June a number of the smaller members of 'the virulently anti-trade union Shipping Federation'[26] were agreeing to meet union demands around wages and recognition. Other workers soon followed the seamen's example.

On Sunday 13 August a peaceful strikers solidarity meeting at St George's Plateau, called by Tom Mann and attended by 80,000 people, was brutally attacked by police, leaving 200 injured, some of them seriously. In response to a call from Mann, and in reaction to police brutality, many more workers, including tramway and corporation staff came out on strike, taking the total to over 66,000. There was now what can best be described as a general transport strike across the city and Birkenhead, with the strike committee controlling the movement of goods and the distribution of food. Extra troops and police in their thousands were drafted in, and on the directions of Home Office Minister Winston Churchill, a gun-boat was placed at the ready on the Mersey adjacent to the Vauxhall Road district.

According to Eric Taplin: 'It was a massive, unplanned, unforeseen revolution, the impact of which none of the combatants could have predicted. Liverpool was never the same again'.[27] Parts of the city became 'no-go areas' for the authorities. Soldiers opened fire on civilians on the Monday and Tuesday following. One of the significant features of the strike was that sectarian differences were for a time put to one side in the interests of a mutual struggle for better pay and working conditions.

On the Wednesday after events at the Plateau a military convoy taking 90 detainees to Walton prison met hostile crowds along Vauxhall Road. The troops opened fire, injuring 13 and killing two; Michael Prendergast, a docker, and John Sutcliffe, a carter. Although some accounts say one was a Protestant, they were both Catholic. However, a large number of Protestant workers attended the funerals, a further sign of the growing solidarity amongst Liverpool workers in spite of continuing sectarian differences. The patterns of rioting which had been established in the previous two summers added to the unrest and disruption. The activities of the more disciplined strikers were augmented by the rowdyism and chaos of local rioters, leading to increased violence and looting. To re-enforce local police, hundreds of officers were drafted in from other areas, and 3,500 troops deployed.

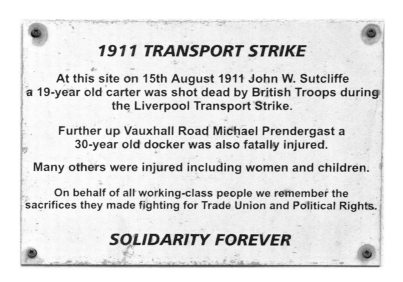

This plaque, in memory of those shot by troops during the Liverpool 1911 General Strike, can be seen at the junction of Vauxhall Road and the former Hopwood Street. Photo: S Rahilly.

Alarmed at the situation, and with the City Council unable to exert control, the government put pressure on railway companies and other key employers to reach agreement with the strike committee. They appointed a Conciliation Committee, with Irish Nationalist T.P. O'Connor and Keffin-Taylor, MP for Kirkdale, taking the lead. O'Connor, with his influence on the Irish, set up shop in the Adelphi Hotel and brokered some agreements between employers and unions. In a separate development the big shipping companies, which had always presented the most resistance to unionisation, and whose vessels were now stranded on the Mersey, succumbed to the joint pressure of the strike in which seamen, dockers and railwaymen were all united. The corporation also drew back from the brink, and began to negotiate with their employees. Arrangements for the re-instatement of workers who had lost their jobs as a consequence of taking part in the strike action were the main sticking point. Although re-instatement in reality was only partially implemented by employers – particularly in the case of tram workers – many of the demands were met. By the end of the year, wages had improved, and union recognition had been granted in many places of work.

During the 72 days of the strike there was a consistent pattern of union representatives negotiating with employers, gaining concessions and then facing the task of persuading workers to accept the terms agreed. There were numerous incidents of workers downing tools on the spot if there was any breach of what had been agreed in the strike settlement.

'A union official, usually Milligan, hurried to the scene to sort out the problem. The men were not prepared to tolerate the slightest subversion of their achievement or any hint of a return to tyranny by the foremen. Neither were they prepared to remain at work if a problem arose; they walked out, much to the alarm of the union officials and the anger of the shipowners …'[28]

There is little evidence of sectarian conflict among the large dock labour force. Whilst there were occasional small incidents, mainly between individuals or small groups, the arena of sectarian conflict in Liverpool was elsewhere. One reason was that there were well defined territories, with Irish Catholic dockers dominating most stands along the North docks, whilst Protestant stands were at Bootle and on the South docks. There were also occupational divisions, with the majority of carters being Protestant. This may well have been because a certain amount of personal capital was required to purchase and maintain not just a cart, but also the horse, which were generally lodged in local stables overnight. The common hardships and the common enemy – the employers – tended to unify dockers at times of workplace tension. The NUDL had a strong Catholic presence in its leadership, and the Mersey Quay and Railway Carters Union was much more Protestant in its membership. In the period from the strikes of 1890 through to 1911 relations between the two had been 'less than fraternal'. However, this did not prevent them working in tandem at times of crisis, most notable in the summer of 1911. Sectarian differences did exist in other occupational areas, such as, for example, between the predominantly Protestant tramway drivers union and the mainly Catholic conductors.[29]

There was a wide spectrum of religious and political views both amongst the Irish leadership of the unions, and amongst their members and their families. The aspiration of national liberation and its associated movements and ideas, introduced Irish people to radical politics. But for most, political consciousness did not go beyond the unifying ideals of Nationalism. Some of the leadership – mostly self-educated – formed a wider view of politics and society, had a knowledge of socialist and syndicalist theory, and were aware of allied movements in other countries. McGhee and McHugh, the original organisers of the NUDL, certainly were in that group. Both had left better paid employment to take up dockland leadership, and were motivated by a combination of humanitarian and socialist ideals.[30] They were aware of and supported the land nationalisation proposals of Henry George, for example, and the Irish land campaign. James Larkin was also in the same category. He was well versed in socialist and syndicalist ideas, read and sold the Clarion, and was an active member of internationalist organisations. James Connolly, a prominent union leader, whose parents were Irish, was not only self-educated, but published his own volumes of history and socialist theory. Michael Davitt, the Irish politician, Land League activist and Home Ruler, also favoured ideas which were much more radical than his electorate would ever envisage, including animal rights and land nationalisation.

There were others who began as radicals and later moved to the right of politics. Those who came into radicalism from the direction of Irish Nationalism, were always more likely to move to the right over time. One such was the MP, T.P. O'Connor, whose low point was perhaps his support for Oswald Mosley. Another was Sexton, who also began as a Nationalist. George Milligan who found himself drawn into trade union activity simply because he was a dock worker with leadership qualities, was a good example of one who took his ideas and world perspective from his Catholicism rather than socialism.[31]

Catholicism in post-famine Ireland was part of both individual and communal core identity. Catholicism, its practice and values were of such importance to those in the dockland communities, that even leaders with radical views had to take it into account. Within Catholic culture and discourse there was a strong current of hostility towards socialism. The conservative attitude of Catholic teaching towards trade unions and to strikes was an influential factor. In addition, any organisation, such as a political party or a trade union, in which the clergy did not have a leading role, was seen as a threat by the Catholic church.

With many union leaders coming from an Irish and Catholic background, and most of the families in local congregations dependent on poorly paid working people for their survival, the Catholic church, whether it chose to or not, was closely involved in the issues of pay, safety at work and job security, which were also the daily concerns of union organisers. The response of churchmen varied from place to place. Cardinal Manning was sympathetic to working men and their families, and became deeply involved in negotiations during the 1889 London dock strike, holding long meetings with the union leadership.[32] In Liverpool in 1911, many clergy were in sympathy with the workers' struggle, but were also wary of the involvement of socialists and others with a creed which might conflict with Catholic authority. Father James Nugent 'mounted a sustained attack on free-thinking outsiders, Socialists and Communists, and men who did not believe in God or hell'.[33]

Yet dockers and their families who were members of the church, had to be supported during strikes, when there was little family income. The St Vincent De Paul Society often helped those in difficulty in whatever way seemed appropriate. In some cases they gave financial assistance to men who wished to purchase the union button, an essential item to ensure employment for certain workers, even though the church was at the time opposed to trade union organisations. The devout Catholic George Milligan stated that: 'In these days when trade unionism is being recognised as the only means left to the poor man for selling his labour at a fair price, I am quite sure this species of collective bargaining will be endorsed by the Catholic Church.'[34] This tension between Catholic teaching on the one hand, and trade union and left-leaning political action on the other, remained a significant factor in Liverpool throughout the following decades.

The persistence of the casual system was a characteristic of dock work. In her report on the subject Eleanor Rathbone identified four categories of dock labourer. There were the indispensible specialists in semi-permanent or permanent employment. There were those who worked regularly, usually in an efficient gang attached to a respected foreman such as Jim Larkin at Harrison's. There were casuals whose work was irregular, and 'casual casuals' who only got work at times of high demand. Union leaders were consistently opposed to the casual system on the docks. However, many of the dockers themselves came to favour the system, with the freedom it gave them to work only on days of their own choosing. This attitude has sometimes been attributed to a culture of the dockland Irish at the time, maintaining they would perhaps have preferred the option of staying in bed on any given morning if they so chose. O'Meara remarked that: 'My father by now was a regular dock labourer, living the usual life of a dock labourer of that period, seeking work when and where he liked and chucking it when he liked.'[35]

A closer examination of the question reveals a very different perspective. Resistance to casual working appears to have arisen mainly through distrust of both the employers and union officials. Men were suspicious – as they so often were when union leadership brought forward the outcome of negotiations – that the hidden hand of the employers was behind proposals to end casualism. Any system which ended casual work would have required registration. This was the nub of the problem – having to hand over personal details. Some feared, for example, that were their true age to be discovered they would have less chance of getting the best paid heavy work. For others it was a matter of losing control.[36] Some were quite well placed as things stood, being members of a group or gang which were known to foremen and got regular work. Another control issue was over days off. Dockers could very easily take days off for, say, family occasions such as funerals, simply by not turning up. There was also the option of taking the extra – and very well paid – work which was sometimes available labouring far into the night and even through to the next morning. Men would then sleep it off, with no obligation to be there the next day. Such independence was rare in the workplace. It is true that overall men would have benefitted from registration, in terms of job security, health and safety, regular pay, and protection from the intrusion of outside workers arriving on the docks, but individuals did not always see it that way, and remained suspicious of employers and their motives. When the Dock Labour Scheme was eventually introduced by a Labour government in 1947, it was seen as 'a two-edged thing'. At the same time as it gave the benefits of a guaranteed minimum sum if you didn't get work, you had to pay for it with a certain loss of liberty.'[37]

In the era following the 1920s those with a connection to Irish Nationalism, Republicanism and Catholicism were less prominent in the leadership of dock workers. Locally born people, though often from an Irish background, were more rooted in local politics, and the labour and trade union movement, as connections with Ireland and Irish politics were severed.

CHAPTER TWELVE

ISOLATION OR INTEGRATION?

The process of Irish integration remained extremely slow. The most disadvantaged amongst the Liverpool Catholic Irish remained an isolated community. There has been much debate as to why this situation persisted. The difficulty in obtaining employment outside of the unskilled casual work in which they were trapped was undoubtedly one factor. Another was the persistent prejudice against Irish Catholics in general, which made it difficult to advance into further education and skilled employment. In many sectors, including housing, education and employment, there was a strict pecking order, and Irish Catholics were at the bottom.

Access to skilled trades was often controlled, with many positions passing from father to son, or being confined to those of a particular religious denomination. Some Irish people managed to find their way into work requiring a level of qualification, whilst others progressed through education or business enterprise. John Pinkman points to one of the difficulties. He obtained a scholarship place for an engineering apprenticeship at Bootle Tech in 1916, but points out that there was stiff competition, as only a small number of Catholics were ever admitted to such places.

'If it was hard enough for non-Catholic lads to get in, it was far worse for us because only three Catholic lads were taken each year.'[1] In time there were networks of Irish Catholic shopkeepers, tailors, grocers, solicitors and so on. Dandy Pat Byrne, an uneducated Irish emigrant who started out as a dock worker, graduated to bar work and management, and finished up a wealthy publican and hotelier, is one example.

In an era where educational opportunity was only for the few, and mainly for males, there were openings for the sons of middle class Irish – who could afford the fees – in professions such as medicine and law. Teaching, nursing and clerical work were seen as providing advancement for women. A minority also found opportunities in the merchant city, working for shipping companies and banks. In Pinkman's words: 'Those were the days when job advertisements in the English newspapers – particularly the Liverpool papers – said: 'No Catholics need apply' or 'No Irish wanted'. Religious discrimination was frequent and vicious. Catholics, especially Irish Catholics, were treated like dirt.'[1] Illiteracy levels in the English language amongst the Irish were twice that of a comparable English group,[2] hardly surprising given that Irish remained the first language for a significant number. The skills they did have were of no use in the urban environment. In the words of one employer they were 'utterly ignorant of the simplest of things.'[3] Many were blighted by ill health and poor diet, rendering them incapable of the more strenuous unskilled work.

Cultural factors, including Irish nationalism, Catholicism and other features of the Irish way of life, contributed to isolation. The Catholic Church was regarded as being allied to France and Spain, enemies of England. Irish nationalism, given impetus by the Famine experience, was committed to the break-up of the United Kingdom and was hostile to the Empire. Their connections to other radical and revolutionary movements were seen as a potential threat.

The arriving Irish, with their religion, politics and institutions, established their own tightly-knit communities based on family and parish networks. This robust structure postponed the process of integration. They had a strong group identity, based on nationalism and Catholicism. Awareness of Irish history, mythology and music were significant. Community organisations such as the Gaelic Athletic Association, the Gaelic League and Church associations, along with the continued national struggle all combined to hold the community tightly together. They felt themselves to be in hostile territory, a place they had come to through force of circumstance, the land of their traditional enemy. Many considered their stay to be temporary. Most lived within a local Catholic parish structure, where their social, educational, welfare and entertainment needs were met without resort to the wider community. They were rural people come to town. They spoke and dressed in a distinctive manner. They had little opportunity for political expression or participation, other than through demonstration and protest. 'These cultural differences in the end proved very difficult to bridge.'[4]

Sectarianism, bordering on outright racism, was another powerful factor holding integration back. In the words of E.D. Steele: 'nowhere else, save in Orange Canada, did the Irish abroad meet with such sustained antagonism as in nineteenth century Britain'.[5]

The Irish came to be regarded as a separate race, with innate characteristics which marked them out as inferior. They were frequently denigrated in the local press. 'The lower order of Irish papists are the filthiest beings in the habitable globe, they abound in dirt and vermin and have no care for anything but self gratification that would degrade the brute creation.'[6] This opinion of the *Liverpool Herald* in 1855, is but one random example.

There are numerous examples of these arguments, including remarks from such men as Frederick Engels, Thomas Carlyle, Benjamin Disraeli, Charles Kingsley and Matthew Arnold.[7] Newspapers and magazines lampooned the Irish, reinforcing popular stereotypes.[8] The power and widespread prevalence of these views should not be under-estimated. There was an almost universal tendency from the 1840s onwards to describe the immigrant Irish and their problems in distinctly racist terms.[9]

Fraser's Magazine referred to one of the most frequently repeated alleged Irish characteristics: 'Now of all the Celtic tribes, famous for their indolence and fickleness as the Celts everywhere are, the Irish are admitted to be the most idle and the most fickle.'[10]

Charles Kingsley, author of *The Water Babies*, wrote in 1860 that: 'I am haunted by the human chimpanzees I saw along the hundred miles of horrible country ... to see white chimpanzees is dreadful'.[11]

Lord Acton wrote in 1862 that: 'the Celts are not amongst the progressive, initiative races.'

Even more Liberal English opinions became infected with these attitudes. Sidney and Beatrice Webb wrote home from Dublin in 1892 that: 'the people here are charming, but we detest them, as we should the Hottentots.'[12] There were even 'scientific' reasons advanced to support these prejudices. The extreme poverty of the Irish in Britain only served to confirm such prejudices and maintain antagonism.

There were vested interests at work in maintaining sectarianism and Irish isolation. It is axiomatic that fear can be an important factor in persuading people to get behind a cause or an organisation, and there were many in politics who used fear of the Irish to maintain the strength of their political or community support. Clergymen spoke out against Catholicism in order to stiffen the resolve and fervour of congregations. Clubs and societies such as the Orange Order and the Working Men's Conservative Association relied on sectarianism as the foundations of their membership and recruitment. And of course, politicians could see the opportunity to hold on to voters who might be tempted to go elsewhere, by raising the fear of the other, in many instances the Irish. At the same time continued Irish isolation served the interests of both the Irish Nationalists and the Catholic Church. The above factors combined to leave the Irish isolated from mainstream Victorian British society. It was to be a long time before these barriers were broken down.

IN HARDSHIP AND HOPE PART THREE
FROM 1914 TO 1960s

CHAPTER THIRTEEN

IRISH INDEPENDENCE AND AFTERMATH

In the years leading up to the Great War of 1914 there was a fresh boost to Protestant fears when government proposals for Home Rule once more came on to the agenda in 1912, the year after the Liverpool general strike. Edward Carson, leader of the Ulster Unionists, and advocate of armed resistance in opposition to Liberal proposals for Irish Home Rule, came to Liverpool and addressed enthusiastic crowds at Sheil Park. He was at first unwilling to respond to Wise's request to address one of his bible meetings, but was strongly advised that it would be unwise not to do so.

In response to the Unionist campaign local branches of the newly founded Irish Volunteers – a drilling and marching organisation – were soon attracting thousands of members in Liverpool, Bootle, Birkenhead and surrounding areas. They supported John Redmond's nationalists by taking part in marches and demonstrations. With the Home Rule Bill coming to parliament, the atmosphere continued to be volatile. Harford and O'Connor addressed 38,000 from platforms in Sylvester Street in support of Home Rule.

The Liverpool Irish and the First World War

When war first broke out, the Irish constitutional leadership in Liverpool – Austin Harford, T.P. O'Connor, officials in the dockers union and the *Catholic Herald* – were enthusiastic in their support for the military and the Empire. They believed that if Irish men fought in the Empire's cause, this would strengthen the case for Home Rule. A large proportion of the Liverpool Irish followed the recommendations of the Nationalist leader John Redmond in the opening phase of the war to join-up.[1] O'Connor was more ambivalent, saying 'that Irishmen have made every sacrifice that could have been asked of us,' but supported the war none the less. He spoke alongside Winston Churchill at a recruitment rally at the Tournament Hall, Edge Lane, in September 1914, praising: 'Our Empire, founded on freedom, on free institutions, on the respect of nationality'.[2] His colleague Austin Harford also endorsed participation in the conflict. Although there were dissenting voices such as Joe Devlin in the north of Ireland, many in the Liverpool Volunteers responded to Redmond's call. The *Liverpool Catholic Herald* reported his observation that in 1915: 'Recruiting had been so heavy in some streets in Scotland division that almost every house had a soldier from it fighting at the front.'[3]

There was little opportunity for the Irish in Liverpool to join specifically Irish regiments. Army policy was firmly opposed. As many Liverpool Irish organisations such as the Volunteers and the AOH got behind the war effort, the Liverpool Irish were, 'simply flooding into existing British units,' during that period early in the war, before the full reality of the high casualty rate became public knowledge. Some estimates put the number as high as 20,000.[4]

There was a specifically Irish Battalion in Liverpool, the 8th 'Irish' in the King's Regiment. This unit became the focal point for Liverpool Irish recruitment and gained much public attention. The unit had a history of Irish connections going back to the 1850s, and was now undergoing a revival. T.P. O'Connor was one of those who supported the unit, and was determined that it should retain its Irish character. New recruits from the Liverpool Irish community soon brought the battalion up to strength. Two additional battalions were recruited, forming the second 8th Irish in October 1914 and the third in May 1915.[5] St Francis Xavier's gave permission for its premises to be used. Their Irish identity was evident in their uniform which included the caubeen cap with a distinctive hackle or feather attached, and in the uniforms of their kilted pipers. The wealthy Irish business man Thomas Ryan provided a supply of Irish wolfhounds.[6] The 8th Irish took part in offensives at Ginchy and at Guillemont in September 1916, and at Ypres in July 1917, sustaining heavy casualties in each case.

On St Patrick's Day 1917, there was a civic reception for 700 battalion soldiers who had been wounded in the war. The Mayor hosted the event and his wife presented bunches of shamrock to the men.[7] Austin Harford, a consistent and articulate advocate of Liverpool Irish integration called for greater recognition of the Irish contribution to the war effort. 'Irishmen have made their sacrifices in this war in no small measure, and those sacrifices should of themselves put an end at once and for all to the hateful policy of the past in dealing with the Irish community – a policy which has been, and still is, a blot upon the municipal and social life of this city.'[8] Amongst the policies Harford was referring to was the annual vote to exclude any Irish nationalist councillors from being considered for the office of Mayor. O'Connor was successful in insisting that casualty lists simply referring to the regiment as, 'the 8th battalion, the King's Regiment', should be amended to include the word 'Irish' in the citation. The War Office conceded and allowed the battalion to be referred to as, 'the 8th Irish battalion'.[9] The experience of the Great War and the common heartache endured by both sides of the Liverpool communal divide was a factor which contributed to the slow process of integration. The battalion itself was disbanded in March 1922 as army numbers were reduced following the war. It was to be reformed during the Second World War.

The Easter Rising, War of Independence and Civil War

Irish nationalist and republican organisations – including the Gaelic League, the Irish Republican Brotherhood (IRB) and the women's organisation Cumann Na mBan – maintained a presence in 20th century Liverpool.[10]

IRB membership included those of Irish descent born in Liverpool along with fresh members from Ireland, who settled in Liverpool.

The Gaelic League (Conradh na Gaeilge) was founded to promote Irish language and culture, and attracted some with a commitment to revolutionary politics. The first branch on Merseyside was formed in 1896. By 1903 there were five branches in Liverpool and two in Birkenhead. The following year Padraic Pearse spoke as their guest at the Picton Library. The network of Irish language speakers was strong on Merseyside at this time, and some of their number – notably Piaras Beaslai (Percy Beasley) Cesca Trench and Norma Borthwick – went on to play important roles in the Gaelic revival movement, in the Gaelic League in Britain and in Ireland itself. Borthwick served on the executive of the League. Beaslai was one of the founders of the Irish Volunteers and took part in the Easter Rising and the War of Independence as a senior officer. Liverpool born Stiofain McEnna was a successful dramatist and journalist, in both Irish and English, who worked for, amongst others, Joseph Pulitzer's New York World.

The Irish Republican Brotherhood, a secret society with a commitment to attaining Irish independence by force of arms, also continued to function, though with a reduced membership, many of them from an older generation.

The Irish Volunteers, formed in reaction to the loyalist Ulster Volunteers, opened several branches in Liverpool, Bootle and Birkenhead. Late in 1915 there was increased talk of revolution in Ireland. At the same time there was the increasing possibility of conscription in Britain. In the spring of 1916 some Liverpool members of the Volunteers began making their way to Ireland. Tom Craven took the lead, and founded the garrison at Kimmage near Dublin.[11] Here Volunteers from England and Scotland, including about 60 Liverpool men, took care of themselves in makeshift circumstances, sometimes relying on money raised in Liverpool for their support. Many – including the Kings, the Kerrs and the Thorntons – travelled in family groups. When the Easter Rising began in April 1916 they were well placed to take part. A detachment was present in the General Post Office at the outbreak of the Rising, and one of their number Joe Gleeson, raised the tricolour over the building.[13] Six members of the Liverpool Cumann na mBan, led by Nora Thornton, and including teenager Rose Anne Murphy (later Morgan) also took part.

For the majority of the Liverpool Irish the Rising came as a surprise. It was at first denounced by Harford as 'insignificant, unrepresentative and irresponsible'.[14] However, the execution of the leadership in the following month changed nationalist attitudes. In the general election immediately after the War in 1918, Sinn Fein won 73 seats out of 105. The Parliamentary Party held on to just six in Ireland, plus O'Connor in Liverpool. Unionists won 22 seats in the north of Ireland. An IRA military campaign began immediately, precipitating the Irish War of

Independence, which was followed by negotiations and a Treaty in 1922. Ahead of the Treaty the Government of Ireland Act had established a parliament in Belfast, in response to demands from Unionists. Following the Treaty civil war broke out over the terms, and lasted until 1923.

Liverpool played a peripheral but significant role in these events. The Irish community in Liverpool, as in Ireland itself, had little engagement with the Rising until the execution of the leadership by a British Army firing squad. The general who issued the order – Maxwell – was from Aigburth in Liverpool.

'During the period 1919 to 1922 the Irish in England identified with the plight of their compatriots across the water as they had never done before, nor were to do so again.'[15] As events unfolded in Ireland, the daily press reports were closely followed by Irish readers in England. 'During the late summer and early autumn of 1920,' for example, 'the attention of many Irish households was focused on the fate of Terence McSweeney, the Mayor of Cork, on hunger strike in Brixton jail.'[15]

From the time of the Rising of 1916 through to the end of the Irish Civil War in 1923, there were a number of overlapping organisations in Liverpool involved in supporting the armed conflict being co-ordinated by Michael Collins in Ireland. There were members of the long-standing IRB. They tended to be older and more settled in employment or with their own businesses. They were well positioned to take part in the covert movement of people and arms.

There was a company of the IRA, manned mainly by younger single men, of both Irish and British birth. They carried out armed actions at regular intervals. The women's organisation, the Cumann na mBan, linked with both, assisted in military operations including arms traffic, and sheltering fugitives. Organisations like the Irish National Foresters, the Sinn Fein clubs and the Irish National Self-Determination League were not committed to armed operations, but had many members who were sympathetic, and could be relied upon to offer assistance on occasions, including the use of premises for concealing weapons or holding meetings. These organisations were occasionally a recruiting ground for the IRA. Liverpool was the most important centre of IRA operations in Britain during the War of Independence.

Any account of secret revolutionary activity faces the challenge of finding evidence. Underground organisations being monitored by the authorities do not keep detailed minutes and records. What evidence is available is often scant, and not always reliable. Oral testimony, police reports and newspaper articles are the most common resources, each with their own drawbacks.

Liverpool activist, John Pinkman, in his autobiography, makes reference to the reliability of oral testimony: 'In later years literally scores of men claimed to have belonged to the 'Liverpool Battalion', or, God help us! the 'Liverpool Brigade' of the Old IRA, and obtained medals and pensions from the Irish government in recognition of their 'service' in the fight for Irish independence. Some even wrote accounts of their 'exploits' in Liverpool for the gullible Irish newspapers. But there was never a battalion of the Old IRA in Liverpool: there was only one undermanned company – and because I was one of its two mobilisers, I knew every man who belonged to it.'[16]

However, it seems likely that Pinkman was not taking into account the many covert operations which were also taking place in Liverpool, including those by older IRB members. Following the Rising in Dublin through until May 1919, Irish republican activity in Liverpool had been in reaction to events, and in particular involved transporting arms and assisting fugitives. These included members of the republican leadership who were returning from Britain to Ireland having escaped from prison, or who were passing through on their way from Ireland to the US. Peter Murphy, proprietor of the '98 Shop on Scotland Road was well known for his leading role in these activities.

Many who had taken part in the Rising had been interned at locations in Britain, including in a camp at Frongoch in north Wales, and prisons such as Lincoln Jail where future Irish President Eamonn deValera was held. The long standing Irish Republican Brotherhood (IRB) network became active in making arrangements for such things as assisting escapees, passing messages and moving weapons and ammunition. The best known safe house was that of Mrs Dan McCarthy the widow of a former IRB centre (leader) in Liverpool. She lived in Guildhall Road, Aintree. Here Eamonn deValera, who had escaped from Lincoln Jail, Cathal Brugha, a leader of the Rising who was recuperating from his wounds, Liam Mellows, Piaras Beaslai and Austin Stack all found refuge. She put herself in great personal danger, and provided for people often at her own expense.[17]

Michael Collins began taking control of IRA activity in Liverpool around May 1919, establishing a military command structure in place of the existing committee system. They were to be under the command of the leadership in Dublin. They were to recruit and train a cadre of activists. Amongst the many who had been interned along with Collins at Frongoch was Liverpool based Tom Craven. Following their release Craven began organising a branch of Collins's force in Liverpool – the Liverpool Irish Republican Army (LIRA). In May 1919 Tom Craven wrote to Collins to inform him that an IRA group had been founded at a meeting in Stanley Road, Bootle. There were 40 members, with Craven as captain, Stephen Lanigan Treasurer, and M. Horan Secretary. Collins replied somewhat gruffly that the IRA did not have secretaries and treasurers. They should appoint a first and second lieutenant.[18] An important function of Collins's organisation in Liverpool throughout the campaign was to enlist seamen who could assist the rebellion by moving personnel to and from Ireland, and by shipping supplies of arms and ammunition. [19]

In the following months Neill Kerr senior played an important role. He was well known in republican circles and had been one of the organisers of the ceremonial funeral of Jeremiah O'Donovan Rossa which had passed through Liverpool in August 1915. He was a trusted friend of Michael Collins, and was in charge of covert activity around Liverpool. Stephen Lanigan was also in regular contact with Collins, as he took charge of the payments for material to be shipped from Liverpool. In those post-war years there were considerable numbers of small arms in circulation. The Liverpool group began sending revolvers, rifles, ammunition and even machine guns, by boat to Ireland. Explosives were obtained through Irish contacts working in mines and quarries. Collins was constantly concerned with the prices being paid, writing on 27 June 1919: 'prices generally speaking are very high and I hope you will succeed in making a reduction.' In July, Collins wrote to Kerr that: 'The 100 rounds of 45 arrived safely … If we get 150 rounds daily, this would be quite alright. Of course the rifles will be more acceptable, and as I have repeatedly said, 45 ammunition is very badly needed.'[20] Collins had a severe supply problem throughout the conflict, and it is evident that supply from Liverpool was steady, but relatively small in quantity.

Collins had an active policy of recruiting those who held key positions in organisations such as the civil service. Lanigan in particular – a senior customs officer – was to prove extremely useful to the IRA in Liverpool, with his organising ability and his knowledge of local day to day customs activity. In order to avoid coming under suspicion, he generally avoided taking part in overt Irish organisations.

The Liverpool-born Irish were especially useful to the organisation, since having local accents and jobs they were less likely to arouse suspicion, and were more difficult to identify. They also knew their way around, had plenty of local contacts and houses where fugitives could reside in secret and comfort. They held positions in local employment, such as on the docks and aboard ship. Many of these were long standing IRB members. A leading figure was Patrick Lively, who had been head of the local IRB since 1906.[20] Irish shipping agents and seamen such as Bernie Kavanagh arranged for the passage of arms and people. A local man with a coal delivery service transported arms around the city in coal bags, without attracting any attention. Liverpudlian John Pinkman was able to introduce himself as a local engineering apprentice – which he was – when persuading a workman to show him the mechanism which operated the dock gates at the Langton dock, in preparation for LIRA actions there.[21]

The IRA's active military organisation remained relatively small, recruiting through local networks and Irish organisations. They were not particularly political in that they were not former activists in such bodies as the Labour Party, the Irish Nationalist Party, or trade unions. A focal point was Peter Murphy's '98 shop in Scotland Place. Potential recruits would have been attracted by the Sinn Fein flags and Nationalist literature available there.

The King brothers, John, George and Patrick travelled from Liverpool to Dublin together and took part in the Easter Rising. John was seriously wounded. Patrick later fought on the Pro-Treaty side in the Civil War. His brother George was killed fighting for the Anti-Treaty forces. Courtesy of the King family.

Under Collins's direction the Liverpool arm began to take shape. He placed a high priority on preventing infiltration by the informers. Liverpool recruitment was strictly controlled, and mainly through friendship networks. New volunteers had to be recommended by an existing trusted member. Where there was doubt, as in the case of men newly arrived from Ireland, applicants were directed to apply to James Moran, the manager of the Irish National Foresters' office on Scotland

Road in Liverpool. He would refer them to his secretary Nan Feeley, who took all personal details and had them sent to the IRA Headquarters in Dublin. Only when a vetting process had been completed would the applicant be admitted to the organisation.[22]

When Tom Craven left for America at short notice, Mike O'Leary took over.[23] However, young activists soon became dissatisfied with his leadership, which was more inclined to lectures on Irish history than to training for direct action. He was replaced by Tom Kerr,[24] – son of Neill Kerr – who was another Liverpool activist who had taken part in the Easter Rising along with his brothers Jack and Neill junior. In addition to these core activists, the organisation in Liverpool relied upon a network of sympathisers; people who would put someone up for the night, no questions asked, or pass a package on to a ship.

From the start of 1920 the war in Ireland had escalated quickly. The British authorities brought in fresh recruits to support the struggling Royal Irish Constabulary. They were predominantly ex-soldiers with recent experience of the brutality of the trenches, and became known as the Black and Tans. As attacks from the IRA multiplied, there were numerous instances of retaliation against property and civilians, such as the Black and Tans' burning of the town of Balbriggan, and their machine gun attack on football supporters in Casement Park, Dublin on 21 November, killing fourteen and wounding 60 more. The local IRA in Liverpool were increasingly keen to see action other than the transport of weapons and personnel. In Dublin Cathal Brugha had decided that the time had come to bring the conflict to England itself, as a response to Black and Tan operations in Ireland.

On 16 November 1920, in a basement hall at 93 Scotland Road, about 30 men from Liverpool, Bootle and the surrounding area met to make preparations for such a campaign.[25] They were addressed by Rory O'Connor, 'Director of Engineering' for the IRA, who had just arrived from Dublin. He told the meeting that whilst Ireland was the front line in the war, Liverpool was deep inside enemy territory, and well positioned to carry out retaliatory actions. Their first action was to be to destroy lock gates and set fire to warehouses. While this meeting was taking place the streets around were watched by members of the Liverpool Cumann Na mBan. Shortly afterwards there was a security disaster for the Liverpool group, when papers discovered in a raid on a house in Dublin were widely publicised in the press. The documents included feasibility plans on the idea of targeting the Liverpool docks and the Stuart Street power station in Manchester. There was a distinct danger that these revelations would jeopardise the far advanced plans for action in Liverpool. The *Liverpool Catholic Herald* ridiculed the revelations as 'fairy tale'.

Members of the Liverpool Company of the IRA were well placed to make their own judgements about the level of police presence on the docks and any heightened state of alert. Additional security at the dock entrance frustrated the main target of the original plan – the gates between the docks and the river. However, the decision was taken to go ahead with the planned diversionary tactic of setting warehouses on fire. On the night of the 28 November, eighteen dockland buildings, mainly cotton and timber warehouses, were set alight. The action caused widespread damage running into hundreds of thousands of pounds, and attracted banner headlines in both local and national press. The report in *The Times* – Sinn Fein plot in Liverpool – was alongside an item on Cardinal Logue's condemnation of the Casement Park shootings.[25]

A civilian, William Ward, was shot dead in Liverpool as he pursued one of the LIRA activists fleeing the scene. The police used what information they had to take people into custody during the following days and weeks. They searched Neill Kerr's house, and in an embarrassing incident for one usually so well organised, they caught him with receipts for materials associated with the raids in his coat pockets. Also in the house was a friend of Kerr's in the uniform of the Irish Republican Army, which he had worn to a local ceili, 'to show people who'd never seen one, what a Volunteer officer's uniform looked like.'[26] Harry Coyle, who used his motor vehicle to run guns and munitions from Glasgow to safe houses in Liverpool, was also apprehended.

Detective work led to the arrest and trial of the Brown sisters, Sheila and Kathleen, members of the local Cumann na mBan. Sheila was a school teacher, and Kathleen worked as a clerk for a local company where Irish republicans often found a job – John Hughes. In their house in Laburnum Grove, Litherland, police found correspondence related to the transportation of weapons such as guns and detonators, along with Sinn Fein membership cards and literature.[27] The effect of these arrests, and the increased police activity following the warehouse fires, was to severely disrupt the traffic of arms through Liverpool, so valued by Michael Collins. 'Edward Brady recorded a reduction in the military wing on Merseyside from five sections to three, with membership down from 150 to 108.'[28]

Some of those arrested 'had no connection whatsoever with the warehouse and timber yard fires.'[29] Those with little evidence against them were interned rather than sent to court. Steve Lanigan and Tom Kerr were both held in the Dublin Bridewell, before being sent to the internment camp at Ballykinlar in County Down. Neill Kerr was convicted of conspiracy to murder and conspiracy to arson.

Following the disruption caused by the convictions and internment, Collins re-organised the Liverpool command, appointing a young medical student, Paddy Daly, to take charge of restarting the flow of arms shipments. Daly arrived from Dublin and obtained a job in a cotton warehouse. Hugh Early, another young man sent over from Dublin, was to take command of what remained of the active service unit, a move greatly resented by locals.

In February of the following year, 'an entirely new form of Sinn Fein activity was put into operation in Liverpool.'[30] Activists posing as police officers confiscated the passports of about twenty emigrants from Ireland with passage booked to the United States. 'The raiders acted with a composure which showed that their parts had been well rehearsed.' The purpose was to confront young men who had arrived from Ireland and were planning to travel to America. Some may well have left Ireland as a result of threats from the Black and Tans, others because they were being pressured to join an IRA unit. They had their passports confiscated, and were forced to listen to a harangue directing them to return to Ireland to take part in the national struggle.

This was followed by action in March, when the plan was to set a 'ring of fire' around Liverpool, by setting farmhouses and buildings alight. This activity was to mirror the continued activity by the Black and Tans in the Irish countryside. The original targets which had been selected by locals such as Pinkman, with their good knowledge of the district, were revised by the new Dublin commander, Early. The new plan was badly flawed. During the operation Paddy Lowe was shot and injured by a farmer. Near Hall Road station on the Southport line Pinkman and four others were arrested and imprisoned for the remainder of the conflict.[31]

In May there was further activity 'in retaliation for Black and Tan activity in Ireland.' In this incident 400 plate glass windows in shops in Liverpool city centre were smashed. On 14 May armed and masked men broke into six houses belonging to army officers, tying up the residents and threatening to set the houses on fire. In June a plan to disrupt local communications was carried out, when 300 telegraph wires were cut. Activists in Huyton were caught and arrested following a gunfight. This was to be the last action in Liverpool, as the Anglo-Irish War came to an end with the truce in July 1921. How well Collins ever managed to restore the shipment of arms through Liverpool during the later part of the conflict is difficult to say.

There was widespread sympathy for the Irish independence movement in Liverpool during the turbulent period just after the Great War. As soldiers returned there was a devastating flu outbreak which killed many. Unemployment was high and the Unemployed Workers Association was very active. In one well-known incident, during a rally at St George's Hall, they stormed the Walker Art Gallery on the opposite side of the plaza and attempted to occupy it. The police response was extremely brutal. The police themselves became involved in industrial action in the police strike in 1919.

The Irish once again took some of the blame for this. General Sir Neville Macready, the Commissioner of Metropolitan Police, was of the opinion that: 'the high proportion of police in Liverpool who went on strike was due to the high proportion of Irish men in the force, a class of men who are always apt to be carried away by any wave of enthusiasm.'[33]

During the course of the strike there was widespread rioting, and gunboats returned to the Mersey. In the midst of all this turbulence the Irish revolutionary movement was organising itself following the Dublin Rising. The dividing line between civilian supporters and active military involvement was not always clear. Peter Murphy who was actively involved in covert activity such as the movement and sheltering of escaped prisoners was also treasurer for a time of the Irish Self-Determination League (ISDL). Another example was Edward Brady, who was Secretary of the Wallasey Branch of the ISDL for a time, but left to join the IRA; 'from the purely political and constitutional side of the Sinn Fein movement, I graduated to the military and secret branch.'[34]

For many, if not most, of the second and third generation the connection with Ireland and Irish culture had weakened over the years. Yet there was a section of the Irish community who were actively involved in Irish organisations of some sort or another. It was from this group that political support for Sinn Fein was most likely to come. The Council of Irish Societies was certainly sympathetic. The Irish Self-Determination League (ISDL),[35] under the leadership of the Nationalist councillor P.J. Kelly, was actively involved in organising meetings, marches and similar events. It had fifteen branches in Liverpool, and considerable political influence within the Irish community. Kelly continued to stand successfully against Labour in local elections. There were a number of emotive issues related to the Irish campaign which re-enforced his position, including the arrest and deportation of activists in Liverpool and the reported actions of the Black and Tans. ISDL meetings in Liverpool were well attended. The Liverpool Stadium (which once stood just north of Tithebarn Street) was a popular venue. The Sinn Fein leader Arthur Griffith was amongst the guest speakers there. These rallies were also fund raising occasions, with the money raised being sent to organisations in Ireland.

It was not long before the authorities began to restrict ISDL activity, including banning meetings at the Stadium and other large venues. The ISDL in Liverpool faced opposition from all sides. One of the concerns was that sectarian tensions were rising in the city as a result of the conflict in Ireland, and ISDL activity was adding to the pressure. The visits of Irish Nationalist leaders to Liverpool in the middle of a revolt against British rule was a nightmare for the authorities and an opportunity for radical Protestantism. Pastor Longbottom had noted the openly seditious content of speeches by the Irish leader Griffith. Protestant counter demonstrations were promised, should another nationalist speaker, Archbishop Mannix, be allowed to address a meeting at the stadium. This Australian based Cork man, who had led the funeral cortege of Terence McSweeney through London, was scheduled to speak in Liverpool. The authorities were so concerned that the Royal Navy intercepted the ship in which he was travelling from the United States, took him into custody and put him ashore in Cornwall, from where he had little chance of making it to the rally in Liverpool.[36]

At the same time, the uneasy relationship between nationalists and Labour persisted. P.J. Kelly – not always the most diplomatic of politicians – had been outspokenly critical of Labour for not getting behind the Irish cause. In April 1920, speaking at a meeting to protest against deportations from Bootle, he said of the conflict in Ireland that: 'it was hypocritical and cowardly of the British Labour Party to blame Mr Lloyd George and Mr Winston Churchill – they did not make the guns; the workers were to blame.'[37] Nor was the ISDL popular amongst trade unionists, many of whom had fought in the War, or had relatives who did so.

During the McSweeney hunger strike P.J. Kelly called for a strike of all Liverpool dockers in support. Although several thousand dockers and coal-heavers responded,[38] their numbers were a relatively small proportion of the estimated 20,000 dock workers of Irish descent in Liverpool. Rising unemployment and lack of job security was certainly a factor in the poor response. The Liverpool Trades Council refused to allow the ISDL a place on the May Day platform at Sheil Park later that year, and had left Kelly and his supporters waiting in the rain.

In 1921 events in Ireland moved on rapidly. Michael Collins was appointed to head the treaty negotiations on behalf of the Irish Government. The settlement reached in the negotiations conceded more than many republicans had ever anticipated. There would now be a sovereign independent parliament in Dublin. But the British required that the new parliament take an oath of loyalty to the British monarch and that the newly established parliament in the north – governing six counties – would remain, thus partitioning Ireland. The republican movement was deeply divided by this settlement, which Collins judged to be the best that could be gained under the circumstances.

In Liverpool as in Ireland, the movement split. Many activists had a loyalty to the military leader Collins, and supported the Treaty. These included Neill Kerr, and John Pinkman, both of whom had been at the centre of activity in Liverpool. Daly, who was still active in running arms to Ireland, came out against the Treaty. Rory O'Connor, who had recently reviewed the situation in Liverpool, also joined the anti-Treaty forces. When Rory O'Connor and others raised the anti-Treaty flag over the Four Courts in Dublin, civil war ensued. Some in the Liverpool company joined this fight in Ireland. The Fleming brothers Denis and Patrick were among their number, as was George King, who was killed in the conflict. Both Flemings returned later in the year, to take charge of the rebel effort in Liverpool. 93 Scotland Road was still a favoured meeting place, as were pubs in the Scotland Place area, where Peter Murphy – who had also joined the anti-Treaty side – had his '98 shop. This group, of around fifty activists, with a reduced level of passive supporters, continued to function, shipping arms to Ireland and planning further actions in Britain. However, the activist group was now smaller, and they were under tighter police surveillance, including interception of communications. Shipping arms to Ireland was made more complicated, since Collins and others, now in the Irish government, were well aware of the methods and routes used, and the people likely to be involved. There were also plans for further actions in Britain, though none ever took place. Concerned at the activities of the group, British authorities arrested 110 Irish men and women who were suspected of being involved in republican activities, and deported them to Ireland, thus eliminating a security risk in Britain, and aiding the Irish Free State. Twenty four of those deported – including five women – were from Liverpool. The deportations were undoubtedly a blow to anti-Treaty activities in Britain in this phase of conflict. The Special Branch was of the view that: 'The recent deportations entirely disorganised the IRA in this country, and completely upset their plans.'[39] The deportations were successfully challenged in court, with the detainees being released, receiving compensation and returning to Britain. The Fleming brothers were re-arrested. Patrick Fleming was convicted and sentenced to twelve months hard labour.

Support for the anti-treaty forces continued in Liverpool in various forms. Permission was sought to carry out collections outside churches after mass on Sundays. Sympathetic priests would sometimes agree, usually with the proviso that collection was not accompanied by any political activity, such as public speeches. The Thomas Ashe Republican Club continued to support the Irregulars, as the anti-Treaty forces came to be called. Arms continued to be transported from Liverpool. In May police seized ammunition and machine gun parts in a raid on the house of John Finn, arresting the new officer in command of the Liverpool Irregulars at this time, William Horan. Following the end of the Civil War in May 1923, there remained a rump of anti-Treaty Sinn Fein IRA in Liverpool, with Peter Murphy a continued prominent member. But they never enjoyed widespread support amongst the Irish community.

The Liverpool Irish community – now dominated by second, third and indeed fourth generations – had become more embedded in British society, as their life experiences became more closely linked to those of mainstream Britain. In particular the widespread participation in the First World War had created common ground with British army colleagues. Many felt ambivalent towards the rebellion which had taken place in Ireland.

There was a further brief outbreak of IRA activity in Liverpool on the eve of the Second World War, when the leadership decided to attempt to cause disruption to the British economy, principally by attacking power supplies. The campaign was largely conducted by activists who came to Britain from Ireland for the purpose. Using mainly gelignite they carried out bombings in London, Manchester and other locations, including Merseyside. In Liverpool they made contact with sympathetic locals. There were attempts to blow up pylons. Bombs were placed in other locations, including railway stations and in post boxes. There was outrage in May 1939 when tear gas was released in two cinemas, the Paramount and the Trocadero.[40]

Amongst those later arrested and convicted were Thomas Kelly, whose premises on Edge Lane were used to store explosives, and three members of the Hannah family of Great Howard Street. The leader of the group, Joe Deegan, a republican from South Armagh, escaped capture. The two principal participants were eventually apprehended trying to make their way back to Ireland. There is no evidence of sympathy for the campaign amongst the Liverpool Irish. The attacks, designed to disrupt, impacted mainly on the local working population, rather than any military target. Besides, since the establishment of the Dublin parliament, there was no longer a broad based campaign around Irish rights in Liverpool. Irish writer Brendan Behan, who arrived in Liverpool in November 1939 on a further IRA bombing mission, testified to the hostility of the local population to his activities. The campaign did succeed in stoking up hostility towards the Irish amongst their traditional foes. Tory Councillor David Rowan's campaign to establish a government agency to monitor Irish migrants began attracting large crowds. However, these events were soon overtaken by the outbreak of the Second World War.

Liverpool nationalists played an important part in Irish revolutionary struggles in the nineteenth and twentieth centuries, and Liverpool's contribution to the success of the War of Independence – a revolution which removed Ireland from the Empire, and established a fully-fledged parliament in Dublin – should be acknowledged. The revolutionary state of mind, and anti-establishment attitude which inspired many, and persisted in each of the episodes recounted above, has survived in Liverpool, to a greater or lesser extent ever since.

CHAPTER FOURTEEN

FROM NATIONALISM TO LABOUR

The Irish community in Liverpool underwent a change in character in the years following the First World War. Migration from Ireland continued steadily, but not in such great numbers as in earlier decades. At the same time, there were large numbers of Liverpool-born Catholics who felt a closer identity with Liverpool than their Irish parents had done. At the same time they did not identify with Britain in the same way as those from a Protestant background. Yet community divisions were reduced as sectarianism began to decline in the generation which had suffered in the war and had less appetite for marching bands and street violence. Industrial unrest, which had continued during the war years, became a more significant issue. Following the Easter Rising and the Anglo Irish war, Nationalism in Liverpool declined as the Labour Party gradually grew in strength. The political and social landscape of the city was changing.

By 1923 the Liverpool Irish community was becoming more detached from events in Ireland. Most Liverpool Nationalists, in contrast to Ireland, were observers rather than participants in the War of Independence and subsequent events. This detachment was reflected in the *Catholic Herald*, when it commented that: 'We want for Ireland what Ireland wants for herself, and not what we think she should ask or take.'[1] Following the chaos and uncertainty of war and the tumultuous events in Ireland, Liverpool political parties and their leaders began to re-organise. As soldiers returned from the trenches, the Labour Party was gaining ground. The Tories and the Liberals were inclined to unite against the ungodly socialist threat. The Irish Catholic voters, once so solidly united behind the Nationalist Catholic cause, were now subjected to pressures likely to divide them.

The Decline of the Nationalist Party
The first of these was attitudes towards Nationalism. Whilst many still adhered to the Nationalist cause, and supported the vigorous IRA campaign in the twenties, many others felt ambivalent about the Easter Rising, which took place while they or their relatives were fighting for Britain in Europe. Such people were inclined to look towards Labour. At the same time a large number of Catholics considered Labour policies to be contrary to Catholic doctrine in a number of significant respects. Whilst the majority of Irish Catholics in Liverpool were undoubtedly to the left, if for no other reason than that they were viscerally opposed to the Tory party, they were not going to flock straight into Labour ranks.

There were certain specific areas where Catholic voters might feel that there was a conflict between their faith and Labour policy. The most important of these was education. As state education expanded, churches were once again concerned to augment their own provision. But how was the cost to be met, especially as standards and expectations rose? In 1925, for example, the Board of Education put four Catholic schools in the category of 'unsuitable for continued recognition and incapable of improvement'.[2] The Catholic Church had in the past found allies in the Anglicans, who joined in a campaign to have tax payers' money utilised to fund denominational schools, while Labour and Liberals were both opposed to funding religious educational institutions from taxation.[3]

There were other areas of Labour social policy which conflicted with church teaching, including divorce legislation, and the expansion of health care to allow state provision of advice on contraception and other family issues. This was territory – Catholic family life – which the church regarded as its own. On such issues as these 'left leaning' Catholics might oppose the Labour Party, which would otherwise have been their natural home.

The new bishop, Keating, though sympathetic to the plight of the working classes, was vocal on these points, and even favoured a Catholic party to represent Catholic interests. There were precedents for such a party in other European countries, such as Germany. There were also those former Nationalists who were influenced by the persistent church teachings on the evils of socialism, 'modernism' and left wing policies in general. For them the state interference was a threat to family life and Christian values. There was also fear that the politics of the left might lead to revolution, as it had done in Russia.

In the post-war era, the Nationalist Party remained exclusively Catholic both in its representation, and in its ethos. In 1918, for example, Austin Harford's nomination papers were signed by four Catholic priests.[4] So when Councillor Walker of the local Protestant Party was re-elected after the war, the idea of a Catholic party did not seem so far fetched. Councillor Taggart – formerly a nationalist – stood on a Liberal platform, and asserted that Irish nationalists would never support Labour. However, the nationalist leadership did just that, recommending voters to support Labour against the Liberals where there was not a Nationalist candidate with a realistic chance. In the post war local elections the Nationalists won sixteen seats, behind Labour on twenty, against an anti-socialist coalition of twenty-five Liberals and eighty Conservatives.[5]

Some of the nationalist group, including P.J. Kelly and M. O'Mahoney, were open in their support for Sinn Fein and the IRA campaign. Others, most notably Austin Harford – who remained a key figure at this time – were more concerned with social issues. He had a solid track record on housing improvement and had worked diligently for slum clearance and the provision of decent municipal housing. In

1916 he had addressed the National Housing and Town Planning Council setting out developments in Liverpool together with his ideas on the provision of 'Homes for Heroes' after the war. *The Daily Chronicle* observed that: 'thanks to the Irish, Liverpool is out and away the leading city of England in all municipal enterprise.'[6] However, his position as Chair of the Housing Committee – a post he occupied for the duration of the war – depended on Tory support. They ousted him unceremoniously in 1919, leading Harford to become a vocal advocate of support for Labour in the local elections, provided there was no Irish candidate standing.

A pact with Labour was negotiated, though it worked mainly to the advantage of the Nationalists. It is indicative of the strength of Nationalist feeling in Liverpool at this time that whilst the vote for constitutional Nationalism collapsed in Ireland, in Liverpool the party increased its representation. Nationalist strength held up for the following two years, perhaps because of the continued conflict in Ireland.

In spite of concerns among sections of the Catholic clergy, many Nationalists were turning to Labour. Prominent Irish Catholics such as Sexton and Morrissey, had already stood under the Labour banner. In 1920 Labour tried putting up candidates against the Nationalists, but Nationalists increased their seats from 16 to 21, 'including Davy Logan's sweet victory over Labour in the South Scotland.'[7] Labour and Nationalists now began regarding each other with caution and suspicion, in preparation for the inevitable combat to come. Labour had been slow to get a foothold in Liverpool, in comparison to other cities. They had much to learn about walking the sectarian tightrope. They worked with Nationalists in some wards, but were concerned that too open a collaboration would alienate Protestant voters. Tory dominance was maintained by Salvidge and the WMCA. Salvidge 'ruthlessly exploited any opportunity to excite the electorate on religious issues.'[8] When the Labour Party began to appear, first in place of the Liberals, and later the Nationalists, Salvidge used the same tactics of distortion and, at times, lies, against them. Socialism was portrayed as an ungodly philosophy, which would promote, in Salvidge's own words: 'free love and the state ownership of children.' The widely distributed pamphlet, *What Socialism Really Means*, asserted that: 'everything would be state planned, state-run, state-crushed.'[9] Lord Birkenhead asserted that 'socialism denied the Bible', even though most of the Labour candidates were practising Christians.

Labour knew that Nationalists were uncertain and divided, and predicted that their own opportunity would soon come. In December 1921 – at the time of the signing of the Irish Treaty – O'Mahoney held South Scotland ward against Labour by just 2,540 to 2,499. The Labour vote was rising in parliamentary elections too. In 1923 they caused an upset by winning Kirkdale in a by-election.

The activities of the Irish Self-Determination League and the Liverpool IRA shored up the Nationalist vote for a time, and raised the sectarian temperature. Again Tory leader Salvidge was not slow to cash in, crying that there was 'a threat of red revolution.' He characterised the issue as 'Consitutionalism versus Revolution and Anarchy and Labour extremists.'[10] Many of the newly enfranchised female voters supported Salvidge's version of stability. The Tories gained ground. By 1922 Labour, squeezed between Tories and Nationalists, was reduced to five council seats, and in 1923 to four. However Labour was to eventually benefit from the disintegration of the Nationalists.

With the establishment of a parliament in Dublin, Nationalism began rapidly disappearing as a local force. If the core of their future platform was to be social policy, then why not join Labour? It took some time for these polarities to be resolved. Seeing the writing on the wall, Harford resigned from the Party, and went in search of a defendable position in the new scheme of things by establishing the Irish Democratic League. He negotiated an understanding with the Conservatives in Exchange in an effort to win a council seat there, but failed.

When Nationalist councillor David Logan – who had so fiercely fought Labour in South Scotland ward – defected to the Labour Party, it was a straw in the wind. Some regarded him as a traitor, who had gone over to a party which was 'neither Catholic nor Irish'.[11] But at Westminster O'Connor – the sole surviving Irish Nationalist – gave his support to Labour.[12]

P.J. Kelly took over as Nationalist leader in Liverpool. The Labour leader Robinson issued an open challenge declaring that: 'We have no quarrel with the Irish party … if objection is taken to the entry of Labour candidates into Irish strongholds we think it is time to ask the Irish party to tell us what is their present policy … do they think they have the right to retain 20 members or more in the city without stating what policy they stand for?' In the post-treaty landscape it was a question Nationalists had difficulty answering. In 1924 Kelly met the Labour leadership, with the intention of coming to an agreement with them, not unlike the days when the Nationalists allied with the Liberals. They would support each other where appropriate, and would not challenge each other in their respective strong-hold seats. But Kelly was not a good negotiator. Instead of conciliation, he went down the route of threatening the Labour leadership. He stated that, in the conflict up until now Labour had lost, whilst the Nationalists had gained. 'If we continue to fight, we can take from you Brunswick and St Anne's. We have no desire to do so, but if the fight continues, we shall not cease reprisals, we can not only lose you seats municipally, we can also take away from you Edge Hill and East Toxteth,'[13] (these last two being Labour held parliamentary seats where the Irish vote was significant). He went on to add: 'We have an extraordinary capacity for destruction, and we are not at all particular when we set out in that capacity.' Another Nationalist councillor pointed out that if the Nationalists folded, Labour would have to fight Catholic candidates directly. Such belligerence only served to antagonise the Labour leadership. Robinson again called publicly for Kelly to state clearly what the policies of the Irish Party were. He did not receive a coherent reply. Kelly's problem was that he was negotiating from a position of weakness. Only days after the bad tempered meeting Labour candidate Davy Logan – a defector from nationalism – took 79% of the vote in the former Irish heartland of North Scotland. The days of Irish Nationalist politics in Liverpool were numbered.

In 1924 two Labour candidates defeated Nationalists in the same heartland area. Kelly, the party leader, lost his seat, whilst other Nationalists joined Labour. 1924 was the last year in which a Nationalist candidate stood in local elections in Liverpool, though T.P. O'Connor was to remain in his parliamentary seat until his death in 1929.

In September 1925 the remaining Nationalists who had not yet come up for re-election, and who had not joined Labour, formed the Catholic Representation Association. There were further defections – including P.J. Kelly – following this change. They had the blessing of Archbishop Keating and met at his rooms, under the chairmanship of Monsignor George, a Catholic priest.

Keating, who had been appointed following Whiteside's death in 1921, was more sympathetic to the plight of working class people, sympathised with the general strike of 1926 and assisted the distressed Lancashire miners. The Catholic Representation Association moved to the left under his influence, though their natural instincts leaned more to the right. He approved of the proposed Nationalist alliance with the Labour Party, but would insist that Catholicism must come first.

For many years the church had had in O'Connor and in the Liverpool Nationalists, a strong voice in both national and local politics. As the Nationalists crumbled, the intention was that this role would now be filled by a Catholic party. In the post war years in Liverpool pro-Catholic sentiment had gained ground against nationalism. In 1922 the *Catholic Herald* was of the opinion that the nationalist question was now settled.[14] Irish Liverpool should move on. Initially the new Catholic Party had success in the old Nationalist wards, with Monsignor George himself spectacularly defeating a Nationalist turned Labour by 3,465 to 617. In 1926 the Catholic Party changed its name to the Centre Party.[15]

The appointment of Bishop Downey in 1928 changed matters. He did not approve of the active participation of clergy in politics, and discouraged the Centre Party's links with the church. Deprived of official church support, the Centre Party nevertheless continued with a handful of seats locally until the nineteen forties.

Downey did take an active part in politics in 1928 when he wrote to all local parliamentary candidates asking them whether they supported equal treatment for denominational schools.[16] That year, in spite of Catholic doubts about their education policy, Labour made two gains, bringing their Liverpool total of parliamentary seats to four.

Harford survived as an independent. A more confident Catholicism, dominated by Liverpool-born Catholics was embarking upon the ambitious project of constructing a cathedral. Harford was appointed chairman. Downey had presided over 400,000 Catholics assembled at Thingwall Park to celebrate the centenary of Catholic Emancipation in 1829, and was convinced that the cathedral project could now be renewed and finally accomplished.[17]

Harford, with his dedication to the housing issue and support for the War had done enough, and indeed more than most, to merit his appointment to the position of Mayor. Tory resistance to the idea of appointing a Catholic to the position (there had already been an Irish mayor) kept him out of the office until he was close to death's door. This sectarian barrier was finally demolished when Harford was appointed Liverpool Mayor, the first Catholic to hold the post, in 1943. He died in office the following year.

There was intense industrial unrest in Liverpool in the immediate post First World War years. Liverpool nationalist politicians frequently became involved in trade union affairs, especially during disputes and arbitration. Michael Davitt and T.P. O'Connor had both been involved in brokering deals involving dock and tramway disputes. O'Connor assisted dockers in the passage of health and safety legislation. P.J. Kelly intervened in support of tramway workers taken on because of staff shortages during the war. These workers were at a double disadvantage, being both Catholic and female.[18] They were poorly paid and badly treated by employers. They met with hostility from Protestant male colleagues with Orange sympathies.[19] Kelly – who sat on the Council Tramways sub-committee – was outraged at what he saw as sectarian victimisation. He encouraged them to join a union and demand better pay and conditions. He worked alongside the Labour leader Robinson in this campaign, which eventually led to inter-union disputes and a tramways strike.[20]

The national police strike in 1919 had greater support on Merseyside than in any other region of the country. Whilst only a small number of police went on strike in other cities around Britain, on Merseyside the majority responded, as more than half the police in Liverpool and Birkenhead struck. In Bootle the figure was 63 out of a total of 77 officers. As a direct result of the strike there were two nights of general disorder in the city.[21]

With the bakers also out on strike there was no bread available. Other workers – including 2,000 painters – joined the ranks of strikers and threats from the trades council to call out even more unions in support of the existing disputes resulted in troops being once again posted on the streets.[22] There were 2,500 in total, including a contingent with fixed bayonets camped out at St George's Plateau in the city centre. Three warships were positioned at the docks.

James Sexton was one of those appointed to the Desborough Commission to come up with a solution to the police strike with recommendations on pay and conditions. Most unions, including the tramway workers, responded by recommending a return to work, though many, especially those in the police, found it hard to gain reinstatement as promised settlements did not always materialise. Two of the police strikers went on to win seats as Labour members on the city council, with one – Jack Hayes – going on to a parliamentary career as MP for Edge Hill.

Workers of Irish descent, including those in the police, were prominent in these strikes. Many still felt themselves to be outsiders with little stake in the mainstream British system. There was a rebellious streak in Irish culture and a longstanding lack of respect for British authority. They were part of a close knit community, where poverty was endemic.

Frank Deegan, who described himself as 'One of the Liverpool Irish' tells how, in the twenties: 'Schooldays were hard; many children, including myself, had no boots or shoes; we went bare foot.'[23] According to his account, families often did not have sufficient food, with parents going hungry in order to feed their children. Nevertheless, wages were reduced. 'Dock labourers suffered three reductions in nineteen twenty-two of one shilling each time. In three years their wages dropped from sixteen shillings a day to ten shillings.'[24]

It was hardly surprising that there were strong feelings of solidarity. There was a tradition of activism through the various political campaigns over the years, in particular the successful campaign for land rights in Ireland. There was a general feeling around the Nationalist cause that 'we are all in this together', which made it easier for politicians such as O'Connor to maintain popularity amongst working class constituents. Nationalists with a social programme such as Harford and P.J. Kelly, felt obliged to take an active part in supporting trade unionists, especially if they were Irish and Catholic, even though neither man was elected on a socialist or labour ticket.

Nationalists in the Labour Party

The majority of Nationalists who went over to the Labour benches in the late 1920s had not come up through the Labour ranks, or through Labour organisations. They had no trade union roots. Labour had merely inherited these seats. Not only that, but their council seats were amongst the safest in the city. In 1929 Labour had 57 council seats, Conservatives 79, Liberals 14, Centre seven and one independent. The Liberals co-operated with the Conservatives to lock Labour out of committee chairmanships.[25] The former Nationalists formed a third of the Labour ranks. Many continued to rely on their Catholicism to get the vote out, at times exhorting voters to support a Labour candidate because he was a frequent attender at mass. During lean years for the party, such as 1924, 1930 and 1936, these secure Nationalists formed the majority of Labour councillors, and were able to consolidate their positions. This situation angered the left, including the Braddocks, as the former Nationalists tended to be on the right. It was said that the labour factions hated each other more than they hated the Tories.

In his biography, *The Greasy Pole*, the former Liverpool Labour councillor Reggie Bevins remarked: 'They were like an exercise in apartheid. The members used to segregate themselves according to their prejudices, and especially according to their religion. In the front two rows sat the left wingers and the militants of those days, the Braddocks and Silvermans and others. Then a no-mans-land of four rows, followed by two straddling rows of middle of the roaders, including myself. Then another no-mans-land, and finally right at the back, a hoard of Irish Roman Catholics. These men knew nothing of Socialism. Most of them had never even heard of it. They were Labour because those who voted for them were poor, and because despite the effluction of time, the Irish Catholics still identified the Conservative Party with the bad behaviour of Oliver Cromwell and William of Orange.'[26] Bevins went on to become Postmaster General in a Conservative government.

A good example of the problems which these divisions could cause came when the former Workhouse came up for sale in 1929. Occupying a nine acre site between Brownlow Hill and Mount Pleasant in the city centre, it was an attractive location. The District Labour Party – Labour's policy making body – had decided by a clear majority that the site should be used for housing. However, the cat was thrown amongst the pigeons when the Catholic diocese applied to purchase the site for a cathedral. With such a large population of Catholics now in the city, and with the growing prestige of the church, the Catholic diocese was intent on building a Cathedral to replace the temporary pro-Cathedral, St Nicholas's, behind the Adelphi Hotel. The Workhouse site was ideal. The site was being sold by the Poor Law Guardians, whose duties were now being taken over by Liverpool Corporation. Their reserve price was £125,000. The diocese was offering £100,000.[27] The Corporation debated how the site might be used. The suggestion of industrial use was rejected, as was the idea that the Corporation could develop the area itself, perhaps for housing. When Archbishop Downey's proposal came before the Council, it was endorsed by eighty-eight votes to twenty-seven. In the end thirty-two Labour councillors voted to accept the offer, in contravention of agreed party policy. Twenty of these – including the party leader Robinson – were Catholics. No Catholic councillor opposed it. The Protestant councillor and chaplain to the Orange Order, H.D. Longbottom, made it clear that he would rather give permission for 'a poison germ factory' than for a Catholic cathedral. One Labour councillor who supported the Catholic bid for the cathedral site was Olive Hughes. She was de-selected in St Anne's ward, and – with Catholic support – stood as an independent. The Labour Party selected an opponent from the left – Bessie Braddock. Braddock carried the seat, under the slogan, 'homes, not priests',[28] but this was Labour's only success in the aftermath of the dispute.

Divisions within the Labour Party were further exacerbated when, at the same time as the Brownlow Hill vote, the Labour Government published its Education Bill. The Bill, which provided for the raising of the school leaving age to fifteen, was once again seen as a threat by the Catholic church. The Liverpool Trades Council insisted that all Labour councillors accept the secular education policy, which was, of course, anathema to the Catholic members. Four Catholic councillors left the party, setting themselves up as Democratic Labour. In the subsequent local elections, Labour did not contest the Democratic Labour seats, and lost five other seats to the Conservatives, as Irish nationalist voters deserted them.

The ex-Nationalists continued to complicate local Labour politics for some time. Later that year the Labour group – that is the elected councillors, rather than the Trades Council – de-selected Robinson as leader. He had been very effective in challenging and defeating the Nationalists just a few years before, and perhaps this was a factor which operated against him amongst ex-Nationalists now in the Labour Party. He was replaced by Luke Hogan, a Catholic from birth, unlike Robinson who was a convert. In addition to his Catholic and Irish background, Hogan was a well established and popular trade unionist, who had been chairman of the Council of Action in Liverpool during the General Strike.

When T.P. O'Connor died in office in 1929 it seemed inevitable that he would be replaced by one of the former nationalists. David Logan – who had astutely moved from the Nationalist to Labour benches some years before – was selected. He had an Irish mother, lived in the area, was well known and was an extremely devout Catholic with a large family. He was a founder member of the Catholic society the Knights of Saint Columba in England. He was to be a good constituency MP, with a genuine concern for the severely disadvantaged area which he represented. He was always strongly opposed to sectarianism. Though holding the secure seat for thirty five years – nine short of O'Connor's total – he made little progress through Labour ranks. He was opposed to contraception, divorce, Sunday opening of pubs, cinemas and playgrounds, and changes to the blasphemy laws. He supported state assistance for denominational education. He announced in his maiden speech that: 'To me God means everything and all things, and I feel that in this House and in the Government of this nation it is essential that we should understand what true religion means.'[29] One of his first actions in parliament was to vote with the Conservatives on education policy. In fact, three local Labour MPs voted with the Conservatives rather than their own party that year, in support of denominational education. They were, predictably, Davy Logan, but also Caine and Gibbins, neither of whom had Catholic connections, but both of whom, as Labour MPs, were well aware of the views of their Catholic constituents.

After the Great War, Protestantism continued as a significant force in Liverpool, but the sectarian enthusiasm for action on the streets subsided. The Protestant Reformers Memorial Church was now under the control of Wise's successor Pastor Longbottom. It maintained a strong membership in a city where church attendances generally were falling, and secularism was becoming the norm. Social issues – particularly unemployment and housing – were returning to the centre of the agenda. The Tories were less keen to use sectarian issues to hammer the Liberals. They were now allied to Liberals in government and increasingly so locally.

The signing of the Treaty and the establishment of the Irish Free State, at long last cleared the way for the greater integration of the Liverpool Irish. Politics, church and the press all played a part. Archbishop 'Dickie' Downey declared in 1928 that Catholic interests were best served in mainstream political parties. By pulling the rug from under the Catholic party he removed one potential focus of sectarian politics from the Liverpool scene. In future Catholic aspirations would be expressed from within established British parties, especially Labour. The movement of former Nationalist leaders into the Labour Party was also significant. From now on they would be working alongside those with the wider interests of labour in general, rather than a narrowly focused Irish agenda, bringing, in time, a broader political perspective to the community. There was little scope left for the old nationalism. Diamond, the influential editor of the *Catholic Herald*, and someone who was a key opinion former, was outspoken in his opposition to T.P. O'Connor's doomed efforts to continue with a political party or organisation based solely on the Irish in Britain. Diamond, acting as spokesperson for a large section of Catholic Irish opinion, made it very clear that, in his view, it was most definitely time to move on. 'After centuries of struggle, Ireland's right to her national life, to her economic, social, educational, religious and political freedom is now a fact. We propose to entirely finish this controversy in the present issue and to get on with other things.'[30]

Persisting Anti-Irish Attitudes

The relative isolation and separateness of Irish Catholicism up to this point had not been solely self-inflicted. The hostility of right leaning politicians and extreme Protestantism persisted. During the hardships of the inter-war period there was moral panic about the numbers of Irish coming to Britain, ostensibly to take jobs from local people. Negative stereotypes of the Irish – many of whom still lived in poverty – persisted.[31]

J.B. Priestley was one of those who explored the Scotland Road area, whilst taking a stroll from his room in the Adelphi Hotel. He called for the deportation of Irish people. 'Liverpool would be glad to be rid of them,' adding that their leaving would be 'a fine exit of ignorance and dirt and drunkenness and disease.'[32] The new Conservative boss in Liverpool, Sir Thomas White, reverted to the attitudes of militant Protestantism by scape-goating Irish Catholics. But his attitudes looked increasingly out of place as the real conflict switched to Conservative versus Labour.

Despite the establishment of Irish independence, under British law the Irish remained British citizens, being regarded as having something akin to dominion status. A free travel area, with passports not being required, was maintained between the now separate jurisdictions. There were contradictions on the Irish side. DeValera's party had been opposed to persons leaving the country during the Anglo Irish conflict, regarding them as traitors. Now, in the twenties and thirties, with Ireland in a prolonged and deep economic recession, the Irish government was content to let them go, relying on Britain as a safety valve against excessive unemployment at home. And they left in their thousands, mainly for industrial centres such as London and Birmingham. Although they did not settle on Merseyside in such great numbers as in previous generations, by the late 1920s there were nevertheless some five thousand arriving annually.[33] The Liverpool born Irish were not necessarily welcoming of these new arrivals. They were protective of their own jobs, which were a precious commodity.

There was a persistent tide of xenophobia in Britain, and on Merseyside especially, directed towards the Irish. Victorian stereotypes were resurrected, and pseudo-scientific theories abounded, as did articles in magazines. G.R. Gair, in the Liverpool Review in 1934, regarded the Irish as 'a real alien menace'. The Irish were still seen as racially inferior by eugenicists, whose theories were gaining in popularity with the rise of the extreme right in Europe.[34]

The Irish were accused of taking jobs which should be going to locals and of claiming benefits to which they were not entitled. Although these allegations were never substantiated, the mood persisted. The Conservative minded regional magazine *Liverpolitan* was consistently anti-Irish, once asking: 'What has England as a whole to say to a system that permits Southern-Ireland to be the breeding ground of redundant low-grade elements, free to cross the channel, to debase the British standard of life?'[35] In 1936 an article expressed concern that there was an economic 'freemasonry' which discriminated in favour of Catholics, alleging that 'Catholics ... are being given preference for employment often irrespective of fitness by officials of departments financed by public funds,' and that there was 'an increasing chorus of complaints that such favouritism is now exceeding the limits that patient Protestant English people ought to tolerate'.[36] The article went on to state that 'Irish medicos and nurses, many of whom fresh from their native land have been given preference over Liverpool-born and Liverpool-trained persons, whose only disability is their Protestantism.'

But there was little beyond anecdotal evidence and rumour. A civil service investigation into benefit claimants found no evidence of Irish 'scrounging'. In fact local rules had made it increasingly difficult to take up certain types of employment, such as local authority posts, where there were now residency requirements in many cases. Councillor Braddock pointed out that as there was a twelve month qualifying period before benefit could be collected, it was unlikely anyone would pay their boat fare and take lodgings for a year in order to claim.

Negative, not to say hostile, attitudes were not confined to politics and the press. The Anglican Bishop David wrote in 1937: 'there are a quarter of a million Irish in Liverpool, and they continue to come over every year for the higher dole. Ireland has discovered a way for England to support her surplus population.' He was concerned that: 'they may gain control of the local Labour party, which in turn may gain control of the local government. In this event Liverpool will be dominated by Roman Catholics.'[37] James Sexton came to the defence of the Irish, pointing out that the large population of 'Irish' in Liverpool owed much to the influx of the nineteenth century, and were not recent arrivals.[38]

In 1939 'the continued influx of labour from the Irish Free state', was the theme of a packed meeting at Picton Hall, so crowded that hundreds were left standing outside. On stage were twenty men who, it was alleged 'lost their jobs at the Speke aircraft factory, only to have those jobs go to Irishmen just arrived in Liverpool.' When Alderman Longbottom entered the meeting he was greeted with loud cheers.[39] The main speaker at the meeting was Conservative councillor David Rowan, who had established the Irish Immigration Investigative Bureau to look into cases in which preference was given to Irish workers.

Pastor Longbottom, having taken over from George Wise, continued to represent his own brand of Protestantism in the local arena, with much Protestant hostility in the political sphere now directed towards Labour. Labour candidates often faced the fury of working-class Protestant councillors. It didn't help that so many ex-nationalists were now in the Labour party, some of them Labour councillors. Even in the 1950s, Labour speakers at St Domingo required a police escort. When the Braddocks held meetings at St Domingo Pit, 'Jack and Bessie, flanked by police, proceeded through this stronghold of Orangeism at their own peril, an army of occupation in hostile territory'.[40] Although the establishment of the Irish state was seen by extreme Protestants as a disaster, there was a substantial victory in the constitution of Northern

Ireland, which was proclaimed, 'a Protestant parliament for a Protestant people', the only one of its kind.

On the Irish Catholic side the feelings of anger and alienation began to fade in the decades after the war. Many found expression of their distinctive identity and history in the practice of the Catholic faith rather than in nationalism. Catholic society went from strength to strength, with a proliferation of social clubs, cultural societies and sporting associations. In this environment the sense of belonging to a distinctive community was maintained. Those with a more political outlook had the option of the Labour Party and the trade union movement, which were both growing in strength. For voters and party members from a Liverpool Irish background Labour now fulfilled many of their aspirations. Catholic Labour councillors could generally be relied upon to support Catholic policy over that of the Labour Party where conflict arose.

On the opposite side of the political divide relations between active Protestants and the Conservative party were not so relaxed. In 1935, Thomas White observed that: 'Whether we like it or no ... there are many thousands of electors in Liverpool who will, if the need arises, put Protestantism before their politics, and it would simply be madness on my part if I told the people of Kirkdale, Everton, or West Toxteth that the Conservative party had ceased to care for their religion or for Protestant interests.'[41]

Protestant candidates frequently stood instead of or against Conservative councillors. Wise himself had been a councillor from 1903-06, and Protestant candidates continued in Liverpool until the nineteen sixties. Although Longbottom never attracted as large a following as Wise had done, he had a dynamic organisation in the twenties at the Reformer's Memorial Church in Kirkdale, where anti-Catholic and anti-Irish views were consistently expressed, though mainly inside the church building rather than on the streets.

The Orange Order in Liverpool also maintained a consistent organisation, with a number of lodges in the city. Fear of the Irish and the need to stand up for the monarchy, the church and the constitution remained important in their minds. At the same time, the Orange tradition of marches, costumes, bands, and celebrations with a strong community base, and special annual occasions such as 12 July, became embedded in local culture and proved resistant to change. Orange Order activity had now become a social and cultural outlet, binding families and generations in the poorer areas of the city.

The presence of the Order as a marching organisation ensured an annual round of predictable sectarian animosity in the city, as opposition regularly turned up to heckle marchers or even attack them. A Protestant presence persisted on the council. Longbottom was elected for Breckfield in 1926. He founded a party newspaper, *The Protestant Times*, and put up six candidates in the local elections in 1930.

Sectarian animosity could surface even amongst senior churchmen. In 1930 the cenotaph outside St George's Hall was first unveiled. The event sparked a sectarian spat between the Anglican and Catholic Bishops. Doctor David, the Anglican, criticised the Catholic clergy for refusing to take part in the ceremony alongside Anglican churchmen.[41] Ecumenism was still a distant prospect. One issue in particular still rankled with Protestants. The Catholic Church was vocal in insisting that the children of 'mixed' marriages – those between a Catholic and a Protestant – should be educated as Catholics. It was a sensitive question in Liverpool, where such marriages were increasingly common.

As the Protestant Party continued doggedly on into the forties and beyond Longbottom himself was elected Mayor in 1950. Whilst animosity never returned to the levels seen in the earlier part of the century, the sectarian trigger could still be activated in Everton. When the Education Act of 1960 allowed aid for the building of Catholic schools, Longbottom won his seat back. He was expelled from the Orange Order in 1961 (he had once been a Grand Master) and died in 1962.

But Protestant issues did not resonate with the wider public as they had done in an earlier generation. Following Longbottom's death the party continued, but without a well known and vocal leadership figurehead there was to be no revival. Protestant support was transferred to the Conservatives, with a steady leakage to Labour. Though the Orange Order remained vigorous on 12 July each year, it became divorced from any influence in local politics, although there were occasional resurrections, such as the Protestant Party's campaign against the threat posed by Catholic Europe, in alignment with other right wing fringe groups, including the Reverend Ian Paisley and the British Constitutional Defence Committee. The result was the continuation into later generations of regressive attitudes and values which often descended into racism and street violence. Sectarian bigotry persisted. The Order remained a recruiting ground for Tory voters, and membership of right wing organisations.

CHAPTER FIFTEEN

COMMUNITY LIFE IN THE INTER-WAR YEARS

For all its hardships and unemployment, there were opportunites for the Irish in Liverpool. There were jobs at sea, on the docks and in industries associated with the docks such as Tate and Lyle and British American Tobacco. The resident population close to the docks was best placed to take advantage. They often had more opportunity than their cousins in Ireland. Catholic education was now well established, and highly valued in the community, which, in conjunction with the local authority, was making such efforts to meet the cost. As the numbers graduating from St Edward's College and other secondary provision increased year by year, the Catholic middle class became stronger, entering professions such as law and medicine, and taking jobs in the local authority, or with shipping and insurance companies in the city.

The parish structure remained robust as those actually born and brought up in the parish – rather then emigrants – became the majority and now raised their own families. The density of population was such that since 1915 there had been sixteen Catholic parishes in the area around Vauxhall Road and Scotland Road, a narrow strip of dockland, housing and industry between the waterfront and Netherfield Road. The Catholic population of the north end of the city remained at around 100,000 in the inter-war years. Parishes were so close together there were points such as Athol Street where four – St Anthony's, St Alban's, St Gerard's and St Sylvester's – intercepted. Another such point was Hornby Street, where St Anthony's, St Brigid's, Our Lady of Reconciliation and St Sylvester's converged. School building continued at the rate of one new school per year between 1902 and 1942.[1]

The leading role of the clergy remained intact. It was to the parish and the clergy that people turned at times of birth, marriage and death. Not only was there the weekly ritual of attendance at mass, but the annual round of ceremonies, processions and celebrations. In addition there were devotional practices such as benediction, rosaries, stations of the cross and novenas. The church asserted its leadership of the community through the grandeur of the church buildings themselves, which stood in contrast to the living conditions of many of the parishioners. Whilst the clergy lived in the community and were closely associated with it, they lived in the comparative luxury of the parish houses built for them.

I am grateful to Frank Boyce who has allowed me access to interviews he conducted with people who once lived in the Scotland Road area of Liverpool. The quotations which follow in this chapter are from his unpublished short study 'Irish Catholic and Scouse' which is based on those interviews.[2] One interviewee, speaking of priests' houses observed:

'We were never admitted into the presbytery. On one occasion I was allowed in through the house to gain access to the church and I just glanced into the dining room. It was like the set of a Hollywood high-society film.'

Each parish had at least four clergy. In addition there were members of religious orders, such as the Jesuits at St Francis Xavier's, Shaw Street, a community of ten Franciscan friars at Fox Street, and the numerous nuns and brothers, teaching in schools and carrying out welfare duties such as at the Women's Refuge in Paul Street, or Father Berry's Homes in Shaw Street.

Although now challenged in politics, the clergy maintained a leadership role in parish life. In the words of one interviewee: 'My parents used to tell me about this parish priest in St Anthony's who used to go around the parish on a Sunday morning knocking people up to go to mass. He would carry a long walking stick and just bang on the doors.' Whilst at St Gerard's from 1923 to 1928, 'Father Hoey was the cause of much comment in the parish when, occasionally, he rode through the streets on a chestnut coloured pony belonging to the late Mr Schumacher.' There were church societies for lay persons in each parish. Some examples were the Catholic Young Men's Society, the Legion of Mary, the Children of Mary for girls, the Pioneer Total Abstinence Association, the Society of St Vincent De Paul, and many others. There were days out, and lavish processions involving ecclesiastical robes, costumes and banners of the various societies, gaudy street decorations, flowers and paper streamers, accompanied by the singing of hymns, and ceremonies, such as the May Queen – dressed as if for a wedding – placing a crown on the head of the statue of Our Lady. The presence of a large Italian community, centred around St Joseph's parish, added colour and variety to Catholic practice.

In addition to church tradition, Irish culture was also embedded in this way of life, with parish ceilis in the hall, where young people could meet under supervision, There were local musicians for such events, 'where the master of ceremonies would announce the dances in Gaelic.' Ceilis often ended with 'The Soldier's Song', which was now the Irish national anthem. There were still such a number of Irish speakers in the area that 'by the end of the 1930s three of the parishes were offering Confessions in the Irish language on Saturday evenings.'

Whilst the number of Irish-born migrants decreased, the link with Ireland was maintained through family holidays and keeping in touch with Irish relatives. A fresh injection of Irish culture often came from Irish clergy who could be posted to Liverpool for a period of up to five years. Their sermons would frequently contain tales of Irish history, and Irish religious practice. 'One of my strongest memories of going to Sunday school … was hearing about Irish families kneeling down every night around their kitchen fires to say the family rosary.' Irish school teachers would also contribute a dose of Irish nationalist history. 'I remember some history and religious lesson where this particular teacher used to 'knock England and the English

… it was a pagan country, … whereas Ireland had kept the Catholic faith.'

Frank Boyce's interviewees confirmed that St Patrick's Day was a major event in the calendar, beginning with mass and the singing of 'Hail Glorious St Patrick' with great enthusiasm and fervour. Girls wore green ribbons in their hair and others wore Shamrock imported from Ireland in great quantities, on their lapel. Later in the day 'from Burlington Street the Irish Foresters, splendid in their colourful regalia marched through to Scotland Road.' The day was completed with events in halls and dining rooms. The Archbishop of Liverpool was usually the guest of honour at an annual dinner at the Adelphi, whilst other venues included the Grafton Rooms, Bootle Town Hall, the Rialto and the Blair Hall.

Each parish had its hall and sports clubs. Inter-parish rivalry in sports such as boxing, billiards and football could be fierce. Two of the most famous rivals were the adjoining parishes of St Anthony's – which straddled Scotland Road – and St Sylvester's. Both took part in the Catholic schools league, which had an eagerly contested cup competition each year, with the final being played at either Anfield or Goodison Park. There was always the possibility that one year they would meet in the final, and when this finally occurred 14,000 spectators attended this primary school football match. When the winners – St Sylvester's – paraded home en masse carrying the cup aloft, they were mobbed at the corner of Hopwood Street by women from St Anthony's. One eye witness remarked: 'They laid into us and there was a helluva fight. The police came and put a stop to it. But as a young girl, I was amazed to watch grown women fighting each other in the street over the result of a kids' football match.' St Sylvester's, incidentally, also had an outstanding tradition of choral singing, and would at times be invited to perform for BBC radio programmes.

A large number of local businesses including pubs, groceries, butchers, and clothing firms, were under Irish ownership. One well known example was the grocer Hughes, which, in the 1920s, found employment for Irish political activists who had slipped out of Ireland to avoid the authorities. Local businesses used their Irish credentials to sell everything from pipe tobacco to shoes, socks and sausages. One typical example was the fish and chip shop in Vescock Street, which had a window display, 'which included a portrait of Michael Collins, neatly surrounded by shamrock, the republican flag and a picture of Pope Pius the XI.' The 98 shop on Byrom Street – which had been the focus of revolutionary activity in the twenties – still sold political and religious objects and newspapers connected to Ireland, whilst nearby Faulkner's, a 'Catholic repository', also sold Catholic religious objects and Irish goods.

But with the passage of time and generations, links with Ireland were weakened and tended to become more romantic and sentimental, finding expression in song and story rather than politics. According to one Irish priest who served in the area during the 1930s: 'I'm not sure how deep the identification with Ireland went. It often seemed a sentimental one to me. The popular Irish songs of the day made a hit with the people of the parish. Singers like Cavan O'Connor and John McCormick. Then some were interested in the Irish poetry of the 'Celtic twilight'. A few were interested in Irish politics. They tended to be the more vociferous of the parishioners. And Irish songs were popular at family gatherings.' Another interviewee remarked that 'as a child I remember my father and others in the family singing Irish songs at 'do's' and get-togethers. Some of them were supposed to be 'rebel songs' like Kevin Barry. Others were lovely ballads like *The Old House* or *The Star of the County Down*. Then there were some phrases that my grandmother used to use, like 'She's coming on a Connemara visit,' which, I later found out, meant that someone was coming to visit us and stay a very long time.' District identity was cemented by a close knit community in which people knew each other and were united by a common culture and communal activity around the parish.

The port and associated industries – all within walking distance of dockland communities – continued to be the primary source of employment. People developed a strong sense both of community and of place.

'There was a family tradition of summer afternoon or evening strolls to the Landing Stage to look at the arrival and departure of ocean liners and cargo ships. Panoramic views of the shipping and the major docks could be had from the ferry to New Brighton or Seacombe, or from a journey on the overhead railway.'

A stronger middle-class culture was also on the rise. An increasing number of Catholics were graduating from Liverpool University and the Catholic teacher training colleges. By 1928 the Irish Society of the University of Liverpool – originally formed in 1911 under Kuno Mayer's chairmanship – was again thriving. Members organised events in the Gilmour Hall in Bedford Street. There were literary and drama sections attached to the Society. The Irish Amateur Players put on regular works, which attracted large audiences from the Irish community. In 1937 there was a proposal to put on the controversial O'Casey play, *Juno and the Paycock*. The society split on the issue, and as a consequence the breakaway Irish Playgoers were established, and continued for many years. The Catholic Secondary Schools Club was set up to provide opportunities for Catholic boys and girls to meet socially, as a means of encouraging 'good Catholic marriages'. There was a wide range of activities in the Club, including drama, whist drives, lectures, and day excursions.

In the post war years in the midst of poverty life had a good deal of colour and dynamism. Local resident Bob Parry, who later became Labour MP for Liverpool Exchange recalled that 'we used to go hunting for brown sugar that had fallen from the bags as they were being hauled up from the docks on carts to the warehouses.'[3] All this was to end as the horses, their stables, manure and carts, were to be replaced by vans from which no bags would fall and later by lorries which would speed through the district carrying sealed containers. Parry recalls collecting 'fades' which were apples that were past their best: 'The stallholders would often give us them for nothing.' Parry remembers his grandmother, 'whose parents were Irish', in traditional dress with a shawl and laced up boots: 'She would go to Great Homer Street late on a Saturday night because that was the time, with the shops being ready to close, when things were cheaper.'[3]

During the 1920s the first signs of profound social change and modernisation began to impact on this close-knit community. Slum clearance was perhaps the greatest factor. There was agreement amongst all groups, political, social and religious, that housing reform was needed, and it was councillors for the Vauxhall and Scotland wards who campaigned for change. The inevitable consequence was to fracture and disrupt the community. Slum clearance, which had been in progress since the turn of the century, gained additional impetus with the Housing Act of 1930, brought in by Labour. With their new powers the council began purchasing land, building municipal housing and demolishing the old slum properties. By 1931 the Corporation housed one eighth of the population.[4] In 1932 they purchased 4,000 acres in Speke and Croxteth. By 1939 one in six was in corporation housing. Between the wars about 140,000 people were re-housed.[5]

The process alarmed the clergy in the Catholic parishes, where they were deeply embedded in the community, and had an infrastructure of churches, parish houses, schools and halls, matched by Catholic welfare networks and social clubs. In the new estates the process of re-building the whole structure would have to begin again. In Holy Cross parish – perhaps the quintessential Liverpool Irish parish – Father James O'Shea was concerned that the parish would be 'left in the midst of a wilderness' and successfully lobbied – with the support of local councillors – for some of the old housing to be replaced on site, retaining the same residents. The result was the building of Fontenoy Gardens in 1935. The parish clergy also negotiated a favourable deal for a school, by taking over the Addison Street Day Industrial School in exchange for land in the area. However, in spite of these efforts, the number in the parish fell from nearly five thousand to less than three thousand. [6]

Modern entertainment ended the communal atmosphere of the League Hall and the music venues such as the Rotunda, where evenings would end with the whole crowd rising to sing the well-known anthem 'A Nation Once Again.' Instead it was the pub which survived as a meeting place and centre of local life. Cinemas were built, and some of the old music halls were also adapted to show films. Here the parish priest or local politician no longer stood up to give a song. The entertainment was by mass media, designed and presented at some distant location and referencing a new international cultural landscape. The local parish entertainments and Irish sentimentality of the district, family stories and 'heroes of renown' were marginalised in this new world.

Modernisation was also impacting on Catholic welfare provision. The welfare state was being built, higher standards were expected, and state provision was destined to become more systematic, better resourced and more comprehensive. Just before the Second World War, Catholic schools again became a bone of contention, raising sectarian tensions. Determined to keep their own schooling system intact, the Catholic authorities requested a substantial grant from the Education Committee in order to meet the new requirement that the school leaving age be raised. The Committee was minded to grant 66%. However, when the matter went to the full council, the Conservatives opposed any grant.[6] Labour favoured a 100% grant, an indication of how strong the Irish Catholic lobby now was inside the Liverpool Labour Party, which earlier in the century had been opposed to state funded denominational education. The Conservatives – using the slogan 'Rome on the rates' – gained eleven seats in the municipal elections. Those who opposed the grants were 68 Conservatives, four Protestants and three Labour. Two of the Labour objectors were from the strongly Orange Garston district. Demanding the grant were 37 Labour members, supported by the Liberals, the Centre Party and five conservatives.

Liverpool under the Conservatives was now the only large authority in England which was not offering assistance to Catholic schools. The surviving sectarian attitudes in the city were now out of step with the rest of the country. The national Board of Education took the decision to withhold grant aid for schools from Liverpool, thus putting additional pressure on the Council.[6] When Labour lost further seats in the next local election, Protestant Labour activists complained to the national executive that actions by the Catholic caucus were causing the party to lose seats. Labour was once again being reduced to the former Nationalist areas. However, the Labour national executive took no action, probably because they were unwilling to take on the entrenched former Nationalists. In the end the Tories relented, with the prospect of a rebellion by enraged ratepayers, who were facing an increased burden as the council continued to lose grants from Westminster. They agreed to build fifteen schools, which would then be leased back to Catholic authorities.

As redevelopment continued, and people were moved out of the old inner city to new estates, they were often shocked at the change. Housing conditions were, of course, much better, with many having indoor toilets, gardens and hot running water for the first time. But there were drawbacks. Pensioners were often in separate bungalows. There were few shops, which for a community accustomed to being able to send a child out to fetch an item from the corner and be back in the space of a few minutes, was a major change. Another significant issue was that extended family networks and local social welfare connections were broken up. These processes accelerated after World War II.

CHAPTER SIXTEEN
AFTER 1945

The way of life which prevailed in the inner-city areas during the inter-war years continued into the post war nineteen-fifties. Whilst there were significant numbers of families of Irish origin in every district of the city, the two core communities were still in the Toxteth/Liverpool 8 district in the south end, and the larger community centred around the area between Vauxhall Road and Scotland Road in the north.

Community feeling in these areas had been cemented by the common struggle through the hardships of war. The intense bombing had claimed many lives, and destroyed not just workplaces, but houses, churches and schools. The districts with an Irish concentration – Bootle, Vauxhall and the north docks – were the hardest hit. Hundreds of homes were destroyed in parishes such as St Alban's.

The feelings of solidarity and common purpose generated during the War not only united the community, but created a common narrative with the wider population. The British aspect of the Liverpool Irish dual identity was strengthened. Links with Ireland had, if anything, been weakened by the experience of war. Whilst large numbers of Irish citizens had once again enlisted in the British army, Ireland itself had remained neutral. And whilst that neutrality can be seen as having been partial towards the allies, the Irish state had taken no active part in the war against the Nazis.

Following the war many social and recreational activities, which had been cancelled for the period of hostilities, were revived. The Gaelic League again opened branches and resumed regular meetings. There were three branches, with Wood Street in the city centre the best known. Ceili dances, especially in parishes where there was an Irish priest, were common. The annual St Patrick's Day parade was also re-established. The Anti-Partition League formed a branch, and put candidates up in local elections in the Scotland Road/Vauxhall area, though with little success.

In the following part of this chapter and throughout the next I have used material gathered in interviews conducted in 2015 and 2017. I consulted over a hundred people with memories of Liverpool in the 1940s through to the 1960s, and carried out more detailed interviews with fifteen of them. The quotations in the following paragraphs are from those discussions. The interviewees were all people who were brought up on Merseyside in a family with Irish connections, either through parents, grandparents or great grandparents. The interviewees were mainly but not exclusively Catholic. There were equal numbers of men and women, with a small number from a background which included both Irish and Caribbean, Arab or Liverpool black ancestors. The topics and questions emerged from discussions conducted during evening classes at the University of Liverpool and at other venues.

Catholicism was strong in post-war Liverpool, and remained a badge of identity for the Irish Catholic community. Amongst the generation born immediately after the war – the 'baby boomers' – regular church attendance remained at a high level, with most churches having to have five masses on Sundays to accommodate the demand.

One interviewee recalled that: 'Catholic practice was very strong in the Dingle where I lived when I was younger. We had Our Lady of Mount Carmel, St Finbar's, St Malachy's, St Vincent's and St Patrick's, all within walking distance of where we lived.'[1] Catholic processions, usually around the streets surrounding the church, continued, demonstrating how the church as an institution remained embedded in the local community. Costumes were worn, bunting put out, and many parishes had their own band. Of those I've interviewed several remember these musicians. 'My grandfather played the concert flute and he used to be invited along to processions, particularly at Holy Cross. There were a lot of processions from there, and they used to be attacked. He got the Benemerenti Medal (a prestigious papal award) for his services.' Another account recalled that: 'St Vincent's were posh. They had their own brass band.' One recalled that: 'as well as our own processions we used to go across to the north end for processions. There they were much bigger.'

Parish clubs each had their own character. 'St Vincent's was well known for billiards, St Malachy's for boxing.' Parish collections were regular, with one interviewee recalling going ahead of the parish priest each week knocking on doors to let people know that the priest would shortly be there. These collections remained the mainstay of church funding even though, in spite of the post war boom, many still lived in poverty. The St Vincent De Paul Society remained very strong, carrying out collections after masses, and administering funding to those referred by the clergy and parish networks. 'My father was that busy with St Vincent De Paul my mother complained that he was never in the house.' Some districts in the north end, such as in St Sylvester's parish, had locations which were '100% Catholic'. 'When I was a boy I only ever met one other boy who was not Catholic. It was solidly Catholic.' Another noted that: 'the 'Bullring area' was Catholic. I can't remember any Protestants'. One interviewee remarked that: 'it was not until I went to University that I met Protestants really'.

In the south end it was more mixed. 'Although we lived in a predominantly Catholic part of Liverpool 8, of course the Orange Lodge was there. There was damage to churches, that sort of thing. There was quite a lot of sectarianism.'

The oppositional nature of local conventions gave religion a greater significance in the minds of children: 'As a child I remember that my mother, when I said I was playing with someone, would ask me what school they went to. And I think it was a way of identifying if I was playing with a Catholic or a Protestant.'

Catholic practice in Liverpool continued to have many Irish characteristics. One interviewee remarked that: 'My father was very keen that the children be raised Catholic. He was very Catholic, but they had a different kind of faith. Whereas my father was from a scientific background, my mother had a strong Irish faith.' There were a number of manifestations of this 'Irish faith'. In particular, wakes were still being held in many families. The body of the deceased was placed in a coffin in the front room, where relatives and neighbours would visit, offer support to the family and say prayers.

'Where I was, most families carried on what I would consider to be an Irish wake. I remember the first one I went to when I was a child, and I was shocked. It was in my own family. It was quite a lively affair actually. The body was in the house. And there were certain women to come in and decorate the room, the crucifix, statues, that was all sorted out by certain women within the Bullring, and that was their role. They'd come in, and they put all white sheets up, and have seats in the room. People would come. They'd have to have a drink. A few drinks really. The first one I went to, there wasn't any praying. A bit like a party. I think people were supporting one another.' In another account: 'If somebody died we would still wake them. All the curtains would be closed, and all the curtains would close along the road. But this practice hasn't carried on into my generation.'

Many interviewees recalled that the Rosary, a form of repetitive prayer typical of Irish practice, was also common. 'We said the Rosary each night before dinner, and after that you could do as you liked.' 'Kneeling down and saying the rosary was very big in our house.' Other religious practices outside of the church included blessing a house or flat before the family moved in, and sprinkling a car with holy water before a long journey. Those who could would often say their prayers in Irish. 'You had people like my father who still prayed in Irish. He had little opportunity to use his language, even though he was a native speaker. My aunts also still prayed in their native language.'

Most interviewees had vivid memories of 'Retreats', where visiting clergy, often from the Redemptorist or Passionist orders, usually Irish, would take over the parish for a week. These clergy continued the fierce Catholicism of Ireland in the late nineteenth century. 'Every five years the Passionists or the Redemptorists would come around. They would frighten the life out of you. Everyone gave up drinking, and everyone was very holy for those weeks.' 'Every parish had its parish retreat, generally conducted by Irish priests. They were very hell fire, very much the Irish Jansenist tradition. Very repressive of sex.'

As was the practice 'back at home' Irish clergy would often take an interest in sports such as boxing and horse racing, and visit the houses of favoured parishioners to relax. 'The priest would come in to watch boxing on the TV on a Saturday night.' 'Father Leahy would have a bottle of Guinness and a whiskey with me dad.' In poorer districts attitudes could be very different.

One interviewee recalled, when referring to the local doctor and the priest: 'they could come into a man's home and turn down the radio, without permission.' Such intrusion was deeply resented by the family.

Much of this was in contrast to the English style of administration and practice, which had learned over generations to keep a lower public profile, and was more influenced by the social conventions of the English upper and middle class. Many of the English clergy remained uneasy about the Irish presence and their association with Irish culture and politics through their affiliation to Catholicism. By one account: 'The only anti-Irishness I came across in Liverpool was from a Catholic priest. What really upset him was when someone approached him and assumed he was Irish.'

But Irish Catholicism in Liverpool had to accommodate itself to the realities of life in the sea port, where attitudes were more liberal than in rural parishes in Ireland. 'It depended on what sort of family you grew up in. I think if the father was a church-goer that was a strong influence. My ex-husband was late for our first date because he was coming from mass.' Within individual families religious practice would differ. Speaking of her grandmother, with whom she lived as a teenager, one commentator said: 'I went to church with her sometimes, but it wasn't regular, whereas my other grandmother never missed.'

Marriage to those of other religions – known in Catholic jargon as 'mixed marriages' – became more common. There was resentment amongst the Anglican clergy that the Catholic Church insisted that in such marriages the Protestant partner convert to Catholicism, and that the children be brought up Catholic. One interviewee speaks of being brought up by a Catholic mother and Protestant father, who was very particular that the family went to mass each Sunday. Others who had one parent from an English background and the other from an Irish family spoke of the contrasting styles of religion.

Unlike Ireland, in Liverpool churches Catholic young men and women might mix with those from other cultures and countries, including Italians, eastern Europeans, people from Africa and later Jamaicans as the number of West Indian immigrants rose into the thousands in the 1950s. Families with a West Indian or African father and Irish Catholic mother became more common. According to Tommy Walsh: 'Often marrying a non-Catholic was seen as a greater problem than marrying a Black person.' In Liverpool there was a significant number of marriages between Irish Catholics and those from Black African, Caribbean or Chinese backgrounds. Socially there were many alternatives to the parish clubs – dance halls and pubs or ethnic centres such as the Caribbean Club – where young people could meet those from other backgrounds. Liverpool was a multi-cultural city long before most other towns. A proportion of the migrants into Liverpool were single young seamen, discharged from a ship, rather than members of family groups. In the absence of strong family links of their own, these young men went in search of a partner from other communities. Such couples and their families would often encounter not only the disadvantage of being Irish, but also the racist attitudes common in Liverpool. In one personal account a family member speaks of her ancestor being refused a wedding in her local Catholic Church, because her partner was Arab. She was told by a priest to 'raise your mongrels somewhere else'. Some from Irish Catholic families were 'ostracised'. One interviewee recalls how her grandmother, an Irish Catholic who married a man from Yemen, was isolated by her family because of it. Others had the experience of being put to the back of the class in school and suffering disadvantage when seeking employment.

In many families two or three generations removed from Irish migration, the cultural link with Ireland persisted. For a minority this link found expression in participation in active Irish clubs and organisations. The various branches of the Gaelic League organised classes and social functions including ceilis, which were strictly Irish language events. There was no concession to dances which were not considered Irish. For this reason waltzes, for example, were not permitted. With the increase in new migrants from Ireland the Gaelic Athletic Association, founded in the 1880s, increased in strength. They promoted Gaelic football, hurling, camogie and handball by organising training and competitions.

Sean McNamara, a Liverpool born traditional fiddle player who later became a leading figure in the tradition internationally, recalled: 'the first ceili band with which I played was a Gaelic League band which played at Sunday night ceilis.'[2] He recalled that in the 1940s: 'there were two other well known ceili bands playing regularly, the Shannon Star and the Brian Boru. When the war ended social activity expanded and there were many more musicians on the scene ... the majority of the Liverpool musicians of the post war period were born there (i.e. in Liverpool) and their ancestors came from different parts of Ireland.'

Also growing in strength at this time was Comhaltas Ceoltoiri Eireann, the Irish music and dance association, dedicated to preserving and reviving Irish traditions. They organised classes and competitions in traditional music, including regional festivals or Fleadhs and a national Fleadh each summer in Ireland. Comhaltas itself had been founded in 1951, with the Liverpool branch starting in 1957. Such was the strength of the Liverpool Ceili Band – a product of the Liverpool music scene where 'we were playing so often at ceilis, we had a great swing and rhythm'[3] – that they became All Ireland champions in 1963 and again in 1964, followed by a tour of the United States and a performance at the London Palladium.

The former Liverpool Irish Centre, Mount Pleasant, which, at time of writing, has remained unused since closure in the 1990s. Photo: G Quiery.

In the post-war years it was easy to pick up broadcasts from RTE – the Irish equivalent of the BBC, known as 'Athlone' – in Liverpool. It was extremely popular amongst the Irish community. 'I never saw the radio tuned to any station other than Athlone.' 'Me mum always tuned in to Irish radio.' Mostly people wanted to keep in touch with music and general news. Irish politics was of little interest. Most families also kept the tradition of singing Irish songs at family parties. 'The Irish connection was still there within the singing. Irish songs. Sentimental. I don't think anyone forgot where they originated from.' Music popular in Ireland but which was not distinctively Irish, such as country music and ballads by the American singer Bing Crosby, were also popular in Liverpool.

Many preferred Irish newspapers if they could get them. 'The *News of the World* and the *Daily Mail* were banned in our house.' The *Catholic Herald* was read widely. Those families in contact with relatives in Ireland would make frequent trips there, especially in the summer. 'I lived all my life in Liverpool, but every time there was a holiday we were on the boat that night. We didn't need money over there. We were on the family farm.'

Tommy Walsh made the observation that the situation of the Irish in Britain contrasted with that in the United States.[4] In the US one could be American and at the same time Irish. People from many European countries had come to the US. They took on a new US identity, whilst at the same time retaining their own national identity. For Irish people in Britain it was not so straightforward. To some extent one had to choose to be either British or Irish. The continued friction over Northern Ireland, the IRA campaign of the fifties, and the eventual advent of the Troubles in the late sixties tended to widen the gulf between British and Irish identities. The Second World War saw a surge in British and English patriotism, essential to the war effort, boosted by the social cohesion and nationwide communal hardships during the war itself.

Whilst there was considerable pressure to maintain Catholic practice – 'It was a mortal sin not to attend mass on a Sunday' – participation in Irish cultural activity was very much a matter of individual preference. There was little social pressure to do so. 'Irish culture was pretty strong for me. My brothers didn't go to Irish events to the extent that I did.' In the fifties many people did indeed opt in to this aspect of their identity. 'I remember that at St Cuthbert's you would get three sixteen-hand reels going.' 'The best ceili by far was at St Alphonsus, corner of Scotland Road, with Father Michael Coleman. There were ceilis at St Aloysius, Huyton, St Monica's, and at St Thomas's where Cornelius McEnroe – cousin of John McEnroe the tennis player – was the priest. On one occasion I was the MC at twenty ceilis on successive nights in Liverpool.' One respondent remembers at St Vincent's in Liverpool 8 the Irish curate coming into the dance and conducting prayers during the break. 'If you had guests – visitors to the area – they would be left wondering what the hell was going on.'

For those in the inner-city areas, educational opportunities remained limited. The Education Act of 1944 and increased public funding gave a greater number access to Catholic grammar schools which were of a very high standard. In the words of Kevin McNamara,[5] 'The Act gave opportunity to the children of working class families who would normally have gone to the parish school. It was a great leap, not only in the quality of the education, but for the opportunities for a scholarship or local authority grant. There was a whole host of people who benefitted.' Kevin's list, people from his own school, included professional people and many who had outstanding academic success in universities around the world. Catholic grammar schools benefitted also, from the generous scholarship schemes offered by local authorities, including Liverpool and Bootle, an essential factor in allowing those from disadvantaged backgrounds to compete with the more fortunate middle class children. Another interviewee, the writer Jimmy McGovern, recalls the harshness of school discipline in his Catholic grammar education. Two of his classmates in particular, 'talented fit young boys you'd expect to do well' were, in his opinion, severly damaged by their educational experiences, resulting in chronic alcoholism and mental illness.

In the 1950s antipathy towards the Irish persisted. Labourers still encountered the notice, 'No Blacks. No Irish' in lodging houses, as several of my interviewees confirmed. There is a lack of research on this topic, but those of an Irish background were at a disadvantage when seeking work. A disproportionate number of the Irish Catholic population remained in unskilled or semi-skilled jobs. Others provided services to the tightly knit community, running market stalls, and corner shops. Although the situation improved during the war and in the boom period just after, unemployment in Liverpool remained at two and a half times the national average.

Following the war there was a fresh influx of workers and families from Ireland. Yet another diaspora was getting under way and young men and women were pouring into Liverpool and into England generally, as Ireland's long period of economic depression continued. Thousands of young people there had little prospect of gainful employment. Post-war reconstruction in industry and housing in Britain, the programme of road and school building, and the openings for nursing staff in the newly established National Health Service all attracted migrants from Ireland. In common with other large cities such as Manchester and Birmingham, a new Irish community was established, many of them taking their place in church pews alongside the longer established families. The fact that Liverpool had daily ferry services directly to Ireland ensured that it remained a popular destination. The extent of this migration was such that many Irish families had the majority of members in England rather than back at home. 'Our parents had brothers and sisters living here in Liverpool. All family members came over here.' And again, speaking of his mother one witness said: 'All her cousins were in Liverpool. They all used to come to our house. I used to sit and listen when they visited. And that was where I learned all about Ireland.'

Since casual work on the docks was not as easily obtained as in the past, male migrants were more likely to find work in the building trade, motorway construction, and factory work. Dock work and older industries such as the Cammell Laird shipyard were declining. Docker numbers had reduced from 21,000 in 1931 to just 12,000 in 1938,[6] and had further reduced by the 1950s. New industries such as telecommunications, motor manufacture, plastics and electronics took their place. Employers such as Dunlop and Plessey continued to employ large numbers of semi-skilled workers on Merseyside. There was also a continued but declining demand for house servants and maids. These new arrivals tended to be more scattered, settling in the large areas between the old decayed city core and the leafy suburbs, in districts such as Old Swan, Bootle, Aintree and Tuebrook. Others found themselves accommodated on the new estates in Huyton, Speke and Croxteth.

Following the war the impetus of redevelopment was restored. As increasing numbers were moved from the city centre, the old communities became hollowed out. It wasn't just the Catholic parishes which suffered. In the 1960s eighteen Anglican churches were closed in the city centre area.

In the Scotland Road district decline continued throughout the 1950s, but it was the decision to site the entrance to the new Wallasey tunnel right at the heart of the area which was the most severe blow. In order to accomplish this project thousands of dwellings were bulldozed, and large numbers of residents – with no prospect of new housing in the area – were moved out. Schools and churches were demolished.

The local community fought back against the brutal re-development, forming the Scotland Road Residents Association to do so. Other local self-help organisations included the Vauxhall Neighbourhood Council, The Eldonians, The Rotunda community education initiative and the community newspaper Scotty Press. But city planners were not to be deterred.

The new transport network included a six-lane dual carriageway, feeder roads, and the four-lane tunnel entrance including a cutting some twenty metres deep. As the geography of the area was transformed, little attention was paid to the structure or needs of the existing community. Business and communication was disrupted, pedestrian access hazardous. The journey for a delivery van from, for example, Juvenal Street to Summerseat, a distance of a couple of hundred yards, would now mean a detour of nearly a mile, through busy traffic. Many historic addresses – such as Sawney Pope Street – and local landmarks – Richmond Square – disappeared. St Bridgid's church, which first opened in the 1870s, had been bombed during the war and subsequently rebuilt and re-opened in 1950; it was demolished again in 1967 to make way for the new tunnel.

The processes of construction and redevelopment caused an extended period of disruption, inconvenience and chaotic management. With the loss of population, community infrastructure declined. Businesses closed down. Many young people who in earlier generations would have remained, now left the area to take up work and residence elsewhere. Large numbers were moved out to new estates and towns such as those in Huyton and Kirkby.

CHAPTER SEVENTEEN
THE NEW COMMUNITIES

As re-development continued, new dwellings were constructed further from the city. Many of those from an Irish background now settled in Speke and Kirkby, each more than five miles from Liverpool centre. These new developments were a mixed blessing. The main objective of providing better housing was undoubtedly achieved. There was now more open space and greenery, but communities which had existed for generations were broken up. Speaking about the effect of the move on his mother, one person I interviewed remarked that: 'We moved to a place called Speke. Me aunty moved first, and then me mum followed, and it was the worst thing she could have done. I think it wiped them out, it killed her. You know, all that travelling, worry. There was no-one dropping in for a cup of sugar or anything.'[1] Waller remarked that: 'Few would recommend life on the new estates at Kirkby, Netherley and other places ... People don't go there, it is said, they are sent.'[2] Another person interviewed remarked that: 'Family and community links in the new areas were fractured.' It was no longer a short walk into town for a tour of pubs, no street markets where 'you could pinch an apple', no walk down to the docks in the evening to have a look at the ships arriving at the Pier Head.

With the Liverpool Irish community structure broken up, Catholicism became the most significant cultural and social remnant of the former Irish identity and way of life. But those who had been brought up in tightly knit, predominantly Catholic communities in the centre, now found that they were in a more mixed community. For example, in St Michael's, Kirkby, in 1965 there were an estimated 2,159 Catholics in the parish, out of a total of 4,250 residents.[3] 'When we moved to the brand new council estate in Aigburth, religion seemed less important somehow. It was a more mixed estate, Catholic and Protestant. But there wasn't the same importance displaying your faith as there used to be in Liverpool 8.' Some saw this as a deliberate policy. 'We were at the back end, when things started changing after the war. I think there was a definite element in the city council with the intention of destroying Catholic communities through redevelopment.'

For some the move to a new area was also a time to break from church practice. 'We got married and moved to Orrell Park, and the priest came knocking on the door. He was a very nice priest and it was all, 'We'll be seeing you at church, etcetera.' Very much wanting to bring us into the fold, and I said, 'No, I don't think so'. And you had feelings of guilt because you knew you'd be bringing the children up to be baptised.'

In areas which did not experience the full impact of re-development, the sense of community persisted for longer. One resident of Old Swan said: 'We were encouraged to play with our relations who lived close around. So many relations, aunties, cousins, grandma, so many children within a short walk.' Such situations did not obtain on the new estates.

As families moved out the Catholic authorities began the massive and onerous task of building new Catholic parishes in each district; schools, churches, accommodation for priests and nuns, church halls. This process was made possible by the post war employment boom, when a large proportion of parishioners were in work. The diocese relied on parish clergy to raise the extremely large sums needed. Each parish was responsible for its own development, and its own debt.

In January 1934 Father Edward Murphy was appointed 'priest in charge' at the new parish of St Aloysius, Twig Lane, Roby. 'This parish had become necessary because of the intensive building of houses in the district by the Liverpool Corporation.'[4] In April 'Canon O'Sullivan was sent to take charge of the infant mission.' The temporary church was completed in June. The priests lived in corporation housing until the church was completed some two years later. The junior and infant schools were completed in 1937, costing £7,600 and taking 450 children. In 1941 the secondary modern school was completed. 'This was the first school in the county to be completed under the 1939 Education Act, 75% of the total cost being met by the Lancashire Education Authority.'[5] By 1949 there were 1,500 pupils in the schools. 'With the school position solved at least for the present, the canon devoted all his energies to accomplishing his greatest ambition; to build a permanent church.'

This was completed in 1952, almost 20 years after the parish had been established. The final cost was £70,000. Canon O'Sullivan had come from a wealthy family in Ireland, who contributed towards his support. The Canon himself purchased the new church organ for £700. Of the £70,000 cost, £23,000 was met from parish funds. The rest was a debt which the parish had to take on. In a diocese which, in the words of Tommy Walsh, was 'run on Bingo',[5] sources of income included weekly collections, home visit collections, pools schemes and whist drives. Parish societies, such as the Catholic Young Men's Society also made large contributions towards paying down debt. In many areas the building of a parish club, which could be adapted for mass on Sundays, was the first step. Clubs with a bar and a network of social activities became an important source of income. Indeed, takings from the bar in the parish club was the most significant source of income for many parishes. St Michael's, Kirkby, in 1976, had an annual income of £16,000. Of this, £9,000 was from the social club, whilst church collections yielded £4,000. The club environment was generally male. In Roby 'women were only admitted on Easter Monday.' Though this parish had a vigorous fund-raising culture, assistance for the parish was eventually required from the curial offices, the central administration of the diocese. At St Aloysius in 1956 alone £7,000 was paid off the debt. While the parish was being established, the county council provided local authority accommodation for nuns until they obtained premises of their own, something which would have been unthinkable in the sectarian environment of Liverpool in an earlier era. By 1961 this parish was out of debt.

Another example of a new parish was St Mary's, Kirkby. Here there was an agreement between the bishop – Derek Warlock – and the Missionaries of the Sacred Heart, setting out details of the number of priests to be appointed, property holdings and settlement of any disputes over jurisdiction.[3] In October 1955 the Liverpool city architect sent the diocese a plan of Northwood, in which areas reserved for churches were identified. A site was selected for the Catholic church. For the first five years the parish priest – Father Taylor – used a school hall for church services. According to a letter from Father Spain – who, incidentally, had been instrumental in setting up the funding for the Liverpool Irish Centre – masses were being said in the church hall, which had been approved for the purpose by the diocese. 'Father Spain more or less built Catholicism in Kirkby. He built the church hall and was in it every night of the week, and on Saturdays they had bingo. On Sunday the curtains were pulled aside and mass was said.' At first masses had been conducted in a Protestant school, until such time as the church hall was ready, another practice which would have been impossible in the old inner-city districts. In parishes outside Liverpool, schools were funded in partnership with local authorities, in an atmosphere which was less fractious than in the twenties and thirties.

In the new parishes those from the former Irish Catholic districts formed new communities. Now the emphasis was on Catholicism, rather than Irishness, since organisations of a specifically Irish character did not become established in the new areas. The church as an institution was strongly present, both in the form of buildings and membership. It was a ready made social structure, where people could meet and make friends. In Holy Angels parish, in 1969, the church estimated that there were 3,700 Catholics, of whom 1,435 on average attended mass. 'On the new estate all my Catholic friends went to church. I did not have one Catholic friend back then who did not go to church.' Another interviewee remarked that: 'When I was young there were still a great number of people who were church attenders.' People continued to find their social life and acquaintances in the parish. In the words of one interviewee: 'Most of my dad's mates went to the parish club, where he went for a drink.' Another recalled that: 'We joined the Catholic youth club and went to Catholic schools.' There were a variety of social activities, often encouraged by clergy who were interested in games such as football and boxing.

Clerical visits to the family home continued. Though this was considered by the clergy as a pastoral activity, keeping in touch with their parishioners, it was also an occasion for collecting money to support the ambitious building programmes. One parish report in Kirkby noted that: 'The parish is well visited by the clergy, but they experience difficulty getting a response from many of the Catholic families who have lapsed.'

Those who could not afford to contribute – and there were many – would often not open the door to the clergy. 'The clergy used to come round regularly in Croxteth, but Croxteth was a poor area. People were moved out. No shops, big families … I think he would have been more welcome if he wasn't collecting. People knew the priest was coming, but they didn't have the money. If they had the money the door was open. But it was a bit of an embarrassment if they didn't have the money.'

Another interviewee from a different parish recalled that: 'There were regular visitations once a month, and I can remember one argument between my father and the priest when the parish introduced its own pools and lottery collection, and father refused to take part, because he would have no say in how the money would be spent, but my mother did sell them, because of the commission.'

During the 1950s many more benefitted from the opportunities in post war Merseyside and the advance of Catholic education and more widespread access to selective grammar schools. In addition to the corporation housing, significant numbers of Catholic families moved out to private housing in suburbs such as Crosby and Formby to the north, Aigburth and Runcorn to the south, and in Wirral on the opposite side of the Mersey. 'And as a result of education, those jobs which went to educated people, teachers, police and senior white collar jobs, those people tended to move into private housing and didn't live in the parish in which they worked.' Although these areas too were more mixed in religion, Catholic parishes with an Irish flavour remained strong. At English Martyrs in Litherland, a district where there was both private and municipal housing, 'we had mass at 7,8, 9, 10 and 11, and the church was always full.'

The sixties also saw a modest but steady revival of Irish cultural activity, centred on the new Irish Centre which opened on Mount Pleasant. Three leading Irish cultural organisations – Conradh na Gaeilge (Gaelic League), Comhaltas Ceoltoiri Eireann (Society of Irish Musicians) and the Gaelic Athletic Association – came together to form the Gaelic Council, to organise major events such as St Patrick's Day celebrations. In 1961, after some members had been impressed by the St Brendan's Irish Centre in Manchester, the proposal to establish a centre in Liverpool was put forward. Soon afterwards the Irish Centre building fund was established with Tommy Walsh as Chair.[6] The GAA and the Gaelic League had reservations about the new enterprise, as it was generally agreed that the Centre would not be exclusively 'Gaelic' in character, but would have to put on more modern entertainment to survive. In addition, the Irish community generally were sceptical about the prospect of raising the necessary funding. Fundraising events were held at parish clubs, mainly Christ the King, Childwall, where Father O'Connor, the original proposer of the idea was based. There were also concerts at the Philharmonic Hall. When they heard that the Notre Dame Sisters on Mount Pleasant were selling the Wellington Rooms, efforts were made to raise the finance to purchase the building. Loans from business and arrangements with the bank – negotiated by Father Patrick Spain, who was very active in Kirkby – led to a successful outcome, with the Liverpool Irish Centre opening in 1965. The magnificent building with its impressive decorative ballroom became a popular venue both for those in the established community and new arrivals.

Decline of Catholic Practice

It was during the 1960s that the most significant legacy of Liverpool's Irish connection – Catholic religious practice and Catholic parish life – began to decline. There were a number of interlinked factors behind this marked reduction in those practising Catholicism. Certainly in the sixties the shackles of conformity were loosened. People felt freer to do as they pleased. At the same time much of the territory which had previously been occupied by religion and by parish life was encroached upon by other disciplines as more people became better educated, reading more widely. Mass media, which at first enabled links with Ireland through RTE radio, and popular Irish singers such as John McCormick, now presented an alternative secular world, an international culture of cinema and music. Politics also was becoming detached from religious loyalties. The churches' sphere of influence was steadily reduced.

There were significant developments within the Catholic church itself, which had the effect of reducing engagement. Undoubtedly people were more inclined to question authority. 'I think also people began to more openly question politicians and church leaders.' Church teaching was challenged across a wide spectrum. 'I remember a big argument one day, with non-Catholics when I was a student, saying, how come you have the Pope in all his finery when there is so much poverty. In my twenties I was very anti-establishment in the Catholic Church.' The Englishness of certain church practices was possibly also a factor. 'As I got older I have taken an interest in Irish politics. But in church there were prayers for The Queen and the royal family, and I didn't agree with that.'

Some felt that matters were not helped by the changes implemented following Vatican Two, which ended many longstanding practices, including the traditional format of the Latin mass. The 'unease among many people at the introduction of liturgical changes was the lack of preparation and proper instruction about the theological reasons behind the changes – it seemed at times to be change for change's sake.' Church teaching on sexuality and matters related to sex was the greatest bone of contention. Modern forms of contraception, which were becoming increasingly available, were forbidden. One option was to abide by church teaching and have large families. The impact was most acutely felt by families on low income. Another option was to simply ignore church teaching, which many did. But this had the effect of loosening their respect for church doctrine and clerical authority in relation to other matters.

Many people just left. 'The growing movement for gender equality, especially after the pill, gave women a sense of independence. The ability of women to control their own fertility meant that they were less dependent on men.' 'The authority of the church was gone. People just said, 'Why should I?''

To Let sign on the former St Austin's parish church, Garston, Liverpool, 2017. Photo: G. Quiery.

For some the manner in which the church wielded its power in the community was a bone of contention. For example, the children of 'mixed marriages' were required to be brought up Catholic. Another question was the attitude towards divorce. 'One thing that did bug me was when I was divorced, the marriage ended and when I do go to church now, I can't take communion, because I am a divorcee, and it is wrong, very wrong. Divorced people turned their back on the church, because they were being treated like lepers.'

I have not investigated the extent of physical or sexual abuse in Catholic institutions on Merseyside. Harsh discipline in institutions and corporal punishment in schools was widespread in state-run, voluntary and religious organisations in the fifties and sixties. A number of my interviewees have vivid memories of harsh school discipline and physical punishment. I have heard one allegation in particular of sexual abuse by an individual teacher in a Liverpool Catholic secondary school run by a religious order in the fifties and sixties. As has so often been the case, these allegations were never taken up by other members of staff, or thoroughly investigated by the institution. In relation to this subject Peter Stanford has remarked on: 'how much Catholic grammar schools from the 1950s through to the 1970s were the route by which generations of working-class Catholic boys and girls got on in life – the Irish Christian Brothers in my own home town of Liverpool boasted that they took the sons of dockers and made them into doctors.' However he goes on to say that it 'remains impossible to know the extent of sexual abuse because every bit of information has to be dragged out of a compulsively secretive Church.'[8]

In Liverpool cases of widespread systematic abuse such as was common in Ireland have not come to light. The Irish church was more closely allied to state power. It had, for example, a monopoly of schools and boarding institutions in many areas. It acted for the state in providing social services, including running residential and penal establishments for children and vulnerable people. It was in a position to exercise social control. In Liverpool the church had less power than in Ireland. Clerical authority was a factor within the domain of parish life, but did not extend far beyond it. For example, clerical pressure to have the Connolly Association banned from the Liverpool Irish Centre – because of its political views – was effectively resisted by the lay management. In contrast to Ireland, those who did not wish to attend a Catholic school or social institution could always make use of nearby local authority provision instead.

The advance of popular entertainment, especially television, also presented fresh challenges to traditional beliefs, which were now being contrasted with new ideas and a strong secular culture which made little reference to religion. Many people remained nominally Catholic, having their children baptised and going to mass on special occasions such as Easter or Christmas, but not otherwise. 'In my own family, none of my children go to mass. They are still Catholic, but say to me , 'Dad, we don't have to go to mass.' Their children are all baptised.'

Continued Integration

As time passed the process of integration became more deeply rooted. As a result the children and grandchildren of Irish migrants had a mixed cultural heritage. Their continued affection for Ireland and its culture remained strong, even as successive generations became more integrated into British society and established customs and practices associated with their Irish heritage were weakened. Regular religious observance declined, and the population became increasingly secular. At the same time, the engines which had driven sectarian animosity were losing their force or had disappeared.

One can find many similarities between Liverpool and both Glasgow and Belfast. All three are sea ports in which extreme poverty was accompanied by sectarian animosity into the first half of the twentieth century. In both Belfast and Glasgow there are important institutions which ensure the continuance of divisions into each succeeding generation. In Glasgow, for example, loyalty to one or other of the city's leading football clubs, Celtic or Rangers, leads each generation into an oppositional culture which stereotypes thousands of their fellow citizens as 'other'. In Liverpool proposals for a Catholic or Nationalist football club never gained traction. In politics the Catholic Party was eventually undermined by Church authorities. Support for Nationalist and Protestant political parties evaporated at the ballot box. Sectarianism was withering.

In the early sixties the city was going into economic decline, and had a poor public image in media across Britain, dominated in particular by news of industrial unrest and dock strikes. The remnants of sectarian division, including disorder on the streets and anti-Irish sentiment could still be found in the city.

Remarkably, it was in these circumstances that a very positive new identity presented itself. It took the form of a cultural renaissance, spearheaded by the success of the many Liverpool bands of the sixties. The best known were The Beatles. Their optimistic sound, light-heartedness and humour gained Liverpool a very positive reputation around the world. They were popular not just in the English-speaking world but also in countries as diverse as Russia, Brazil and Japan. Young people in other countries began imitating the Liverpool accent and foreign media celebrated the Liverpool sense of humour as expressed by The Beatles. The resulting transformation in Liverpool itself is analysed by Keith Roberts: 'This era coincided with the gradual sloughing off of the more unpleasant aspects of the past and an anticipation of a future in which the prejudices and bitterness between Catholic and Protestant were forgotten.'[9] He continues, 'People began to look past the constraints of low living standards and take solace in the intrinsic worth of the city. The development of shared customs and a unique brogue extended this commonality to their neighbours regardless of their creed.' He goes on to point out that: 'Music was an extremely important component of this new Scouse identity. The bands of the Merseybeat promoted 1960s Liverpool under a common badge.'[10]

Success for the city in popular music was accompanied by achievements in other creative fields, including comedy, television, screen writing, drama and poetry. Distinguished writers whose work is directly inspired by the cultural milieu of the working-class culture of Irish Liverpool include James Hanley and George Garrett. Romantic novelists Maureen Lee and Lynn Andrews are also from this background, as are film and television dramatist Jimmy McGovern and the poet Roger McGough. Arguably work for television and theatre by Alan Bleasdale and Carla Lane also take this way of life as an inspiration as did Liverpool comedians of the sixties and seventies such as Tom O'Connor. Other well known figures from the sixties with Irish roots include entertainer Cilla Black from Scotland Road, Arthur Dooley, sculptor and raconteur, artist Sam Walsh, boxers John Conteh, Shea Neary and Andy Holligan, and many footballers.

The success of these prominent individuals has been matched by the contribution of those from an Irish background to every aspect of life in the city. They have played a leading role in trade union leadership. Their number included Jack Jones – full name James Larkin Jones – from Garston, veteran of the Spanish Civil War and for many years the combative General Secretary of the Transport and General Workers Union. They have been prominent in every aspect of life on Merseyside, including civic institutions, business, media and social care.

Increasing civic pride and rising self-esteem became important factors in the outstanding success of two local institutions - Liverpool and Everton football clubs. In an article in the Irish Post, Tony Birtill reflected on the decline of sectarianism in Liverpool, where the experience has contrasted with both Glasgow and Belfast: 'Soccer, a divisive force in Scotland, helped bring people together in Liverpool, with Everton FC and Liverpool FC enjoying support from both Catholics and Protestants.'[11] This point of view is reinforced in Robert's research. In his words: 'Despite the city's downturn, the city's two football teams became key repositories of loyalty and red and blue began to eclipse orange and green, amid broader societal processes of secularism, even if the outright repudiation of religion was less marked in Liverpool.'[12]

The decline of sectarian animosity continued into the seventies. The Anglican bishop, David Sheppard (appointed in 1975) and the Catholic Derek Warlock (appointed in 1976) led the way in collaboration across the former divide. The improving relations were symbolised by the visits to both cathedrals of Queen Elizabeth II in 1978 and Pope John Paul II in 1982.

As anti-Irish attitudes declined in Liverpool racism and antagonism towards other groups became more evident. The question of the extent to which the city's new unity and inclusivity was extended to black and other minority communities is explored in detail by Keith Roberts.[13]

The Irish presence in Liverpool was undoubtedly a significant ingredient in the development of the distinctive Liverpool sense of identity. Many of the characteristics of that revival are also evident in Irish culture, including humour, a love of music and ballad melodies, literature and poetry, and the enthusiasm for sporting rivalry, as found in football in particular. Other influences were past hardships and the related sense of solidarity it generated, attitudes to authority, the international dimension related to the port and the multi-cultural nature of the city at a time when most of Britain was relatively homogenous.

And Finally ...

My account of the Liverpool Irish concludes in the nineteen sixties. However, the city today still has a significant number of Irish born residents. There is a steady flow of Irish students attending the city's three Universities. Many remain after graduation to take up employment in the city or establish their own businesses. The city is home to a number of institutions with an Irish focus. Following the closure of the original Irish Centre on Mount Pleasant in the 1990s, the Liverpool Irish Centre in Boundary Lane was founded under the leadership of Tommy Walsh and continues to be a social and cultural hub of Irish activity. The Institute of Irish Studies at the University of Liverpool was founded in the eighties to promote and develop the study of Irish history, culture and society. It now enjoys a world-wide reputation whilst retaining close links with the local community. The Liverpool Irish Festival, now in its fourteenth year, has a reputation for providing a broad and imaginative programme which includes both contemporary and traditional music, drama, literature, film and local heritage. Irish Community Care Merseyside is a dedicated social service for vulnerable members of the Irish community in the region. Other active organisations include Conradh na Gaeilge, the Gaelic Athletic Association, Comhaltas Ceoltoiri Eireann and a number of Irish dance schools. The city also has a good number of Irish theme pubs and an annual St Patrick's Day parade.

I hope that this book has helped explain the story behind this thriving Irish culture in a British city. It is for each reader to draw their own conclusions from the history of the Liverpool Irish. I have tried my best to tell their story as objectively and fairly as possible. I have had to be selective in the use of material; there is just so much of it. I hope that some of those who have read this book will follow the story in greater detail in the works of Frank Neal, John Belchem, Michael Kelly, Tony Birtill and the many others who have written on the subject. I would also recommend the adventure of delving into the wealth of material in local libraries and archives, especially the Liverpool Record Office at Central Library. It is open to the public and contains so much interesting material, not just in newspaper accounts, but in the records of local public bodies, organisations and societies.

The Irish migrants who came to Liverpool included not only economic migrants, but many who – just like those modern migrants driven by catastrophic circumstances – foresook their homeland in order just to survive. Liverpool is a city which has experienced the disruption, hardship and conflict which arises from migration in such large numbers. There are certain patterns of behaviour which are likely to occur wherever migration takes place. In Liverpool it is certainly true that fear and suspicion of the migrant population, and their position in the economic and social hierarchy, was vigorously exploited by politicians and religious leaders for their own ends. It is also evident that both local and national politicians failed in their duty to address the housing crisis, which had to await the arrival of a Labour administration at Westminster in the twentieth century before effective action was taken.

Another challenge for migrant communities is integration into the social and economic structures of their new homeland. In Liverpool this process took much longer than was the case elsewhere. I hope that in this book I have managed to cast some light on the reasons why.

There are places where religious and cultural organisations, marching traditions and sporting allegiance operate to renew and feed sectarian divisions in succeeding generations. In Liverpool such engines of prejudice have not survived on any significant scale into the present century. This is one respect in which Liverpool is fortunate and perhaps exceptional. From the nineteen-sixties a new and confident Liverpool identity began to establish itself. This was a positive force which emerged even as the city struggled economically and suffered from a poor reputation in national media. From the city's dynamic and colourful social environment, cultural and sporting success stories with national and international reach, sprang up. The city quite rightly claimed these as a confirmation of an exceptional identity, which is a source of recognition and pride.

The people of Liverpool and Merseyside have shown great generosity of spirit, to create a city in which animosity and sectarianism are being replaced by a common and heartfelt identity, which puts emphasis on those factors which unite rather than the sterile divisions and bigotry of the past. Most, I believe, are of one mind in addressing the remnants of prejudice and the problems of poverty which still persist.

It is to their credit.

'When a story is told it is no longer forgotten. It becomes something else. The memory of who we were. The hope of what we can become.'

Tatiana de Rosnay from *Sarah's Key*

This Celtic Liver Bird can be seen in Granby Street, Liverpool 8, Liverpool's most culturally diverse district. Originally created by Fred Brown it was erected by community activist Joe Farrag and is held in trust for the local community by SHAP Ltd.

REFERENCES

CHAPTER ONE
THE FIRST ARRIVALS

1. Muir, R. *A History of Liverpool.* (University of Liverpool Press, 1907. Re-published. p.68. Quote from Leland.

2. Ibid. p.132.

3. Troughton, T. *The History of Liverpool from the Earliest Authenticated Period Down to the Present Time.* Liverpool, 1810. p.104.

4. For an explanation of the Penal Laws see Beckett, J.C. *The Making of Modern Ireland* p.151. Also Beresford, Ellis P. *A History of the Irish Working Class.* pp.55, 57, 60.

5. Smithers, H. *Liverpool; Its Commerce, Statistics and Institutions with a History of the Cotton Trade,* 1825. p.97.

6. Ascott, Lewis and Power. Liverpool, 1600-1750. Referred to in Birtill, Irish in Liverpool p.15.

7. Howley, P. *Slavers, Traders and Privateers.* p.189.

8. Burke, T. *Catholic History of Liverpool.* p.13.

9. Smithers, H. Op cit. p.91.

10. Muir. Op cit. p.181.

11. Smithers. Op cit. p.93.

12. Gore's Directory, 1807. p.94.

13. Muir. Op cit. p.244.

14. Troughton, T. *The History of Liverpool from the Earliest Authenticated Period Down to the Present Time.* Liverpool, 1810. p.198.

15. Gore's Directory, 1807.

16. For discussion on the growth of the city see: Power, M.J. The growth of Liverpool. In Popular Politics, riot and labour. Essays in Liverpool history 1790-1940 Belchem, J. Ed. LUP. 1992. p.21. ff.

17. Beckett, J.C. *The Making of Modern Ireland. 1603-1923.* (Faber, 1966). p.292.

18. *Liverpool Mercury,* 9 July 1824. p.10. Col 2. For discussion of this issue see R.F. Foster. *Modern Ireland 1600-1972,* p.320. Peter and Fiona Somerset Fry. *A History of Ireland.* (Routledge, 1988). p.228.

19. O'Tuathaigh, M.A.G. *The Irish in Nineteenth-century Britain: Problems of Integration of the Irish in the Victorian City.* Swift and Gilley (Eds). (Croom Helm, 1985). p17.

20. Aughton, P. *Liverpool: A People's History.*

21. British Parliamentary Papers (Commons) Select Committee on Settlement and Poor Removal, 1847. Vol. XI. p.47. Q.4370. Evidence of Rushton.

22. Denvir, J. *The Irish in Britain.* p.153.

23. Papworth, J.D. *The Irish in Liverpool, 1835-71: Segregation and Dispersal.* Unpublished PhD thesis, University of Liverpool, 1982. p.47.

24. Jackson, J.A. *The Irish In Britain.* Routledge and Keegan, Paul. p.7.

25. Smithers. Op cit. p.199.

26. Burke,T, *Catholic History of Liverpool.* p.31.

27. Papworth, J.D. Op cit. p.95.

28. Ibid. p.129.

29. Ibid. Table 2.1.

30. Melville H. Redburn. *His First Voyage.* Chapter XXXIX. Can be found at http://www.gutenberg.org/files/8118/8118.txt.

31. Taylor, I. *Black Spot on the Mersey.* Unpublished PhD thesis. University of Liverpool, 1976. p.104.

32. Stephen, Leslie. *Dictionary of National Biography 7. Brown, William (1784-1864), London.* (Smith, Elder & Co).

CHAPTER TWO
LIFE IN THE IRISH COMMUNITY

1. For biographical details of Cornwall Lewis see, https://en.wikisource.org/wiki/Lewis,_George_Cornwall_(DNB00)

2. P.P. 1836 (40) XXXIV. Royal Commission on the Condition of the poorer classes in Ireland: Appendix G: State of the Irish poor in Great Britain. Evidence of William Parlour. p.20.

3. Ibid. p.54. Evidence of the Reverend Mr Murphy.

4. Ibid. p.23. Evidence of Reverend Fisher.

5. Ibid. p.24.

6. Ibid. p.26. Evidence of Doctor Collins.

7. Ibid. p.22. Evidence of Vincent Glover.

8. Ibid. p.23.

9. Woodham-Smith, C. *The Great Hunger.* (Old Town Books, 1989). p.25.

10. Condition of the poorer classes in Ireland. Op cit. Evidence of William Parlour. p.19.

11. Ibid. p.20.

12. Belchem, J. *Irish Catholic and Scouse. The history of the Liverpool-Irish, 1800-1939.* (LUP, 2007). p.101.

13. Denvir, J. *Life Story of an Old Rebel.* p.10.

14. Burke. Op cit. p.66.

15. Denvir. Op cit. p.48. Ch. IV. p.48. (Can be obtained free on-line from the Gutenberg Project).

16. *Liverpool Mail.* 25 November 1841.

17. Birtill, T. *A Hidden History. Irish in Liverpool – An Ghealige I Learpholl.* (Liverpool Irish Festival). *2012.*

18. Ibid. p.17.

19. Doyle. P. *Mitres and Missions in Lancashire,* (Bluecoat Press, Liverpool, 2005). p.41.

20. Hume A. *Missions at Home, or a Clergyman's Account of a Portion of the Town of Liverpool,* referenced in Birtill. Op cit. p.31.

21. Denvir. *Life Story of an Old Rebel.* Op cit. p.15.

22. Murphy. Op cit. p.17.

23. Frazer, W.M. *Duncan of Liverpool.* (Carnegie publishing, 1997). p.28.

24. Report Liverpool Inquiry, 1833. Evidence of Dr Collins. p.461.

25. *Liverpool Mercury.* 23 September 1831.

26. Poor Enquiry, Ireland,1836. Appendix G. Op cit. p.29.

27. Poor Inquiry Ireland. Op cit. p.29.

28. For an account of Kitty Wilkinson's life, see Kelly, M. *Mothers of the City.* (AJH Publishing, 2007).

29. Fraser, Op cit. p.32.

30. Ibid. p.32.

31. Ibid. p.26.

32. For descriptions of diseases common in Liverpool at this time, see Appendix 2.

33. Frazer, Op cit. p.18.

34. Poor Inquiry (Ireland) Op cit. Appendix G. p.23.

35. *Liverpool Mail,* 14 July 1837.

36. *Liverpool Mail,* 14 March 1837.

37. Neal F. *Sectarian Violence: The Liverpool Experience. 1819-1914.* (Manchester University Press, 1988). p.51.

38. Ibid. p.37.

39. Burke. Op cit. p.78.

CHAPTER THREE

THE REFORM ACT 1832

1. *Liverpool Mercury,* 17 July 1835.

2. Neal, F. Op cit. p.42.

3. *Liverpool Mercury,* 17 July 1835.

4. Murphy, J. *The Religious Problem in English Education.* LUP, 1959. p.13.

5. *Fraser's Magazine for Town and Country.* January 1839. p.31.

6. Murphy. Op cit. p.76.

7. Trevalyn, C.E. *The Liverpool Corporation School: No Popery Agitation.* 1840. p.6.

8. *Liverpool Standard,* 30 September 1840.

9. Neal. Op cit. p 64.

10. Murphy. Op cit. p.83.

11. Neal. Op cit. p.56.

12. *Liverpool Mercury,* 16 July 1841.

13. Neal. Op cit. p.59.

14. Ibid. p.60.

15. Murphy. Op cit. p.246.

16. *Liverpool Mercury,* 2 July 1841. p.6.

17. Midwinter, E.C. *Liverpool and the New Poor Law, in Old Liverpool.* (Devon, David & Charles, 1971). p.74.

18. Burke. Op cit. p.79.

19. Neal. Op cit. p.60.

20. McCabe, A.T. in *Victorian Lancashire.* Bell S.P. (Ed)

CHAPTER FOUR

THE IMPACT OF THE IRISH FAMINE

1. *The Times*. London. 24 December 1846.

2. Woodham, Smith. *The Great Hunger*. (Old Town Books, 1962). p.210-11.

3. Report of Liverpool Chief Constable. 16 February 1847. LRO.

4. BPP. (Commons) Select Committee on Poor Removal, 1854. Q.4270. Evidence of Edward Rushton.

5. Letter from Mr Rushton, stipendary magistrate to Sir George Grey, Home Secretary, 21 April 1849. Reproduced in Minutes of evidence of Rev. Augustus Campbell, Select Committee on the Removal of the Poor, 1854. BPP. Vol. XVII. p.357.

6. PP Commons. Select Committee on Emigrant Ships.(1854) Evidence of J. Bensard. Q.4896-7.

7. *The Times*, 7 December 1848.

8. Death of Luke McCoy. *Liverpool Mercury*, 27 November 1846, is but one example. Also *Manchester Guardian*, 27 January 1847.

9. Neal, F. Op cit. p.84.

10. Ibid. p.87.

11. Evidence of Campbell. Select Committee on Removal of the Poor. Op cit. p.357.

12. *Liverpool Mercury*, 15 January 1847.

13. Select Committee on the Removal of the Poor, 1854. Vol. XVII. Q.835.

14. Papworth. Op cit. p.48.

15. Evidence of Augustus Campbell, Chairman of Select Vestry to Select Committee on the Removal of the Poor, 1854. Minutes of evidence. BPP. Vol. XVII. p.357.

16. Frazer. Op cit. p.57.

17. *Liverpool Mail*. 26 December 1846.

18. Duncan, W.H. *First Annual Report of the Medical Officer of Health*. p.8.

19. Neal. Op cit. p.91.

20. Frazer. Op cit. p.58.

21. Select Committee on Poor Removal, 1854. Appendix G. Irish Poor in Great Britain.

22. Papworth, J.D. Op cit. p.48.

CHAPTER FIVE

ON THE WATERFRONT

1. Proceedings of the Select Committee on the Passengers' Act, HC, 1851. Vol. 19. Q.2869. Stephen, Sir G.

2. Ibid. Q.2865.

3. Ibid. Q.2883.

4. Ibid. Q.2883.

5. Ibid. Q.2875.

6. Coleman, T. *Passage to America*. (Hutchinson, 1972). p.77.

7. Proceedings of Select Committee on the Passengers' Act, Op cit. Q.2872

8. Ibid. Q.2768.

9. Coleman. Op cit. p.72.

10. Ibid. p.71.

11. Proceedings of the Select Committee on the Passengers' Act. Op cit. 3738.

12. Coleman. Op cit. p.81. Letter from Vere Foster in correspondence on the treatment of passengers on board the emigrant ship, *Washington*. HC. 1851, Vol.40. p.434.

13. Proceedings of the Select Committee on the Passengers' Act. Q.2884.

14. Quote from The Emigrant's Manual in Coleman. Op cit. p.85-86.

CHAPTER SIX

THE LIVERPOOL IRISH COMMUNITY FROM 1850-1914

1. Papworth, J.D. *The Irish in Liverpool 1835-71: Segregation and Dispersal*. Unpublished PhD thesis. University of Liverpool. 1982. p.14.

2. Papworth, J.D. Op cit.

3. Ibid. p.129.

4. Ibid. p.65.

5. Ibid. p.177.

6. Report of Medical Officer of Health 1847. Or Mr Thomas Fresh. Health Committee minutes, 1849. *Liverpool Mercury*, Friday 18 January 1850.

7. *Liverpool Mercury*, 8 May 1846. p.226.

8. Taylor, I. *Black Spot on the Mersey*. Unpublished PhD thesis. University of Liverpool, 1976. p.93.

9. Ibid. p.164-165.

10. Finch, John. Statistics of Vauxhall Ward, Liverpool compiled by John Finch. Facsimile reprint prepared and introduced by Harold Hikins. *The Condition of the Working Class in Liverpool in 1842*. (Toulouse Press, 1986). p.30.

11. Klapas, J.A. *Geographical Aspects of Religious Changes in Victorian Liverpool. 1837-1901*. Unpublished M.A. Thesis, 1977, Liverpool.

12. Taylor. Op cit. p.89.

13. Dowling. Evidence to Select Committee on Railway Labourers, 1846. BPP. Vol.xiii. Q.3042 to 3059.

14. Select Committee on the Removal of the Poor, 1854. BPP. Vol.xvii. p.370.

15. Taylor. Op cit. See chart after p.59.

16. Select Committee on Girls, 1883. Evidence of Fr. Nugent. Q.99.

17. Letford, L. *Irish and Non-Irish Women Living in their Households in Nineteenth Century Liverpool*. Unpublished PhD, University of Lancaster, 1996. p.232.

18. Kanya-Forstner, M. *The Politics of Survival*. Unpublished PhD thesis. University of Liverpool. 1997. p.95

19. *Liverpool Mercury*, 31 January 1854.

20. *Liverpool Mercury*, 9 September 1853. p.7.

21. Kanya-Forstner. Op cit. p.88.

22. In his evidence to the Select Committee in Intemperance in 1877, PP, 1877 (418) XI. Evidence of James Nugent.

23. O'Mara. Op cit. p.49.

24. Kanya-Forstner, Martha. *The Politics of Survival: Irish Women in Outcast Liverpool, 1850-1890*. Unpublished PhD thesis. University of Liverpool, 1997.

25. Kanya-Forstner. Op cit. p.104.

25. Ibid. p.124.

26. *Liverpool Mercury*, 3 June 1851. Quoted in Forstner. p.130.

27. Ibid. p.138.

28. PRO HO 144/32/78794. See Kanya-Forstner p.142. ff.

29. Kanya-Forstner. Op cit. p.114.

30. Ibid. p.117.

31. Select Committee on Intemperance. Third Report. Minutes of Evidence. F.J. Nugent. Q.8216. PP, 1877. (418) Vol. XI. 759.

32. Kanya-Forstner. p.187. Op cit. Evidence of Rev. Campbell to Select Committee on Poor removal. 1854.

33. Lownes, F.D. *Prostitution and Venereal Disease in Liverpool*. pp.3, 4.

34. Shimmin. Liverpool Life, Its Pleasures, Practices and Pastimes. *Liverpool Mercury*, 1856. p.vii.

35. For Josephine Butler see Biography. Appendix One.

36. Select Committee on the Protection of Young Girls. PP. 1882 (344) XIII. Evidence of Nugent. Q.99.

37. Ibid. Q.147.

38. LRO. Liverpool Borough Prisons. Prison Minister's Report. Liverpool Council Proceedings, 1866.

39. Kanya-Forstner. Op cit. p.174.

40. *Liverpool Mercury*, 31 October 1851.

41. *Liverpool Mercury*, 31 January 1854.

42. Dowling Evidence to Select Committee on Railway Labourers, 1846. BPP. xiii. Q.3042 to 3059.

43. Evidence of Rev Campbell Select Committee on Removal of the Poor. Op cit. pp311-312.

44. *Liverpool Mercury*, 20 February 1855.

45. Dr. Buchan. Report on an Epidemic of Typhus in Liverpool. Appendix to 7th Report of the Medical Officer of the Privy Council. Parl Papers (1865). Vol. XXVI. p.468.

46. O'Tuathaigh, Op cit. p.17.

47. For an account of his life, see Kelly, M. *Liverpool's Irish Connection*. (Ribcar, 2007).

CHAPTER SEVEN

THE CATHOLIC CHURCH IN THE IRISH COMMUNITY

1. De Beaumont, Gustave. *Ireland: Social, Political and Economic*. Edited and translated by W.C. Taylor. pp.90, 91.

2. Klapas, J.A. *Geographical Aspects of Religious Change in Victoran Liverpool, 1837-1901*. University of Liverpool. Unpublished M.A. thesis, 1977. Fig. 29.

3. Burke, T. Op cit. p.126.

4. Liverpool Metropilitan Cathedral Archive. St Alban's parish box. Envelope. 13 October 1889.

5. Burke. Op cit. p.87.

6. Doyle, P. *Mitres and Missions: The Roman Catholic Dioceses of Lancashire. 1850-2000.* (Bluecoat Press, 2005). p.72.

7. Samuel, R. *The Roman Catholic Church and the Irish Poor in the Irish in the Victorian City.* Swift and Gilley (Eds). p.275.

8. Mayhew, H. *London Labour and London Poor*, Vol. 1. p.114.

9. Kanya-Forstner, Op cit. p.220.

10. Lowe, W.J. *The Lancashire Irish and the Catholic Church, 1846-71: The Social Dimension. In Irish Historical Studies, 20.* 1976. p.129.

11. Burke. Op cit. p.124.

12. Doyle. Op cit. p.88 gives the figure 177,893 for 1887. Lowe, p.114 gives a lower figure of 120,000.

13. Kanya-Forstner. Op cit. p.249.

14. Belchem. *Irish Catholic and Scouse.* Op cit. pp.76, 77.

15. Samuel. Op cit. p.281.

16. Belchem. Op cit. p.76.

17. Lowe. Op cit. p.113.

18. Doyle. Op cit. p.125.

19. LRO. SVP Minute book, 1870. 361/Vin/1. p.96.

20. Kanya-Forstner. Op cit. p.276.

21. LRO. Liverpool Borough Prison, Prison Minister's Report, Liverpool Council Proceedings, 1886.

22. LRO. SVP Minute book, 30 November 1870. 361/Vin/1.

23. Simey, Margaret. *The Charitable Effort in Liverpool.* p.111.

24. Burke. Op cit. p.104.

25. Ibid. p.70.

26. Ibid. p.107.

27. John, Denvir. *The Life Story of an Old Rebel.* Op cit. pp.13, 14.

28. O'Meara. Op cit. p.103.

29. Burke. Op cit. p.76.

30. Ibid. p.108.

31. Doyle. Op cit. p.157.

32. Boyce, F. *City of Story Tellers in Merseyside Culture and Place.* Mike Benbough-Jackson and Sam Davies (Eds) p.202.

33. Bennett, Canon B. *Father Nugent of Liverpool.* (1973). p.30.

34. P.P. 1882. (344) XIII Report of the Select Committee of the House of Lords on the Relating to the Protection of Young Girls. June 1883. Q.108.

35. *The Tablet.* 13 January 1894. p.15.

36. For a short account of the Clarence see: Runaghan, P. *Fr Nugent's Liverpool.* (Countyvise, 2003). p.33. For more detail see Hope University Library. Nugent archive. NCA 068. The Clarence.

37. *Liverpool Catholic Herald,* 8 August 1908.

38. Library of Liverpool Hope University. Father Berry's Homes. Annual Reports and balance sheets, 1892-1904. Balance sheet 1892.

39. *The Tablet,* 13 January 1894.

40. Annual Reports of the Catholic Children's Protection Society (1884), p.1.

41. For discussion of this issue see: O'Tuathaigh M.A.G. *The Irish in Nineteenth-century Britain: Problems of Integration. In the Irish in the Victorian City.* Swift and Gilley eds, p.13. ff.

CHAPTER EIGHT

THE IRISH NATIONALIST PARTY

1. Burke. Op cit. p.80.

2. Waller, P.J. *Democracy and Sectarianism. A Political and Social History of Liverpool, 1868-1939.* Liverpool University Press, 1981. p.29.

3. Burke. Op cit. p.209.

4. Waller. Op cit. p.30.

5. O'Connell, B. *The Irish Nationalist Party in Liverpool 1873-1922.* Unpublished MA thesis. University of Liverpool, 1971. p.179.

6. Ibid. p.45.

7. Ibid. p.46.

8. *Liverpool Daily Post,* 29 November 1879.

9. Rathbone, E.F. *William Rathbone: A Memoir,*1905. p.308.

10. O'Meara. Op cit. p.50.

11. O'Connell. Op cit. p.56.

12. Ibid. p.82.

13. Waller. Op cit. p.39.

14. Burke. Op cit. p.244.

15. Belchem. Op cit. p.142.

16. *Daily Post*, 11 November 1885.

17. *The Times*, 22 September 1885.

18. *The Porcupine*: quoted in Waller, Op cit. p.513.

19. O'Connell, B. *The Irish Nationalist Party in Liverpool*. Op cit. p.65.

20. Ibid. p.67.

21. *Daily Post*, 24 November 1890.

22. *Daily Post*, 29 October 1882.

23. Waller. Op cit. p.141.

24. *Liverpool Courier*, 29 October 1895.

25. Waller. Op cit. p.161.

26. Waller. Ibid. p.141.

27. O'Connell. Op cit. pp.75-79.

28. *Liverpool Mercury*, 28 November 1898.

29. Belchem. Op cit. p.145.

30. Belchem. Ibid. p.146.

31. Brady, L.W. *T.P. O'Connor and the Liverpool Irish*. p.151.

32. O'Connell. Op cit. p.75.

33. For a biographical summary see Appendix One.

34. Belchem. Op cit. p.150.

35. *Liverpool Catholic Herald*, 9 August 1901.

36. O'Connell. Op cit. p.84.

37. Waller. Op cit. p.136.

38. Waller. Op cit. p.217.

39. Sexton, J. *Sir James Sexton, Agitator. The Life Story of the Docker's MP.* (1936). p.204.

40. Waller. Op cit. p.234.

41. Sexton. Op cit. p.204.

42. Waller. Op cit. p.234.

43. O'Connell. Op cit. p.48.

44. *Liverpool Catholic Herald*, 15 January 1910.

45. *Liverpool Catholic Herald*, Friday 14 April 1905.

CHAPTER NINE
IRISH REVOLUTIONARIES

1. Moore, Kevin, in Belchem (ed) *Popular Politics Riot and Labour*. Ch.3. This whig and Tory ridden town. Page 49 discusses the amount of repeal rent collected in Liverpool.

2. Belchem, J. (ed) *Popular Politics Riot and Labour*. Ch.4. p.72.

3. Ibid. p.70.

4. Ibid. p.96.

5. Ibid. p.87.

6. Ibid. p.88.

7. Ibid. p.96.

8. Ibid. p.94.

9. Belchem, J. *Irish Catholic and Scouse.* Op cit. p.163. His burial in Glasnevin, Dublin, though opposed by Cardinal Cullen, attracted large crowds.

10. HO. 45/7799. 1. Letter from Mayor, 26 September 1865.

11. PP. 1864 XXXV. pp.585-7.

12. PRO. HO. 45. Nos/7799/135. McHale to Inspector General, 18 October 1866.

13. HO. 45/7799 p.893.

14. HO. 45/7799. p.1453.

15. Frank, Neal. Op cit. p.180.

16. *The Times*, 18 May 1881.

CHAPTER TEN
PERSISTING SECTARIANISM

1. Burke. *Catholic History of Liverpool*, p.132.

2. Ibid. p.140.

3. Ibid. p.229.

4. *Liverpool Mercury*, 18 October 1862.

5. Burke. Op cit. p.181.

6. *Liverpool Mercury*, 27 April 1868.

7. Waller. Op cit. p.16.

8. Waller. Ibid. p.63.

9. *Liverpool Courier*, 25 May 1893.

10. Waller. Op cit. p.141.

11. Waller. Ibid. p.140.

12. See for example *Liverpool Weekly Albion*, 17 July 1886.

13. *Liverpool Daily Post*, 8 April 1901.

14. *Liverpool Daily Post*, 27 May 1901.

15. Neal. Op cit. p.208.

16. Ibid. p.209.

17. *Liverpool Echo*. 10, 13, 15, 17, November and 8, 9, 10, 11 and 12, December 1902.

18. Neal. Op cit. p.215.

19. Ibid. p.217.

20. Ibid. p.225.

21. HO 144/1050/186261, Report of Inquiry Commissioner, under the Police (Liverpool Inquiry) Act, 1909. Q.11937-54.

22. Ibid. Q.1402-3.

23. Neal. Op cit. p.226.

24. HO 144/1050/186261, Report of Inquiry Commissioner, under the Police (Liverpool Inquiry) Act, 1909. p.3.

25. HO. 144/1050/186261. Op cit. p.14.

26. Neal. Op cit. p.230.

27. Ibid. p.231.

28. *Liverpool Daily Post*, 23 June 1909.

29. Ibid.

30. HO. 144/1050/186261, Report of Inquiry Commissioner. Op cit. Q.9815. ff.

31. Ibid. 20180-405.

32. HO. 144/1050/186261 Report of Inquiry Commissioner. Op cit. p.81.

33. Neal. Op cit. p.232.

34. HO. 144/1050/186261, Report of Inquiry Commissioner Police (Liverpool Inquiry) Act 1909. Report by Arthur Ashton.

35. Ibid. p.66.

36. Ibid. p.67.

37. Neal. Op cit. p.238.

38. HO. 144/1050/186261. Op cit. p.61.

39. Ibid. p.63.

40. Ibid. p.67.

41. Ibid. p.67.

CHAPTER ELEVEN

THE IRISH ON THE LIVERPOOL DOCKS

1. Larkin, E. *James Larkin. Irish Labour Leader.1876-1947.* (Pluto, 1989). p.4.

2. For description of dock occupations see Towers, Brian, *Waterfront Blues.* (Carnegie, 2011). pp.101-104.

3. Towers, Brian. Op cit. p.105. Also Taplin, *The Dockers' Union.* (Leicester University Press, 1985). p.21.

4. Towers. Op cit. p.104.

5. Ibid. p.109.

6. Taplin. Op cit. p.51.

7. Towers. Op cit. p.70.

8. Rathbone, E. Report on the results of a Special Inquiry into the conditions of Labour at the Liverpool Docks, 1905. Transitions of the Liverpool Economic and Statistical Society, 1903-04. p.20.

9. The desperate situation of casual dock workers was highlighted by a number of authors, including Mayhew in *London Labour and London Poor,* and Charles Booth in *Life and Labour in the East End of London.* See Mayhew in *London Labour and London poor.* p.259. ff.

10. Towers. Op cit. p.118. ff.

11. Ibid. p.121.

12. Taplin. *The Dockers Union.* Op cit. p.25.

13. McCarthy, T. *The Great Dock Strike,* 1889.

14. Taplin, E. *The Liverpool Tramways Agitation of 1889.* Hikins Ed. *Building the Union* pp.55-76.

15. Waller. Op cit. pp.102-103.

16. Bean. *The Liverpool Dock Strike of 1890.* p.60.

17. Taplin. Op cit. p.14.

18. Larkin. Op cit. p.10.

19. *Liverpool Weekly Courier,* 1 June 1905.

20. Taplin. Op cit. p.70.

21. Larkin, E. Op cit. p.61.

22. Ibid. p.12.

23. Taplin. Op cit. p.98. Eleanor Rathbone found that whilst a dock labourer might expect to take home about £60 per annum, a lower middle class clerk had an income of around £300.

24. Taplin. p.87.

25. Ibid. p.85.

26. Ibid. p.93.

27. Davies, S. *A Stormy Political Career. P.J. Kelly and Irish Nationalist and Labour Politics in Liverpool, 1891-1936.* p.162. ff.

28. Taplin. Op cit. p.28.

29. Ibid. p.97.

30. McCarthy, T. Op cit. pp.201-2.

31. Belchem. *Irish, Catholic and Scouse.* Op cit. p.50.

32. Milligan. Article in *Liverpool Catholic Herald,* 18 October 1913.

33. O'Mara. Op cit. p.40.

34. Taplin. Op cit. p.111.

CHAPTER TWELVE

ISOLATION OR INTEGRATION?

1. Pinkman, J.A. *In the Legion of the Vanguard.* Maguire, (Ed). (Mercier Press, 1998). p.13.

2. Steele, E.D. *The Irish Presence in the North of England.* (Northern History, Vol.12). p.224.

3. O'Tuathaigh, M.A.G. *The Irish in Nineteenth Century Britain: Problems of Integration.* In , *The Irish in the Victorian City.* Swift and Gilley, (Eds). p.13.

4. Royal Commission on Children's Employment, PP. 1863, XVII. p.447. Evidence of George Evans.

5. Steele, E.D. Op cit. p.226.

6. *Liverpool Herald,* 17 November 1855.

7. O'Tuathaigh. Op cit. p.23.

8. Curtis, L. *Nothing But The Same Old Story.* (Information on Ireland, 1984). pp.57-64.

9. Ibid. pp.59, 60.

10. O'Tuathaigh. Op cit. p.21.

11. Curtis. Op cit. p.51.

12. Curtis, L.P. *Anglo-Saxons and Celts. A Study of Anti-Irish Prejudice in Victorian England.* (USA Conf of British Studies, Connecticut, 1968). p70.

CHAPTER THIRTEEN

IRISH INDEPENDENCE AND AFTERMATH

1. *Liverpool Catholic Herald,* 20 March 1915.

2. Whitting Jones, Barbara. *Liverpool Politics,* 1936. p.128.

3. *Liverpool Catholic Herald,* 20 March 1915.

4. Brady, L.W. *T.P. O'Connor and the Liverpool Irish.* (Royal Historical Siciety, 1983). p.223.

5. Fitzsimons, Jim. *A Personal History of the 8th Irish Battalion: The King's Liverpool Regiment.* (Liverpool Starfish Multimedia, 2002).

6. *Liverpool Catholic Herald,* 10 February 1917.

7. *Liverpool Catholic Herald,* 24 March 1917.

8. *Liverpool Catholic Herald,* 17 November 1917.

9. *Liverpool Catholic Herald,* 31 July 1915.

10. Birtill, T.A. *Hidden History. Irish in Liverpool.* Op cit. p.58.

11. See: http://www.bureauofmilitary history.ie/reels/bmh/BMH.WS0367.p df p.8. Also Craven, T.A. *Narrative of the Six Days Defence of the Irish Republic.* p.3.

12. Ibid. p.4.

13. Irish Bureau of Military History. Witness Statement 497. p.7. Eamonn Bulfin.

14. Brady, L.W. *T.P. O'Connor and the Liverpool Irish.* p.226.

15. Fielding, S. *Class and Ethnicity. Irish Catholics in England.* OUP, 1993 p.102.

16. Pinkman, J. Op cit. p.22.

17. Ibid. p.108-109. See also, Belchem. Op cit. p.265.

18. University College Dublin (UCD) Archives. Michael Collins Correspondence. Liverpool. 57. Tom Craven to Michael Collins. 25 May 1919.

19. See: http://www.bureauofmilitary history.ie/reels/bmh/BMH.WS0797.p df p.37.

20. UCD archives. Op cit. Collins to Lanigan, 23 July 1919.

21. Pinkman. Op cit. p.33.

22. Ibid. p.21.

23. See: http://www.bureauofmilitaryhistory. ie/reels/bmh/BMH.WS0797.pdf

24. Pinkman. Op cit. p.34.

25. Ibid. p.33.

26. Ibid p.40.

27. Ibid. p.42.

28. Belchem. Op cit. p.273.

29. Pinkman. Op cit. p.28.

30. *The Times.* 21 February 1921.

31. Pinkman. Op cit. p.53.

32. UCD. Mulcahy Papers P7/A/29 Dept of Engineering report on visit to Britain, September 1921.

33. McCready, Sir N. *Annals of an Active Life,* 1924. p.411.

34. Belchem. Op cit. p.282.

35. Davies, S. Op cit. p.172.

36. Ibid. p.173.

37. *Liverpool Courier*, 12 April 1920.

38. *Liverpool Daily Post*, April 1937.

39. Davies. Op cit. p.170.

40. Belchem. Op cit. p.279.

41. Evans, B. *Fear and Loathing in Liverpool: The IRA's 1939 Bombing Campaign on Merseyside.* Published in Transactions of the Lancashire and Cheshire Historical Society, Volume 162, 2013.

CHAPTER FOURTEEN
FROM NATIONALISM TO LABOUR

1. Belchem. Op cit. p.260.

2. Waller. Op cit. p.298.

3. Ibid. p.231.

4. Belchem. Op cit. p.260.

5. Waller. Op cit. p.285.

6. *Liverpool Catholic Herald*, 2 February 1918.

7. Belchem. Op cit. p.291.

8. Hachey, T.E. *British and Irish Separatism in Liverpool.*

9. Waller. Op cit. p.234.

10. Waller. Op cit. p.285.

11. Belchem. Op cit. p.291.

12. Waller. Op cit. p.293.

13. *Liverpool Daily Post.* 3 July 1924. Davies, S. Op cit. p.176.

14. *Liverpool Catholic Herald*, 11 February 1922.

15. *Liverpool Catholic Herald*, 14 November 1925.

16. *The Times.* 8 March 1928.

17. Davies. Op cit. p.163.

18. Davies. Op cit. p.162.

19. Ibid. p.166.

20. Waller. p.284.

21. Ibid. p.285.

22. Ibid. p.284.

23. Deegan F. *There's No Other Way.* p.6.

24. Ibid. p.7.

25. Waller. Op cit. p.324.

26. Bevins R. *The Greasy Pole. A Personal Account of the Realities of British Politics.* (Hodder and Stoughton, 1965). pp.12-14.

27. Waller. Op cit. p.324.

28. Ibid. p.325.

29. Ibid. p.324.

30. Davies. Op cit. p.180.

31. *Liverpool Catholic Herald*, 11 February 1922.

32. See material in HO 45/14634.

33. Priestly, J.B. *English Journey.* (London, 1994). pp.249-284.

34. Parker. H.A. *Study of Migration to Merseyside with Special Reference to Irish Immigration.* 1931. Quoted in Belchem. Op cit. pp.304-5.

35. Gair. G.R. *The Irish Immigration Question.* 1-3, *Liverpool Review,* Jan-Mar 1934.

36. *Liverpolitan, Between Ourselves.* June 1938.

37. *Liverpolitan, Between Ourselves.* January 1936.

38. 'The Irish in Liverpool', Liverpool Diocesan Review, April 1937.

39. *Liverpool Daily Post.* 19 January 1939.

40. Toole, H. *Mrs Bessie Braddock, MP. A Biography.* 1957. p.56.

41. Waller. Op cit. p.339.

42. Ibid. p.326.

CHAPTER FIFTEEN
COMMUNITY LIFE IN INTER-WAR YEARS

1. Doyle. *Mitres and Missions.* Op cit. p.152.

2. Boyce, F. *Irish Catholic or Scouse?* Unpublished essay. A copy of this essay can be accessed for academic purposes at the McLua Library at the Institute of Irish Studies, University of Liverpool.

3. *Scottie Road. A City Within a City.* (Trinity Mirror). p.34.

4. Waller. Op cit. p.288.

5. Belchem. Op cit. p.321.

6. Waller. Op cit. p 342.

CHAPTER SIXTEEN
AFTER 1945

1. A record of these interviews entitled *In Hardship and Hope interviews,* Quiery, G. 2017. can be accessed for academic purposes at the McLua library, Institute of Irish Studies, University of Liverpool.

2. Newsletter article accessible at Liverpool Comhaltas files in wordpress.com

3. McManus, Kevin. *Ceilis, Jigs and Ballads.* IPM. p.19.

4. Walsh, T. Interview conducted in 2007. See *In Hardship and Hope interviews.* Op cit.

5. Dr Kevin McNamara (1934-2017) was born in Bootle, was Labour MP for Hull North (1966-2005) and Labour Shadow Northern Ireland Secretary (1987-94).

6. Waller. Op cit. p.302.

CHAPTER SEVENTEEN
NEW COMMUNITIES

1. The quotations in this chapter are from interviews referred to earlier, in the document entitled *In Hardship and Hope – interviews, Quiery, G. 2017*, which can be accessed for academic purposes at the McLua Library, Institute of Irish Studies, University of Liverpool.

2. Waller, Op cit. p.352.

3. Liverpool Metropolitan Cathedral. Archive. Parish Box 161.

4. Ibid. Box 193.

5. Interview conducted with Tommy Walsh, 2007, included in *In Hardship and Hope – interviews.* Op cit.

6. Walsh, T. *Being Irish in Liverpool.* p.91. ff.

7. Doyle. Op cit. p.335.

8. Stanford, P. *The New Review, The Observer,* 6 August 2017.

9. Roberts, Keith Daniel. *Liverpool Sectarianism. The Rise and Demise.* (LUP 2017).

10. Ibid. p.290.

11. Ibid. p.291.

12. *Irish Post,* 27 January 1996.

13. Ibid. p.292.

14. Roberts. Op cit. Chapter 7.

BIBLIOGRAPHY

Secondary Sources

Aughton, P. *Liverpool: A People's History*. (Carnegie Publishing Ltd, 2008).

Bean, R. *The Liverpool Dock Strike of 1890*. (AO-L).

Beckett, J.C. *The Making of Modern Ireland 1603-1923*. (Faber and Faber, 1981).

Belchem, J. *Irish Catholic and Scouse:The History of the Liverpool-Irish,1800-1939.* (LUP, 2007).

Belchem, J. (Ed). *Popular Politics, Riot and Labour*. (LUP, 1992).

Bennett, Canon J. *Father Nugent of Liverpool*. (L.C.C.P.S. 1974).

Berresford Ellis, P. *A History of the Irish Working Class*. (Pluto, 2007).

Birtill, T. *A Hidden History. Irish in Liverpool. An Ghaeilge I Learpholl*. (Liverpool Authors, 2013).

Brady, L.W. *T.P. O'Connor and the Liverpool Irish*. (Royal Historical Society, 1983).

Burke, T.A. *The Catholic History of Liverpool*. (1910).

Chandler, G. *Liverpool*. (Batsford, 1957).

Coleman, T. *Passage to America*. (Hutchinson, 1972).

Curtis, L. *Nothing but the Same Old Story*. (Information on Ireland, 1984).

Doyle, P. *Mitres and Missions in Lancashire*. (Bluecoat Press, 2005).

Fielding, S. *Class and Ethnicity: Irish Catholics in England, 1880-1939*. (OUP, 1993).

Fitzsimons, Jim. *A Personal History of the 8th Irish Battalion: The King's Liverpool Regiment*. (Liverpool Starfish Multimedia, 2002).

Frazer, W.M. *Duncan of Liverpool*. (Carnegie Publishing , 1997).

Furnival. J. *Children of the Second Spring*. (Gracewing, 2006).

Hachey, T.E. *Britain and Irish Separatism: From the Fenians to the Free State, 1867-1922*. (Catholic University of America Press, 1984).

Hikins, H. (Ed). *The Liverpool Tramways Agitation of 1889*. (Toulouse Press).

Hikins, H. *Strike – 1911*. (Toulouse Press, 1980).

Howley, F. *Slavers, Traders and Privateers*. (Countyvise, 2008).

Hunter, B. *They Knew Why They Fought: Unofficial Struggles and Leadership on the Docks, 1945-1989*. (Index Books, 1994).

Jackson, J.A. *The Irish in Britain*. (Routledge and Paul, 1963).

Kelly, M. *Liverpool's Irish Connection*. (AJH Publishing, 2006).

Kelly, M. *Mothers of the City*. (AJH Publishing, 2007).

Larkin, E. *James Larkin: Irish Labour Leader, 1876-1947*. (Pluto Press, 1989).

Lowe, W.J. *The Irish in Mid-Victorian Lancashire: The Shaping of a Working Class Community*. (Lang, 1989).

MacRaild, D.M. *Irish Migrants in Modern Britain, 1750-1922.* (Palgrave, 1999).

Mayhew, H. *London Labour and the London Poor, Vol. IV*. (Dover, 1968).

McCarthy, T. *The Great Dock Strike 1889*. (Weidenfeld and Nicolson, 1988).

Muir, R. *A History of Liverpool*. (1907, Republished by LUP).

Murphy, J. *The Religious Problem in English Education*. (LUP, 1959).

Neal, F. *Sectarian Violence: The Liverpool Experience, 1819-1914*. (MUP, 1998).

O'Brien, R.B. *The Life of Charles Stewart Parnell, 1846-1891*. (Harper, 1898).

Rathbone E. *Report on the results of a Special Inquiry into the conditions of Labour at the Liverpool Docks*. (1905).

Runaghan P. *Father Nugent's Liverpool*. (Countyvise, 2003).

Sexton, J. *Sir James Sexton, Agitator. The Life of the Dockers MP: An Autobiography*. (Faber and Faber, 1936).

Simey, M. *Charity Rediscovered: A Study of Philanthropic Effort in Nineteenth-century Liverpool*. (LUP, 1992).

Stephen, L. *Dictionary of National Biography 7. Brown, William (1784-1864)*. (Smith, Elder).

Swift, R. (Ed). and Gilley, S. (Eds). *The Irish in the Victorian City*. (Croom Helm, 1985).

Swift, R. *Irish Migrants in Britain: a Documentary History*. (Cork University Press, 2002).

Taplin, E. *The Dockers' Union: A Study of the National Union of Dock Labourers, 1889-1922*. (Leicester University Press, 1985).

Towers, B. *Waterfront Blues: The Rise and Fall of Liverpool's Dockland*. (Carnegie, 2011).

Troughton, T. *The History of Liverpool from the Earliest Authenticated Period Down to the Present Time*. Liverpool, 1810.

Waller, P.J. *Democracy and Sectarianism*. (LUP, 1981).

Whittingham-Jones, B. *The Pedigree of Liverpool Politics: White, Orange and Green*. (1936).

Wilcox. A. *Living in Liverpool: A Collection of Sources for Family, Local and Social Historians*. (Cambridge Scholars, 2011).

Woodham-Smith, C. *The Great Hunger*. (Old Town Books, 1989).

Contemporary Accounts

Bevins, R. *The Greasy Pole*. London, 1965.

Craven, T. *A Narrative of the Six Days Defence of the Irish Republic*. (Liverpool 1916 Commemoration Committee, 2016).

Deegan, F. *There's No Other Way*. (Toulouse Press, 1980).

Denvir, J. *The Life Story of an Old Rebel*. 1910. Reprinted1972. Republished at Gutenberg.org 2005.

Denvir, J. *The Irish in Britain*. 1892. Reprint 1982.

Duncan, W.H. *First Annual Report of the Medical Officer of Health*.

Finch, J. *Statistics of Vauxhall Ward, Liverpool compiled by John Finch. Facsimile reprint prepared and introduced by Harold Hikins, The Condition of the Working Class in Liverpool in 1842*. (Toulouse Press, 1986).

Hume, A. *Missions at Home, or a Clergyman's Account of a Portion of the Town of Liverpool*.

Hume, A. *Condition of Liverpool, Religious and Social*. Liverpool, 1858.

Lowndes, F.D. *Prostitution and Venereal Disease in Liverpool*. London, 1886.

McCarthy, J. *Story of an Irishman*. London, 1904.

Macready, Sir N. *Annals of an Active Life*. see: https://archive.org/details/in. ernet. dli.2015.536843

McGrath, T.F. *History of the Ancient Order of Hibernians*. Cleveland, Ohio, 1898.

O'Mara. P. *The Autobiography of a Liverpool Irish Slummy*. London, 1934.

Pinkman, J.A. *In the Legion of the Vanguard*. Edited by F.E. Maguire. (Mercier Press, 1998).

Priestley, J.B. *English Journey*. London, 1994.

Rathbone, E.F. *William Rathbone*. 1906.

Salvidge, S. *Salvidge of Liverpool: Behind the Political Scene*. 1934.

Sykes, A.H. *Squalid Liverpool*. Liverpool, 1883.

Shimmin, H. *Liverpool Life, its Pleasures Practices and Pastimes*. Liverpool Mercury, 1856.

Trevelyan, C.E. *The Liverpool Corporation School: No Popery Agitation*. 1840.

Walsh, T. *Being Irish in Liverpool*. (St Michael's Irish Centre, Liverpool).

Whitty, M.J. *A Proposal for Diminishing Crime Misery and Poverty in Liverpool*. 1865.

Essays

Belchem, J. (Ed). *Merseypride: Essays in Liverpool Exceptionalism*. (LUP, 2000).

Boyce, F. *City of Storytellers, in Merseyside Culture and Place*. Edited by Mike Benbough-Jackson and Sam Davies. (CSP 2011).

Curtis, L.P. *Anglo-Saxons and Celts: A study of anti-Irish prejudice in Victorian England*. (USA Conf of British Studies, Connecticut, 1968).

Davies, S. *A Stormy Political Career: P.J. Kelly and Irish Nationalist and Labour Politics in Liverpool, 1891-1936*. Transactions of the Historical Society of Lancashire and Cheshire (THSLC). Vol.148. (1999-2000).

Evans, B. *Fear and Loathing in Liverpool: The IRA's 1939 Bombing Campaign on Merseyside*. THSLC. Vol. 162. (2013).

Lasek, J.A. *Liverpool and the 1851 Census of Religious Worship.* University of Liverpool Geographic Society Journal.

Lowe, W.J. *The Lancashire Irish and the Catholic Church 1846-71.* Irish Historical Studies, 20. 1976.

Moore, K. in Belchem (Ed) *Popular Politics Riot and Labour. Ch..3. This Whig and Tory-ridden Town.*

Neal, F. *The Birkenhead Garibaldi Riots.* THSLC, Vol. 131. 1982. p.87. ff.

Neal, F. *A Criminal Profile of the Liverpool Irish.* THSLC, Vol. 140. 1991. p.161.

O'Tuathaigh, M.A.G. *The Irish in Nineteenth-century Britain: Problems of Integration.* In *The Irish in the Victorian City.* Swift and Gilley eds. (Croom Helm, 1985).

Parker, H. *A Study of Migration to Merseyside: With Special Reference to Irish Immigration.* University of Liverpool, 1931. The Social Survey of Merseyside No.2.

Power, M.J. *The Growth of Liverpool.* In *Popular Politics, Riot and Labour: Essays in Liverpool History, 1790-1940.* Belchem, J. (Ed). (LUP, 1992).

Samuel, R. *The Roman Catholic Church and the Irish Poor.* In *The Irish in the Victorian City.* Swift and Gilley, (Eds). (Croom Helm, 1985).

Swift, R. *The Outcast Irish in the British Victorian City: Problems and Perspectives.* Irish Historical Studies. Vol.25, No.99 (May 1987). pp.264-276.

Lowe, W.J. *Lancashire Fenianism 1864-71.* THSLC. Vol. 126. 1976. p.156.

Steele, E.D. *The Irish presence in the North of England 1850-1914.* (Northern History, 1976).

Parliamentary Papers

Royal Commission on Children's Employment. PP 1863 XVII.

Royal Commission on the Conditions of the Poorer Classes in Ireland: Appendix G. Report on the State of the Irish Poor in Great Britain. PP 1836 XXXIV.

Proceeds of the Committee on the Passengers Act. 1851.

Select Committee on Emigrant Ships.(1854) BPP. Commons 1854.

Select Committee on the protection of young girls. PP 1882 (344) XIII.

Select Committee on Railway Labourers. 1846 BPP XIII.

Select Committee on Intemperance. Third Report. Minutes of Evidence. PP 1877 (418) Vol XI.

Select Committee on Settlement and Poor Removal. British Parliamentary Papers (Commons) 1847.

Kew National Archives

HO 45/184 Ribbonism 1841.

HO 45/7799 Fenianism. 1. Letter from Mayor 26 September 1865.

HO 45/9339/21762 Precautionary stationing of troops.

HO 45/11032/423878 Disturbances. Liverpool Unemployment Riots.

HO 45/9604/A1370 Explosives. Protection of Mersey Powder Hulks.

HO 144/704/107039 Disturbances. Anti-Catholic Disturbances at Liverpool. Imprisonment of Pastor George Wise.

HO 144/1044/184061 Disturbances. Sectarian Disturbances in Liverpool,1911.

HO 144/1050/186261 Report of Inquiry Commissioner, under the Police (Liverpool Enquiry) Act 1909.

Liverpool Public Record Office

Liverpool Borough Prisons. Prison Minister's Report. Liverpool Council Proceedings 1866.

Liverpool Mortality sub-committee. Report and evidence, 1866.

Report of Liverpool Chief Constable, 16 February 1847.

Report Liverpool Inquiry, 1910.

Report of Medical Officer of Health, 1847.

352 CLE /CUT1 Liverpool Corporation: Town Clerk's Newscuttings 1867-1967.

361 VIN Society of T Vincent De Paul: Conference of St Mary's Highfield Street. 1868-77.

Unpublished PhD Theses

Kanya-Forstner, M. *The Politics of Survival: Irish women in Outcast Liverpool 1859-1890.* Unpublished PhD thesis. University of Liverpool, 1997.

Klapas, J.A. *Geographical Aspects of Religious Changes in Victorian Liverpool. 1837-1901.* Unpublished MA thesis. University of Liverpool, 1977.

Letford, Lynda. *Irish and Non-Irish Women Living in Households in Nineteenth-century Liverpool: Issues of Class, Gender and Birthplace*. Unpublished PhD thesis. University of Lancaster, 1996.

O'Connell, B. *The Irish Nationalist Party in Liverpool 1873-1922*. Unpublished MA thesis. University of Liverpool, 1971.

Papworth, J.D. *The Irish in Liverpool 1835-71: Segregation and Dispersal*. Unpublished PhD thesis. University of Liverpool, 1971.

Taylor, I. *Black Spot on the Mersey*. Unpublished PhD thesis. University of Liverpool, 1976.

Other

Annual reports of the Catholic Children's Protection Society (1884).

Gore's Directory.

Irish Bureau of Military History.

Liverpool Albion.

Liverpool Catholic Herald.

Liverpool Daily Post.

Liverpool Mail.

Liverpool Mercury.

Melville, H. *Redburn: His first voyage.*

Metropolitan Cathedral Archive, Liverpool.

The Porcupine.

Library of Liverpool Hope University.

University College Dublin. Mulcahy Papers P7/A/29.

On-line sources

http://www.brad.ac.uk/acad/diaspora/guides/brit.shtml

For material related to Irish settlement in Britain, see: http://www.movinghere.org.uk/galleries/histories/irish/settling/settling.htm

For a brief introduction to the history of Liverpool, see: http://www.local histories.org/liverpool.html

http://www.liverpoolinpictures.com/History_of_Liverpool.htm

For photographs of Liverpool courts and other dwellings, health issues and local history: http://www.mersey-gateway.org/server.php?show=nav.001

BIOGRAPHICAL NOTES

Archdeacon, George Active in O'Connell's repeal movement in Liverpool and Manchester. Was a repeal warden, until expelled for advocating physical force. Later joined the Fenians.

Béaslaí, Piaras (1881-1965) (Percy Beasley) Born Liverpool. Educated at St Francis Xavier. Joined Gaelic League. Fluent Irish speaker. Left for Ireland where he worked with Richard Mulcahy and Padraic Pearse in Gaelic League. Founder member of Irish Volunteers. Fought in both the Rising and the War of Independence. Helped facilitate a mass escape of rebels from prison in Manchester. Director of publicity for IRA. Elected to Dail Eireann (the Irish parliament). Took the pro-Treaty side. Recounted his experiences in *Michael Collins and the Making of a New Ireland* (Dublin.1926).

Beavan, Margaret (1876-1913) Born Liverpool. First woman to be Mayor. Pioneer of Child Welfare Association. Founded Liverpool Open Air Hospital. Elected as councillor for Liberals in 1920s, later switching to Conservatives.

Berry, Father John Catholic clergyman, who was rector of St Philip Neri, Catharine Street. 1892: Opened refuge for boys off Williamson Square. 1894: Opened night shelter for boys sleeping rough who could not afford basic accommodation.

Bligh, Dr Alexander (1834-1922) Born Galway. Educated Galway, Dublin and London. Qualified as doctor. General practitioner for many years in Liverpool. Irish language activist. Founder of Irish Home Rule movement in Liverpool. 1876-1902: Nationalist councillor.

Bligh, Dr John Born Tuam, Co Galway. Educated, Galway. Active in Liverpool mid-Nineteenth Century. Medical practitioner. Lived at 117 Mount Pleasant. President of Abercromby Branch of Irish National League. Irish language activist.

Borthwick, Norma (1862-1934) Born Bebington, Wirral. An artist and Irish speaker. Leading member of Gaelic revival, and Gaelic League, serving on the executive. Won prize for her essay in Irish. Taught Irish to Lady Gregory. Buried on Skye.

Braddock, Elizabeth (Bessie) Margaret (née Bamber) (1899-1970) From 1920 was member of ILP and then Communist Party. 1924: Joined Labour Party. MP Liverpool Exchange. 1945-70: Council member. 1930-61: Forthright campaigner on housing, health and other social issues. Strongly opposed to sectarianism. Frequently conducted election meetings in Protestant heartland of Everton where she was threatened by crowds. Opposed strong Catholic Nationalist influence on Labour. Opposed purchase of Cathedral site, calling for 'more homes, not priests'. Campaigned for slum clearance.

Braddock, John Known as Jack. (1893-1963) Born Hanley. Moved to Liverpool 1915. Wagon repairer, insurance agent. Had extended period of unemployment. 1922-24: Active Communist Party member. From 1929: Labour councillor, Everton. 1935: Deputy Leader Liverpool Labour Party. From 1948: Leader. 1922: Married Bessie Bamber.

Brown, Sir William (1st Baronet) (1784-1864)
Born Ballymena, Co Antrim. Member of Parliament, merchant and banker. Arrived in Liverpool from United States in 1809. Dealer in linen and cotton. Soon developed the business into one of general trade and finally banking. Brown became one of the leaders in Liverpool commerce. In 1860 he gave Liverpool the William Brown Library at a cost of over £42,000. Buried Childwall, Liverpool.

Browne, Edward (1825-98) Born Co Meath. Became a prosperous corn merchant. Liberal Unionist. 1870-79: Catholic member of School Board.

Burke, Thomas (1865-1943) Born Connemara. Nationalist councillor, Vauxhall ward 1899-1921. Specialised in education matters. Alderman. Kept poultry stall in St John's Market. Active in Irish Language and Ancient Order of Hibernians. Author of *The Catholic History of Liverpool.*

Butler, Josephine Elizabeth (née Grey) (1828-1906) Feminist and social reformer who was especially concerned with the welfare of prostitutes. Evangelical Anglican. Led the long campaign for the repeal of the Contagious Diseases Acts both in Britain and internationally from 1869 to 1886. The acts harmed and unfairly imprisoned young women who were suspected of being prostitutes. Repealed 1886.

Byrne, Patrick (1850-90) Known as Dandy Pat. Born Wexford. 1863: Came to Liverpool. Worked as a docker at first but later became a successful businessman running pubs, the best known being the Morning Star, Scotland Road, and the Tatlock. 1883: First elected as councillor for brief period. 1885: Elected Nationalist councillor for Scotland Ward. Generous to employees, schools and Catholic charities. Took up the cause of low pay of scavengers, who emptied the waste from poor housing. Suffered from sectarian beatings. The remains of the monument erected in his memory at Scotland Place now stand behind St. Anthony's Church, Scotland Road. Buried St Aidan's, Wexford.

Cain, Robert (1826-1907) Born Spike Island, Co Cork. Father a soldier. Family moved to Liverpool around 1828 to live in Islington. 1848: Began brewing on Limekiln Lane, Scotland Road district. 1858: Moved to larger operation, Stanhope Street. 1900: Constructed the red brick brewery in Grafton Street. Built the iconic pubs The Philharmonic and The Vines. Property developer who became one of Britain's richest men. Strong supporter of the Conservative Party, especially in elections in Toxteth.

Carling, James William (1857-87) Born 38 Addison Street, Liverpool, to Irish mother. Family thought to possibly be descendants of Turlough O'Carolan, harper and Ireland's national composer. He became a pavement artist known as 'The Little Chalker'. Went to America in 1871. Successful artist whose illustrations for Edgar Allen Poe's work, though not used by Poe, are in Museum of Richmond. Returned to Liverpool 1887. Buried in Walton. The James Carling International Pavement Art Competition has taken place on Bold Street, the very street where, in his own lifetime, he was forbidden to work.

Chadwick, Edwin Compiled *The Sanitary Report, 1842*, following a detailed investigation into conditions in Liverpool, relating lack of sanitation directly to disease, high mortality and low life expectancy. The Report sold 30,000 copies and formed the basis for the 1848 Public Health Act. Frederick Engels used material from the Report for his book *Condition of the Working Class in England* (1844).

Chambre Hardman, Edward (1898-1988) Born Leopardstown, Co Dublin. Military service with 8th Gurka rifles. Established photographic studio in Bold Street. His work is an important part of British photographic history. His residence at 59 Rodney Street is now a National Trust property.

Clancy, Joseph Hotel owner. Chair of Irish National League, St Anne's branch. Criticised Labour left as 'Socialist-Atheist'. 1924-25: Leader of the remaining Liberal-Catholic councillors who formed the Catholic Representation Association when most others joined Labour.

Commins, Andrew (1832-1916) Born Co Carlow. Barrister. Educated Queen's College, Cork and London University. 1870: Co-founder of Home Rule Confederation (HRC). 1875-76: President of HRC. 1876-92: Liverpool councillor. 1892-1913: Alderman. 1880-1900: Nationalist MP for various Irish constituencies. According to John Denvir: 'there was a general belief amongst Liverpool Irishmen that he knew *everything*'.

Connolly, Lawrence (1828-1903) Born Dublin. Came to Liverpool 1857. Fruit merchant. 1875: Challenged the hegemony of Catholic Club by standing as first Home Rule candidate and winning. Was a property developer in New Brighton, where he lived. Like so many Liverpool Irish Nationalist councillors, went on to a parliamentary career as MP for Longford South (1885-88). Retired through ill health.

Corbally, Christopher James (1802-88) Born Ireland. Member of the Catholic Club. 1857: Liberal councillor. Magistrate. Treasurer of Catholic Benevolent Society for 30 years. Treasurer of Catholic reformatory ship 'Clarence'. Buried Anfield cemetery.

Cotter, Joseph Born Liverpool, 1877. Irish father and English mother. Orphaned at age of two, worked as coal miner in his teens. Went to sea as a cook. Was a steward on Cunard's *Mauretania*, Founded Ship's Cooks and Stewards Union. Member of Liverpool Strike Committee, 1911. Vice President, Liverpool Trades Council, 1913. CBE (1920).

Crilly, Alfred (1840-85) Irish born journalist. Became first official leader of Irish Nationalist Party in Liverpool, 1873. Suffered from poor health.

Deegan, Frank (1910-92) Born Bootle. Father an Irish immigrant labourer. Active member Liverpool Unemployed Movement. Fought in International Brigade, Spanish Civil War, 1937. Published a memoir, *There's No Other Way*, 1980.

Denvir, John (1834-1916) Born in Bushmills, County Antrim. Moved to Liverpool in childhood. Managed and edited *The Catholic Times*, *The United Irishman*, and *The Nationalist*. He was prominent in the Fenians and later amongst Irish Nationalists in Liverpool. 1870: published *Denvir's Penny Library*, a series of books on Irish poetry, history and biography, and a pamphlet *The Catalpa*, in 1877, *The Irish in Britain* in 1892, and in 1910 his autobiography, *Life Story of an Old Rebel*.

Diamond, Charles (1858-1934) Born Derry, Ireland. Journalist and founder of 37 weekly newspapers. Founded *Liverpool Catholic Herald* in 1887. Remained editor until his death. 1920: arrested and charged with encouraging assassination in Ireland. Anti-Parnell Nationalist MP for Monaghan, 1892. Unsucccessful Labour candidate in 1918 and 1922 general elections. Well travelled, outspoken and controversial.

Doran, Felix Eighteenth century Liverpool merchant, born in Ireland. Lived in Lord Street. Partner in a slave ship called *The Bloom*. In a single voyage made a profit of £28,000 (equivalent to over £2 million in 2016) from selling 300 Africans as slaves.

Downey, Richard (1881-1953) Nick-named 'Dickie Downey'. Born Kilkenny. Educated St Edwards College, Liverpool. Archbishop of Liverpool, 1928-53. Presided at Thingwall rally on centenary of Catholic Emancipation in 1929, which an estimated 400,000 attended. Preached against 'the Godless soulless philosophy of Karl Marx.' Purchased the cathedral site, Brownlow Hill.

Duncan, William Henry (1805-63) Born Liverpool, to Scottish parents. Qualified from Edinburgh University. Following the Liverpool Sanitary Act of 1846, he was appointed Medical Officer of Health for Liverpool, the first appointment of its kind. Worked alongside Thomas Fresh, Inspector of Nuisances and James Newlands, Borough Engineer, to research and highlight the notorious living and sanitary conditions in Liverpool, and to implement measures to improve life in the city. His incisive and detailed annual reports are a rich source for historians. Buried in Westpark, Elgin.

Dunning, Leonard (1860-1941) Born London. Educated Eton and Oxford. 1888-95: District Inspector in the Royal Irish Constabulary. 1895-1902: Assistant Head Constable in Liverpool. 1902-1911: Head Constable. George Wise took a particular dislike to him, accusing him of anti-Protestant bias. Following the 1909 sectarian disturbances he remarked that 'life had been hell,' and that if he had realised the difficulties he would never have come to Liverpool. 1912-30: HM Inspector of Constabulary. 1917: Knighted.

Egerton, 'Ma' (1863-) Well known Dublin born Liverpool publican. Licensee of American Bar in Lime Street and Eagle in Pudsey Street, behind the Empire Theatre. Played a part in bringing Crippen to justice for murdering his wife.

Ewart, Louis Protestant preacher and anti-ritualist, who worked for the Kensit campaign in Liverpool, organising parades and outdoor meetings when the Kensits were absent. Took over the Kensit campaigns after 1904. His organisation was particularly strong in Garston.

Fletcher, Ralph (1757-1832) Born Bolton. Wealthy family. Father a coal merchant. 1797: Justice of the Peace. Colonel in Bolton Volunteers. Active opponent of worker combinations (trade unions). Was 'an inveterate Orangeman, and consequently illiberal in his religious feelings' (*Bolton Chronicle,* 1832). Was a driving force in establishing the Orange Order in Lancashire towns and military units during early nineteenth century, when first Orange marches were held in Liverpool.

Forwood, Arthur Bower (1836-98) Influential Liverpool Conservative. 1871: Elected to council. 1878: Mayor. 1885-98: MP for Ormskirk. Was effectively the leader of Liverpool Conservatives. 1880: Became chairman of the Liverpool Constitutional Association. Forthright in his views, was a populist, anti-Irish, who was willing to socialise across all classes in order to get the vote out. He was so long in local politics that when he was eventually elected to parliament he is said to have once addressed the Speaker of the House as 'Mister Mayor'. His position can be summed up as a one nation Tory: The Union, monarchy, empire and the Church. Merchant ship owner. His statue stands in St John's Gardens, Liverpool.

Gamble, Sir David (1823-1907) Irish Presbyterian who worked with James Muspratt, establishing chemical manufacturing (forerunner of Proctor and Gamble). Contributor to Irish Famine Relief Fund. 1903: Founder member of Liverpool Unionist Free Food League.

Garrett, George (1896-1966) Born Seacombe, Wirral. Father Orange Lodge Grand Master, mother Irish Republican Catholic. Lived in Park Lane district. Merchant seaman. Joined Wobblies in USA. Communist. Took part in 1922 Hunger March. Writer and dramatist. Founder member of Merseyside Left Theatre (forerunner of Unity). Work included account of unemployed workers struggle Liverpool 1921-22.

Gladstone, William Ewart (1809-98) Born Rodney Street, Liverpool into a wealthy establishment family. Became Prime Minister four times. Introduced Irish Home Rule Bill in 1886 and again in 1893, when it was heavily defeated in the House of Lords.

Goss, Alexander (1814-72) Born Ormskirk. English aristocracy. Educated Ushaw and Rome. 1856: Appointed Catholic Bishop of Liverpool. Opposed Home Rule. 1861: Supported Conservatives. Instructed Catholics not to attend 1867 Manchester Martyrs demonstration. Put much effort into schools.

Grogan, William (1871-1928) Nationalist councillor from 1920. Supported working class causes, then switched to Labour.

Hanley, James (1901-85) Probably born Liverpool into a seafaring Irish family. Grew up in Liverpool. Went to sea aged 14. First novel *Drift* (1930) followed by 48 other works including radio plays for BBC. Much of his work set in Irish Catholic Liverpool. His work is realist and often dark. Never accepted by literary establishment.

Harford, Austin (1863-1944) Cloth and woollen merchant, Richmond Street. 1899: Nationalist councillor. With brother Frank, broke Lynskey's hold of Nationalists. 1900: Challenged O'Connor for nomination, but withdrew following promises from party leadership nationally. 1907-24: Deputy Chair of Housing Committee. Campaigned for slum clearance. Took charge of Cathedral fund-raising. Good singer. First Catholic Mayor of Liverpool, 1943-44.

Hogan, Luke Trade Union official. 1929: Chair of Liverpool Council of Action during general strike. 1930: Leader of Liverpool Labour Party following ousting of Robinson who had opposed Catholic diocese purchase of cathedral site. Sociable and eloquent. Closely identified with the Catholic caucus on council. Opposed grants to birth control clinic. 1945-46: Lord Mayor. Resigned from Labour 1950, following dispute with national party over closure of Liverpool Cotton Exchange. Sat as independent Catholic councillor.

Holme, Samuel (1800-72) Wealthy Liverpool builder and Tory politician, who started out as bricklayer. Main contractor for St George's Hall. Prominent Tory. 1852: Mayor of Liverpool.

Hughes, John Born Ireland. Came to Liverpool in 1880. Founded grocery business which eventually grew to more then 60 shops. Nationalist, active in support of Irish culture. Actively supported Irish republicans in 1920s, often finding jobs for activists coming to Liverpool under cover.

Hume, Abraham (1814-84) Born at Hillsborough, County Down to Scottish parents. Educated Glasgow University, and Trinity College, Dublin. Taught at Liverpool Institute and Liverpool Collegiate Institution. 1847: Appointed vicar of the new Anglican parish of Vauxhall. Was a prominent liberal Anglican clergyman. Hume took part in most of the public, scientific, educational, and ecclesiastical events in Liverpool. A founder of the Historic Society of Lancashire and Cheshire. Conducted a series of social and statistical inquiries in his parish and other Liverpool districts. A student of the Irish language. A fellow of the Royal Statistical Society. Buried at Anfield cemetery, Liverpool.

Jacob, Albert Edward (1858-1929) Dublin born. Biscuit manufacturer. 1902-12: Liberal councillor Aigburth. 1924-29: Conservative MP, Toxteth.

Jones, Agnes (1832-68) Born Cambridge, to Irish parents. Father was an army officer. Brought up near Fahan, Co Donegal. 1862: Studied under Florence Nightingale. 1864: Appointed Lady Superintendent at Infirmary of Liverpool Workhouse. Introduced radical changes to humanise the institution and worked tirelessly to improve conditions. 1868: Weakened by long working hours fell ill with the infectious disease typhus. Died shortly afterwards. William Rathbone paid for a statue in her honour, known as *The White Angel*. Now stands in The Oratory next to Liverpool Anglican cathedral. Buried in Fahan churchyard.

Keating, Frederick William (1859-1928) Born Birmingham. 1882: Ordained. 1921-28: Bishop of Liverpool. Sympathetic to the poor and the working class. Approved of Labour Party and advocated Nationalist alliance with them. Influenced Catholic Representation Association towards the left. Supported striking Lancashire miners and was sympathetic to the General Strike, 1929.

Kelly, Margaret Born Dublin 1912. Moved to Liverpool during turmoil of Easter Rising 1916. Lived in West Derby. Became a dancer. Founded The Bluebell Girls dance troupes in Paris.

Kelly, Patrick J (1869-1928) Irish born. Settled Liverpool 1880s. Nationalist councillor 1914-1924. Pro Labour. Organised dockers demonstrations in support of Irish War of Independence. Imprisoned for Sinn Fein activity 1921. Supported tramway workers in strike over pay and conditions. As Nationalist leader attempted to negotiate election pact with Labour shortly before Nationalist wipe-out in 1920s.

Kensit, John (1853-1902) Born London. 1889: Founder of the Wycliffe Preachers and the Protestant Truth Society. Vocal and active opponent of excessive ritual in the Anglican Church. Opposed Oxford movement. Organised anti-Catholic rallies on Merseyside. Died several weeks after being struck by a metal object at ferry terminal on his way back from a meeting in Birkenhead.

Kerr, Neill Lived Bootle. Along with his sons Tom, Jack and Neill junior, took part in the 1916 Rising in Dublin. Leader of IRB in Liverpool. Following waterfront attacks in November 1920 was sentenced to two years. Supported Collins and the Treaty.

Langan, Jack (1798-1846) Born Ireland, he was a sailor who later became a boxer, known as 'The Irish Champion'. He had a public house and music venue near the Clarence Dock, which was one of the first premises Irish migrants would see as they arrived in Liverpool. Died in Cheshire on St Patrick's Day.

Lanigan, Stephen Born Liverpool. Senior customs and excise officer. Member of the IRB. Acted as an undercover agent for Michael Collins' operations in Liverpool during Irish War of Independence. Co-ordinated smuggling of weapons and ammunition to Ireland and the transport of persons. 1922: Interned in Belfast.

Larkin, Delia (1878-1949) Born Toxteth, Liverpool. Trade union organiser, journalist and actress. Organised drama groups in Liverpool and Garston, before leaving to join her older brother, James, in Ireland. She went on to found the Irish Women's Workers Union, and was prominent in the 1913 Dublin Lockout.

Larkin, James (1876-1947) Born Combermere Street, Liverpool, to Irish parents. Brought up in Toxteth. Began work aged eleven. 1893: Stowaway on a ship when a teenager, working his way through north and south America. Became involved in radical politics in Liverpool, and joined ILP. 1903-05: Foreman for Harrison Line. Known as 'The Rusher'. Came to leadership of the Harrison Line dispute over trade union recognition. Friend of Fred Bower, with whom he placed a time capsule underneath the Anglican cathedral foundation stone in 1904, documenting conditions of the poor at the time. Active in charitable work. 1905: Was election agent for Sexton in Toxteth. 1906: Officer of National Union of Dock Labourers. Founded the Irish Transport and General Union. 1913: Leader of the epic Dublin lockout. 1914-23: In America, spent time in prison for union activity and was finally deported. Self-educated, non-smoker, Catholic, Teetotaller.

Lee, Maureen Born in Bootle, during World War II. She attended Commercial College and became a shorthand typist. She published over one hundred and fifty short-stories, before publishing her first novel *Lila* in 1983. Since 1994 she has continued to publish dramatic historical sagas mainly set in her home city of Liverpool. In 2000, her novel *Dancing in the Dark* won the Romantic Novel of the Year Award from the Romantic Novelists' Association.

Logan, David Gilbert (1871-1964) Born Liverpool. Scottish father, Irish mother. Pawnbroker. Union organiser. 1920-23: Nationalist councillor. 1924: Became one of the first Nationalists to jump ship and join Labour. 1929: Nominated to succeed T.P. O'Connor and, like O'Connor, held the seat until his death. Devout Catholic. Opposed Sunday opening of cinemas and playgrounds.

Longbottom, H.D. (1886-1962) 1913: Assistant to George Wise. Later took over as pastor of the Protestant Reformers Memorial Church. 1931: Elected to City Council as Protestant candidate. Blamed unemployment and slums on Irish immigration. 1950-51: Lord Mayor. 1946-56: Member of Orange Order, Grand Master. 1961: Expelled.

Lowry, James Born Belfast. Established business as a grocer in Liverpool. Temperance worker. Methodist. President Liverpool Trades Council. Active in WMCA 1870s and 80s.

Lynskey, George Jeremy (1861-1921) Born Galway. Liverpool solicitor. Secretary of Young Ireland Society. Irish National League organiser. 1889: Elected councillor. Leadership role in Liverpool Nationalist Party. Councillor during the brief Liberal/Nationalist administration in Liverpool in1892-95. Was discredited amongst Nationalists for attending Queen Victoria's jubilee banquet. Returned to popularity for his role in supporting striking dockers and defending Catholics during the Wiseite disturbances around 1909.

McArdle, Charles (1833-1906) Cotton merchant. Nationalist councillor 1876-84.

McArdle, John Nineteenth century Ulster born Catholic. Publican in Crosbie Street. His pub hosted Ancient Order of Hibernians lodge.

McCarthy, Justin (1830-1912) Born Cork. 1852-60: Journalist on *Liverpool Daily Post.* 1864-68: Editor of Liverpool paper *Morning Star.* 1878-1900: Nationalist MP.

McCarthy, Mrs Lived in Aintree. Husband Dan McCarthy. Provided a safe house for fugitives during Irish War of Independence, including Cathal Brugha who recuperated there after the 1916 Rising, and future President Eamonn DeValera, following his escape from Lincoln jail.

McCracken, Thomas (1850-1917) Born Belfast. Wine and spirit merchant, Myrtle Street. Orangeman. Freemason. 1880: Co-founder of Junior Conservative Club. Contributed to Catholic charities. At various times fell out with Conservatives and Orange Order.

McHugh, Edward (1853-1915) Born Ireland. Land reformer and trade unionist, Founded National Union of Dock Labourers. 1890: Came to Liverpool to oversee strike arrangements. He and his colleague Richard McGhee were deposed as union leaders shortly afterwards, in favour of James Sexton, who was better known in Liverpool.

McKinney, James (1848-1918) Born Co Tyrone, Ireland. Anglican clergyman, who came to Liverpool. Vicar St Silas from 1893, where he increased the congregation to nearly 2,000. Orangeman. Outspoken in support of Empire and Boer War. Quarreled with George Wise.

McNeile, Hugh (1795-1879) Born Balycastle, Co Antrim. Educated at Trinity College Dublin and Cambridge University. Ordained Anglican minister. Appointed to St Jude's, Liverpool in 1834. Founder member of the Liverpool Protestant Association in 1835. Led the campaign against Liberal measures to introduce inter-denominational education to Liverpool Corporation schools, enlisting Conservative support. Renowned and inflammatory public speaker, pamphleteer and demagogue who was a vocal and relentless opponent of Roman Catholicism. Resisted attempts to introduce reforms in education, and to allow Catholic services in workhouse. Opposed Maynooth grant. Dean of Ripon (1868-1875).

McManus, Terence Bellew Born Fermanagh. Wealthy shipping merchant. Leader of Liverpool Confederates in 1840s. 1848: Took part in Rising in Ireland. Deported to Van Diemens Land, escaped to USA where he died in poverty. 1861: Buried in Glasnevin, Ireland following large public funeral.

McNamara, Sean (1928-2012) Born Toxteth, Liverpool. Traditional fiddler. Founder member of the Liverpool Ceili Band, which was All-Ireland Champion band at Fleadh Cheol na hEireann in 1963 and again 1964. He was one of the leading Irish traditional musicians of his generation.

Madden, Thomas John (1853-1915) Born Belfast. Anglican clergyman. Came to Liverpool 1879. Parishes included St Luke's and Christ Church, Everton. 1906: Archdeacon of Liverpool. Spoke out against George Wise's 'bastard Protestantism'.

Mahon, Simon (1914-86) Born Liverpool to Irish Catholic family. General contractor. Labour councillor. Chairman, Housing committee. 1955-79: Labour MP Bootle. Papal Knight. Wrote to Ladbrokes in 1978 objecting to their 'appalling taste' in taking bets on the outcome of the papal conclave electing a pope in Rome.

Milligan, George Jardine (1868-1925) Born Liverpool. Barman, docker. Leader of the North End dockers. Deputy to James Sexton. Catholic. Self-educated. Anti-Socialist. 1917: Awarded OBE. 1924: Appointed Justice of the Peace. 1911: Published: *Life Through Labour's Eyes*.

Morrissey, Alice Fabian and active member of ILP. Founder of Women's Social and Political Union in Liverpool. Jailed (Strangeways) for suffragette activity. Organised Liverpool WSPU. Died suddenly 1912.

Morrissey, John Wolfe Tone 1901: Elected city auditor. 1905-08: Liverpool's first Labour councillor. Made radical change to the role of auditor, subjecting city accounts and councillors' personal expense claims to meticulous scrutiny. Pacifist. Teetotaller. Devout Catholic.

Murphy, Peter For many years the proprietor of Irish Depot and Repository, also known as the '98 shop at 13 Scotland Place, where political literature, religious items, Irish goods and newspapers were on sale. Took active part in Nationalist politics, especially during the War of Independence. Supported the anti-Treaty side.

Murphy, Rose Anne (1898-1984) Joined Cumann na mBan, the women's section of the Irish armed revolutionary movement. 1915: Attended funeral of O'Donovan Rossa at Glasnevin. Trained with Cumann na mBan in Duke Street, Liverpool and took part in the 1916 Rising. Later married Henry Morgan and raised family in Liverpool.

Muspratt, James (1793-1886) Born Dublin. 1819: Married Julia Connor. They had ten children. 1822: Moved to Liverpool and began manufacture of chemicals on a large scale, using the LeBlanc process. 1828: Opened plant in St Helens in partnership with another Irish chemist, Josiah Gamble (of Proctor and Gamble). Prosecuted for pollution on several occasions. His chimney on Vauxhall Road, 150 foot high, was visible from the sea. Built a large house at Seaforth. Descendents remained influential in Liverpool. Founder of the Liverpool Institute for Boys. Buried at Walton.

Nugent, James (1822-1905) Born 22 Hunter Street, Liverpool. 1847: Ordained as Catholic priest. Founder of a number of Catholic social service organisations and education establishments, for which he was a very effective fundraiser. 1849: Started Ragged School in Spitalfields. Worked with John Denvir raising funds through the Save The Boy campaign. 1850: Opened Middle School for Boys in Rodney Street along with Fr Worthy. 1851: Brought Sisters of Notre Dame to Liverpool. They took charge of St Nicholas's School, Copperas Hill, and went on to found secondary school and teacher training college. 1853: Founded Catholic Institute, Hope Street, later to become St Edwards College. 1856: Became secretary of Catholic Reformatory Association. 1860: Founded *The Catholic Times*. 1860: Appointed the first Catholic Chaplain to Walton Gaol. His reports highlighted the deprivation endured by women. Was a witness to parliamentary Select Committees. 1875: Funded and built the League Hall (capacity 2,000) with support of Denvir, providing regular alternative entertainment to pubs in order to promote temperance. 1881: Nugent and Bishop O'Reilly jointly founded the Liverpool Catholic Children's Protection Society, which sent children to homes in Canada, a policy now largely discredited. 1891: Opened a refuge for women in Paul Street, Liverpool. His statue in St John's Gardens is said to be the only statue to a Catholic clergyman on public land in England.

O'Connell, Daniel (1775-1847) Born Co Kerry, Ireland. Barrister, and wealthy Catholic. Known as 'The Home Ruler'. Led the campaign for Catholic Emancipation (the right of Catholics to sit in parliament). The campaign was successful when in 1829, Catholics and other non-Anglican Christian denominations including Presbyterians were admitted to parliament. Was a frequent visitor to Liverpool where he attended mass in St Nicholas's Church and addressed crowds from the balcony of Adelphi Hotel. In 1840 led a campaign for Home Rule, a parliament in Dublin, holding monster meetings around Ireland including at Tara. Fell ill after imprisonment for leading the campaign. Died while in Rome. His body was returned to Ireland via England. Fearing disorder in Liverpool the authorities retained his body for a night in Chester before transport to a ship on the Birkenhead side of the Mersey, where crowds came to pay their last respects before the corpse was transported to Ireland.

O'Connor, Thomas Power (1848-1929) Born Athlone. Known as Tay Pay. Journalist. Graduated from Galway. 1885-1929: Nationalist MP for Scotland constituency, Liverpool. At first spent little time in Liverpool, but was forced to pay more attention to his constituency when challenged by Harford in 1900. From then on proved popular in the area. Arbitrated in 1911 union employer disputes. Continued as a Nationalist in Liverpool long after the party had disappeared. Was unopposed in 1918, 1922, 1923, 1924 and 1929 general elections. Father of the house. Buried Kensall Green cemetery.

O'Mara, Patrick (1902-83) Born Liverpool. Author of *The Autobiography of a Liverpool Irish Slummy*, an unflinching account of the hardships and social deprivation of his Liverpool family; domestic violence, family conflict and the struggle for survival. Migrated to USA in 1920, first to Baltimore, where he worked as taxi driver, then Arizona. Joined Marines during World War Two. Continued to write. Reputedly married German baroness.

O'Reilly, Bernard (1824-93) Born Ballybay, Monaghan, Ireland. Educated at Catholic seminary at Ushaw. 1847: First Catholic parish, St Patrick's, where he became seriously ill after contracting infectious disease through ministering in the deprived district nearby. 1873: Appointed Bishop of Liverpool. 1883: Founded seminary at Upholland.

O'Shea, William (1840-1905) Home Rule MP, 1880-85. His wife Catherine (Kitty) had a long relationship with Parnell, culminating in O'Shea's divorce. 1885: Stood as Liberal candidate, Liverpool Exchange after Parnell stood down. Narrowly defeated.

Parker, Father (1804-47) Rector of St Patrick's, Park Place for seventeen years until his death from typhus, an infectious illness, probably contracted by visiting the sick in his parish. Became embroiled in controversy on a number of occasions. An English Catholic, he was unsympathetic to O'Connel's Repeal the Union campaign, and refused permission for Repealers to have a table outside his church after mass. Buried in the crypt under St Patrick's.

Parnell, Charles Stewart (1846-91) Charismatic and radical leader of the Irish Parliamentary Party. Frequent visitor to Liverpool, where he addressed crowds at St George's Plateau, the League Hall and other venues. 1885: Stood as candidate in first election under the new wider franchise, when Liverpool Nationalists hoped to win two or three seats. Forced the choice of T.P. O'Connor, Galway, as the candidate for the safest seat, Scotland division. He stood for Exchange where there was also a strong possibility of a Nationalist victory. Withdrew at last minute, and recommended voters supported Captain O'Shea, a Liberal, in contradiction to party policy. What was not publicly known at the time was that Parnell was having an affair with O'Shea's wife, Kitty and was trying to persuade O'Shea to allow a divorce. O'Shea was narrowly defeated. When the scandal finally broke, he faced stern clerical opposition, but the party radicals, including several Liverpool branches, supported him and opposed resignation. He was finally forced to stand down and died shortly afterwards.

Patterson, John (1822-90) Corn merchant. Leader of Ulster Presbyterians, Liverpool. Temperance campaigner.

Pinkman, John (1902-70) Born and educated in Liverpool. 1918: Joined Sinn Fein. 1920: Joined Liverpool company of the Irish Volunteers (the IRA) and took part in Liverpool actions. Convicted and imprisoned in Dartmoor until the treaty of 1921. Fought on Treaty side in Civil War. His memoir *In the Legion of the Vanguard* is a detailed and informative account of his experiences.

Rathbone, Eleanor Florence (1872-1946) Daughter of William Rathbone sixth and Emily Lyle. Long-term campaigner for women's rights. 1903: Published the detailed and insightful *Report on the results of a Special Inquiry into the conditions of Labour at the Liverpool Docks.* 1909-1934: Independent councillor for Granby. 1929: MP for Universities. President National Union of Women's Suffrage Societies. Founder of Liverpool Personal Service Society. Campaigned against female genital mutilation, and for Family Allowances. Opposed Boer War.

Rushton, Edward (1795-1851) Barrister. Son of Liverpool poet and human rights campaigner of same name, Edward junior became a prominent figure in Liverpool politics. 1839: Appointed Stipendiary Magistrate. Prominent during the influx of Irish migrants in 1840. He ordered the police to keep a record of the numbers arriving, providing historians with much useful and accurate information. Vocal in highlighting the challenges local administration faced during the Famine years. Opposed Orange presence in the police.

Russell, Charles (Baron Russell of Killowen) (1832-1900) Born Newry, Co Down. Practised in the Liverpool. Lectured on the life of Daniel O'Connell. Liberal MP. 1886: Appointed Lord Chief Justice by Gladstone administration. First Catholic since the Reformation to hold that office.

Salvidge, Archibald Tutton (1863-1928) Managing director of Bent's Brewery. 1888-92: Vice chairman of Working Men's Christian Association. 1892-1928: Chairman. 1896: Conservative councillor. 1919-1928: Chairman of Liverpool Consitutional Association. Mobilised the WMCA to support the Tory cause, and controlled the local party for a generation. Maintained a populist Tory stance in Liverpool, often using antipathy towards the Irish and loyalty to Crown, Bible and Empire as election themes.

Scott, Elisha (1839-1959) Born Co Antrim. Played in goal for Linfield FC, Belfast. 1913-35: Liverpool FC goalkeeper. 1934-49: manager of Belfast Celtic. 31 Ireland caps. 429 league appearances for Liverpool.

Sexton, James (1856-1938) Born Newcastle upon Tyne. Worked Pilkington's Glass, St Helens. Seaman. Docker. Incapacitated in severe accident to face and arm. 1893: Defeated James Larkin in election for Gen Secretary, NUDL. Held post until 1922. 1905: Founder member of ILP. 1905-38: Liverpool Labour councillor. 1918-31: Labour MP St Helens. 1931: Knighted.

Sheil, Richard (1791-1871) Born Tipperary, Ireland. Merchant and town councillor. Elected to Council 1835 as a Liberal, and was the only Catholic on the Council. Campaigner for Catholic rights. Sheil Road and Sheil Park in Liverpool are named after him. Buried Anfield cemetery.

Stones, Albert Hired by George Wise in 1903 to look after the Wise Crusade while Wise was in prison. Took over south end activity when Wise was released. Following a rift, and accusations of financial impropriety, he split with Wise in 1904 and set up his own organisation.

Taggart, John Gregory (1861-1925) Born Tyrone. Moved to Liverpool 1866. Worked as miner in North East. Returned to Liverpool as labourer in Tate and Lyle. District Secretary Gasworkers and General Labourers Union. 1888: Became Liverpool's first working class councillor. Home Rule supporter. Thought to be 'the ablest of the Irish Nationalists. Gained his education through evening classes, winning prizes in many subjects, including chemistry, mathematics, physics and physiology. Accomplished musician. Teetotaller.

Tapscott, William American packet ship broker, with offices on Regents Road, Liverpool, and Eden Quay, Dublin in 1840s and 50s. He worked in conjunction with his brother James, who looked after the New York end of the business, and specialized in selling pre-paid passages to successful immigrants who now wished to bring their families to America. Eventually went bankrupt. Served three years penal servitude for fraud of shipping passengers.

Taylor, Frances (known as Mother Magdalen Taylor) (1832-1900) Born Lincolnshire. 1854: Went to Crimea with Florence Nightingale to nurse sick and wounded soldiers. 1855: Converted to Catholicism. 1869: Founded Poor Servants of the Mother of God. 1891: At request of Fr James Nugent established shelter for women in Liverpool, near Sylvester Street, and later at Paul Street.

Thom, Hannah May (1817-72) Born into the wealthy Rathbone family. Married Reverend Thom an Ulsterman and Unitarian. Was for many years nurse superintendent at Marybone and became well known in the area around Holy Cross Catholic parish and Vauxhall. Worked for 20 years in the area where poverty and disease were extreme and endemic. Statue erected in her memory by local subscription after her death, restored in 1987, now stands in the gardens of a residential home Mazenod Court, in Addison Street, Liverpool.

Trench, Cesca (1891-1918) Born in the vicarage of St John the Baptist Church, Tuebrook, Liverpool. She was the granddaughter of Richard Chenevix Trench, the Archbishop of Dublin. Irish speaker and language activist. Studied art in Paris and Dublin. Member of Cumann na mBan. Designed posters for Gaelic League paper An Claidheamh Soluis, edited by P.H. Pearse. An associate of Claude Chavasse.

Walsh, Tommy (1939-2010) Born Liverpool. Worked in retail. Manager of the Liverpool Irish Centre from 1963 to 1993. Dynamic personality at heart of Irish community both in Liverpool and Britain. First Chairman of Federation of Irish Societies in Britain. 1974: Irishman of the Year. Member Irish Commission for Prisoners Overseas. 1964-67: President of GAA in Britain. Founded St Michael's Irish Centre, now Liverpool Irish Centre. His autobiography *Being Irish in Liverpool* gives a unique insight into Irish Liverpool in 20th century.

White, Thomas (1877-1938) Born Liverpool. Cabin boy, later ship's steward, licenced victualler. 1919: Elected Conservative councillor. Supported Salvidge. Orangeman. 1928-38: Leader of Liverpool Conservatives. 1929: Managing director of Bent's Brewery. Buried at sea.

White, Rev Verner Irish Presbyterian who opposed accommodation with Catholics on Select Vestry Board in 1870s.

Whiteside, Thomas (1857-1921) Lancashire family. Pro-Unionist. Clashed with Irish Nationalists over School Board election. 1894-1921: Catholic Bishop of Liverpool. 1906: Led public demonstration against Liberal education proposals. 1909: Led Catholic deputation to Council protesting against Wiseite crusades. After 1911 blamed drunkeness and squalor amongst Irish for 1911 violence. Supported the Centre Party.

Whitley, Edward (1825-92) Influential Liverpool Conservative. 1865-92: Conservative councillor. 1880-92: Conservative MP for first Liverpool, then Everton district. Sunday school teacher. Opposed Irish Nationalists, suggesting that Liberals and Tories unite to ensure government by 'respectable people'. Influential in Tory leadership.

Whitty, James (1813-76) Born Co Wexford, prosperous woollen merchant first in Bradford and then Liverpool. President, Irish Catholic Club. Friend of Rathbones. Liberal Member of Town Council, School Board and Select Vestry. Challenged Poor Law Guardians, refusal to allow services for Catholics in the Workhouse. Active in advocating for Catholic rights. Buried at Ford.

Whitty, May (1865-1948) Grand-daughter of M.J. Whitty (see below) she was a stage and film actress, best known for her part as Miss Froy, in Alfred Hitchcock's *The Lady Vanishes* (1938). Married Ben Webster. Awarded DBE in 1918.

Whitty, Michael James (1795-1873) Born Co Wexford, Ireland. Came to Liverpool from London in 1830 to take up post of editor of *Liverpool Journal*. 1833: Appointed first Chief Constable. Founded Liverpool police and went on to found the fire service. A powerfully built man, he often took a 'front line' approach to riot control. After leaving his post as Chief Constable, returned to journalism. In 1851 challenged Judge Ramshay's negative views of Liverpool people and was imprisoned as a result, following which the judge was dismissed. In 1855, after a successful campaign to have the tax on newspapers reduced, went on to found the *Liverpool Daily Post*, an affordable newspaper. Buried Anfield cemetery.

Wilcock, Father October 1832: laid foundation stone of St Anthony's Church, Scotland Road. 1842: Protested against corporation schools regulations which effectively excluded Catholics. 1844: Retired from St Anthony's.

Wilkinson, Kitty (1785-1860) Born Co Derry/Londonderry, Ireland. Came to Liverpool with parents aged nine. Father and brother drowned in shipwreck near Liverpool. 1797: Aged twelve, went to work in a mill at Caton in Lancashire. At 20 she returned to Liverpool to be with her mother. Both worked in domestic service. Married seaman Emanuel Demontee. They had two sons. He was lost at sea. Married Tom Wilkinson, and lived in Dennison Street near the Clarence Dock. When cholera broke out in 1832, her method of washing and disinfecting clothing protected those in the neighbourhood from infection. Came to the attention of Liverpool philanthropist William Rathbone, and his wife Elizabeth, who were active in the District Provident Society. Her work became widely recognised, and resulted in Liverpool Corporation opening a public baths and wash house, the first of its kind, in Upper Frederick Street in Liverpool in 1842. Kitty and her husband Tom were the first superintendents, appointed at William Rathbone's instigation, in 1846. That same year the Mayoress presented Kitty with a silver teapot, a gift from Queen Victoria. Gravestone stands in St James's cemetery at the side of Liverpool Anglican Cathedral. She is remembered in a stained-glass window at the entrance to the Lady Chapel in the Cathedral. In 2010 she became the first woman to be represented by a statue in Liverpool's St George's Hall. Liverpool historian Michael Kelly has produced an excellent biography of Kitty. A short film, *Saint of the Slums* can be found on YouTube. 'Through rising from abject poverty to achieve lasting reforms in public health Kitty Wilkinson is a real inspiration for every woman in this city.' Councillor Flo Clucas, 2010.

Wise, George (1856-1917) Born Bermondsey. 1888: Arrived Liverpool. Worked for Christian evidence and YMCA. Later became Protestant Fundamentalist Crusader. 1903-06: Councillor Kirkdale Ward. Pastor of Protestant Reformers Memorial Church. Vehemently anti-Catholic. Held regular outdoor meetings at St Domingo's Pit, Everton and other venues. Agitated against Catholic processions. Was imprisoned for refusing to be bound over to keep the peace. Commission of Inquiry into 1909 disturbances found against all his allegations.

Yates, John (1807-87) Born Haslingden. Solicitor. Convert to Catholicism. 1844: Liverpool Liberal who was first Catholic member of the Select Vestry. 1870: Was elected to Town Council and also first School Board. Contributed generously to Catholic charities and building funds. Buried St Oswald's, Liverpool.

APPENDIX TWO
DISEASES REFERRED TO IN THE TEXT

In nineteenth century Liverpool there were recurring epidemics of the following highly infectious diseases.

Cholera. An infection of the small intestine that is caused by bacteria. The main symptoms are profuse watery diarrhoea and vomiting. Transmission is primarily through consuming contaminated drinking water or food. The severity of the diarrhoea and vomiting can lead to rapid dehydration, and the passing of blood.

Dysentery (formerly known as flux or the bloody flux). An inflammatory disorder of the intestine, especially of the colon, that results in severe diarrhoea containing mucus and/or blood in the faeces with fever and abdominal pain.

Typhus. The name comes from the Greek *typhos* meaning smoky or hazy, describing the state of mind of those affected, and describes a number of related diseases. It is spread by mites, fleas and body lice, and progresses quickly when people live in overcrowded conditions. The symptoms are abdominal pain, backache, a dull red rash (which begins on the middle of the body and spreads) extremely high fever, hacking dry cough, headaches, joint pain, nausea and vomiting. Typhus and the accompanying lethargy and hazy state of mind, was endemic in Liverpool's poorer districts throughout the nineteenth century. Typhus should not be confused with typhoid fever, as the diseases are unrelated.

Typhoid fever is characterized by a slowly progressive fever as high as 40 C (104 F), profuse sweating and gastroenteritis. Less commonly, a rash of flat rose-colored spots may appear. It is transmitted by the ingestion of food or water contaminated with the faeces of an infected person. The course of typhoid fever is divided into individual stages, each lasting approximately one week. In the first week, there is a slowly rising temperature with headache and coughing. Blood may be coughed up and abdominal pain is also common. In the second week there is high fever with patient unable to remain standing. In the third week a number of complications can occur, including internal bleeding and perforation of the intestines, often leading to septicaemia, which can be fatal. Another common outcome is encephalitis (inflammation and swelling in the brain).

DO NOT MIX UP YOUR RATHBONES!

William Rathbone 2nd came to Liverpool in 1742. He was married to Sarah Hyde. He founded the merchant firm Rathbone Brothers. He joined the Society of Friends (Quakers).

William Rathbone 3rd (1726-89) Married Rachael Rutter. He was a wealthy merchant and ship owner. A Quaker, he opposed the slave trade. They had eleven children.

William Rathbone 4th (1757-1809) Married Hannah Reynolds. They had eight children. They left the Quakers following a dispute about religious prejudice in Ireland, and became associated with the Unitarian church. Was a founder of the Liverpool Committee for the Abolition of the Slave Trade.

William Rathbone 5th (1787-1868) Married Elizabeth Greg. Elected to city council in 1835, following the Great Reform Act. Was Mayor 1837. He and Elizabeth supported Kitty Wilkinson in her work to prevent the spread of cholera. Was instrumental in the pioneering work of founding the public wash houses and baths. Resident at Greenbank House, near to Greenbank Park in Liverpool. Distributed the New England Relief Fund during the Irish Famine of 1840s.

Hannah May Thom (nee Rathbone) (1817-1872) A daughter of William and Elizabeth, she married a Unitarian, the Reverend Thom. In spite of her wealthy background, she dedicated her life to nursing the poor, elderly and infirm of the district around Holy Cross parish. She was held in such high esteem by local Catholics that a statue, funded by public subscription, was erected in her memory. It was restored in 1987 and stands today in grounds to the side of Addison Street.

William Rathbone 6th (1819-1902) Worked with Florence Nightingale to found the Liverpool Training School and Home for Nurses, and to found the district nursing service in 1860s. Campaigned for, and met the cost of, the nursing post at the infirmary in the Liverpool Workhouse. The first appointee was Agnes Jones. Commissioned the statue, *The White Angel*, in her memory. Associated with the founding of University of Liverpool. MP for Liverpool 1869-1880. MP for other seats until 1895. He died at Greenbank House. He is remembered by a statue in St John's Gardens.

Eleanor Rathbone. Daughter of William Rathbone 6th, independent member of Liverpool City Council in 1909 for the seat of Granby Ward, a position she maintained until 1934. The same year she published her first book *How the Casual Labourer Lives*, casting light on the financial realities for Liverpool workers for the first time. MP: 1929-1946. Successfully campaigned for Family Allowances.

THE IRISH GREAT HUNGER

Why did the crop failures of the 1840s lead to mass starvation in Ireland? The potato has always been susceptible to blight, and there had been regular crop failures in the decades before 1845, causing severe regional famines in parts of Ireland. But there were other significant factors involved. Following the completion of British colonisation in the 1600s, many in the native population were displaced, and land in Ireland was divided into large estates in the possession of a small number of wealthy landlords. The Penal Laws enforced taxation without representation, excluding Catholics from many areas of public life – such as access to the professions, courts, and parliament – and compromising their property rights. By the early nineteenth century many of these laws had been repealed and there was a thriving middle class, some of them big farmers, others merchants and business people. But the greatest proportion were languishing in extreme poverty. The landed estates were still there, but rather than building up a wealthy agricultural economy, they had become mired in debt and dedicated to growing cash crops to meet the needs of absentee landlords.

Following the Act of Union (1800), Ireland remained in a state of political and economic crisis. Issues such as Catholic Emancipation, and later Home Rule rankled, as did the questions of land reform, tithes and the rural unrest related to both. Tithes involved annual payments, often in the form of crops from the land, to the local established Anglican church. It was greatly resented by Catholics. Evictions continued. Anticipated British investment in Ireland did not materialise. Rather Irish capital was exported. Although some absentee landlords, such as the Duke of Devonshire, were prepared to reinvest income from rents in their Irish estates, the majority preferred to spend their Irish incomes on lavish lifestyles elsewhere. Some estimates put the export of capital in the early 1840s as high as £6 million per annum. Since the rebellion of 1798 the edifice was more reliant than ever on coercion and the British military presence.

Following the conclusion of the Napoleonic Wars there was a slump in corn prices, bringing about an agricultural crisis. Irish industry was also in difficulty, as manufacturers tried to compete with cheap imports from the better capitalised British producers. The results were that 'Irish industry collapsed, unemployment was widespread and Dublin … became a half-dead city.'[1]

The population was increasing rapidly, from an estimated 2.5 million in 1767 to 5 million in 1800 to 6.75 million in 1821 and finally to about 8.25 million in 1841, four years before the potato crop failure, and much greater than the 5.5 million in Ireland at the present day.[2] Those most vulnerable were the subsistence farmers. They were numerous. Displaced from the land, they lived on the margins, without fixity of tenure or protection from rent rises. The price they could get for produce had fallen. In a non-cash economy produce was often given up as rent. There were no industrial centres to which they could flee. The potato was not suitable as a cash export item. Yet it gave a large crop on little space, and storage and preparation did not require anything more than the most basic equipment – a spade and a cooking pot. It became the staple diet of the poor.

There had been over a dozen potato famines in Ireland during the first four decades of the century. One was documented in the *Liverpool Mercury:* 'We regret to state that in Galway, Clare and several other counties, famine has again appeared with all its horrors. During this awful visitation grain, oatmeal and corn continue to be shipped off to England in large quantities. Meanwhile there is every prospect of an abundant harvest; but the population of the country will, it is apprehended, derive no advantage from this abundance.'[3]

The Duke of Wellington, who in addition to his many other occupations, was an Irish landlord, declared that: 'there never was a country in which poverty existed to the extent it exists in Ireland'.[4] Following the 1841 census the Irish Census Commissioners reported that: 'nearly half the families of the rural population are living in the lowest state', meaning that they existed in the fourth class of housing, windowless mud cabins of one room. In the western counties, more than three fifths of the population lived this way. Many women suffered from blindness because of the constant smoke inside the cabins.

Whilst discussion continues as to the proper weight to attach to the various causal factors, in the words of Foster: '... no amount of disagreement can conceal the devastating extent of depopulation or the horrific conditions in which lives were lost'.

Throughout the Famine years agricultural produce, including grain and livestock, continued to be exported from Ireland in large quantities. Many landlords adopted a policy of getting rid of their tenants, evicting en masse, often making use of bailiffs in the most brutal of circumstances. Having nowhere else to go, many of the victims made their way to Liverpool.

We will never know how many perished in the Irish famine. Census returns for the western counties in 1841 may well have underestimated population totals considerably. Furthermore, records were not kept of the dying or those emigrating. Hundreds of thousands died from starvation. Hundreds of thousands died from disease, including typhus, relapsing fever and cholera. Estimates of the total deaths from these combined causes vary from 750,000 (Foster) to, 'not far short of a million' (Beckett) to a million (Fry. Woodham-Smith). In addition about 1.5 million emigrated in these years. The population of Ireland was cut by one third in six years, and was to continue to decline for the remainder of the century, until it reached a figure of just over 4 million. Ireland remains one of the few countries anywhere in the world with a population today which is significantly less than it was in the 1840s.

The crop first failed in the autumn of 1845. Peel, Prime Minister at the time, was alert to the dangers, and responded vigorously. In the words of one commentator: 'He stands out as one of the very few Englishmen who showed something other than callous indifference to the plight of the victims of the famine.' He instituted a programme of public works, and distributed corn purchased in the United States. In the words of Daniel O'Connell's Freeman's Journal: 'No man died of famine during his administration, and it is a boast of which he might well be proud.'[5]

His successor was Lord John Russell who asserted: 'It must be thoroughly understood that we cannot feed the people'.[6] Charles Wood, the Chancellor of the Exchequer, and his first Secretary, Charles Trevelyan, were of the same mind. Charles Trevelyan stated that: 'the Famine reflected the wishes of an all wise

Providence.'[7] In other words, famine was the will of God. They believed that the market forces were sacrosanct and ought not to be interfered with; the doctrine known as laissez faire, in modern parlance free market economics. It is remarkable that many of the landed aristocracy who advocated the lasez faire doctrine also supported the corn laws legislation, which was used to tax imported grain, in order to keep the domestic price high, a measure which favoured the landed classes.

The reply to this from Ireland was that: 'You cannot answer the cry of want by a quotation from political economy.'[8] Government aid was to be restricted to the provision of public works. They would not buy food. The food would have to be provided by private business.

Catastrophes as great as that of 1845 were to follow. The potato crop failed again in the autumn of 1846. This disaster, coming on top of the failure of the previous year, and coupled with the new policy of not buying supplies of food to distribute in aid, left hundreds of thousands facing destitution, and death from starvation and disease. By January 1847 the government began to recognise that people would have to be fed, and that the expense would have to be borne by the public purse. By August over 3 million, 'were being fed daily at public expense.'[9]

The impetus of emigration was not inhibited by landlords. Many were glad to get rid of their impoverished tenants who could no longer afford rent, and might at any moment become a charge on local rates. The Chief Constable of Liverpool referred to one instance which he knew of as an example, in which 1,400 tenants had been served with eviction notices, with 900 of them leaving soon afterwards.

'An application of this kind is known throughout the barony as soon as it takes place, and when known the cottier and his family, without hesitation, put everything portable on their backs and make their way towards Dublin or some other seaport, determined to reach England where they understand they will not be allowed to starve ...'[10]

Furthermore, certain land-lords used the money raised in England for the relief of the starving to pay ferry companies to ship their tenants from Ireland to Liverpool instead.

'A few weeks ago, I saw a number of poor people taken on board one of the Shannon boats to be conveyed to Dublin, from which I know their passage was continued in the company's boat to Liverpool. From the manner in which they came on board, no question being put to them as to their ability to pay their passage themselves, it seemed to me very likely to be one of those contract cases which I often heard of as between shipping companies and relief committees ... They were paupers from the estate of the Marquiss of Clanrickard, and they were sent away at the expense of a relief fund, a considerable part of which I knew to have been contributed by ... the Society of Friends in England ... I saw with my own eyes the miserable poor being taken off it (*The Estate*) and boated off to infest Liverpool, partly at the expense of money raised in England to give them food.'[11]

At the same time landlords were exporting cash crops in large quantities, much of it coming through Liverpool. Huge quantities of grain were exported during 1846-47,[12] frequently under armed guard.[13] One observer reported in 1846 that: 'barges leave Clonmel once a week for this place, with the export supplies under convoy which, last Tuesday, consisted of two guns, 50 cavalry and 80 infantry escorting them ...'

Although the quantity of food being exported would not have fed the population, it might at least have relieved the misery of some. We should also note that in the 1840s people in all parts of Britain, including the south of England, experienced hunger and food shortage, though not to anything like the extent of the Irish. There were attempts to storm food warehouses not just in England but on the continent as well.[14]

The root cause of the Famine was the failure of the potato crop. The agricultural, economic and political system established following the conquest of the sixteen-hundreds, and later the Act of Union, had left millions in extreme poverty and precarious conditions. Had government taken effective action earlier, lives would have been saved. Had land reform – which was only achieved following bitter campaigns later in the century – been introduced, those living on the land would have had a better chance of survival. The Famine, known in Ireland as the Great Hunger, is often blamed on 'England'. It was more accurately the British establishment and landed classes which were to blame. The British aristocracy believed in their right to rule. They would only ever introduce reform when under extreme pressure. They adopted an economic philosophy – laissez faire (let markets decide) – which conveniently favoured their own interests. Their incompetence, unwillingness to act and callous disregard for the welfare of the poor under their governance were important contributory factors to the tragedy Great Hunger.

References

1. Woodham-Smith, C. *The Great Hunger.* Signet. London, 1964. p.16.

2. Somerset-Fry, P. and F. *A History of Ireland.* Routledge. London, 1991. p.228.

3. *Liverpool Mercury*, 9 July 1824. p.10. Col.2.

4. Woodham-Smith. Op cit. p.20.

5. Beckett, J.C. *The Making of Modern Ireland.* Faber and Faber. London, 1981. p.338.

6. Beckett. Op cit. p.339.

7. Somerset-Fry. Op cit. p.233.

8. Beckett. Op cit. p.338.

9. Beckett. Op cit. p.341.

10. Report of Liverpool Chief Constable, 16 February 1847.

11. *Manchester Examiner.* Reported in *Liverpool Mercury*, 18 May 1847.

12. Woodham-Smith. p.75.

13. Op cit. p.77.

14. *Liverpool Mercury,* 18 May 1847.

INDEX

251

ABOUT THE AUTHOR

Greg Quiery – from Newtownards in Co. Down – was a community development worker in Belfast during the early years of the Troubles, before coming to Liverpool in 1974. He has worked as a teacher in secondary education, a Head-teacher and later as Head of the Virtual School, Liverpool's Education Service for Looked-After Children. Greg – one of the first to introduce locally the study of Irish history and culture – was a Fellow at the University of Liverpool's Institute of Irish Studies in its formative years, and still conducts occasional courses on local history in the Continuing Education Department at Liverpool. In 1998, as Chair of the Liverpool Great Hunger Commemoration Committee, he was closely involved in creating the Memorial to the Irish Famine in St Luke's Gardens, Liverpool. Greg is a Liverpool Irish Festival board member, conducts local heritage walks, has written the Irish Trail for the Museum of Liverpool, and – as a member of the Liverpool 1916 Commemoration Committee – produced, in partnership with the Museum of Liverpool, the display '1916 – the Liverpool Connection.' He is a traditional musician, has made an album of his own songs, and is active in environmental campaigns.